BRAZIL AND SOUTH KOREA:
ECONOMIC CRISIS AND RESTRUCTURING

Brazil and South Korea:
Economic Crisis and Restructuring

Edited by
Edmund Amann and Ha-Joon Chang

Institute of Latin American Studies
31 Tavistock Square, London WC1H 9HA
http://www.sas.ac.uk/ilas/publicat.htm

Institute of Latin American Studies
School of Advanced Study
University of London

British Library Cataloguing-in-Publication Data
A catalogue record for this book is available
from the British Library

ISBN   1 900039 51 6

Institute of Latin American Studies
University of London, 2004

TABLE OF CONTENTS

NOTES ON CONTRIBUTORS

Edmund Amann is Senior Lecturer in Development Economics at the University of Manchester. He has been Research Fellow at the University of Oxford Centre for Brazilian Studies and Lecturer at the University of London Institute of Latin American Studies. His publications include *Economic Liberalisation and Industrial Performance in Brazil* (Oxford University Press, 2000) and various articles in economics and area studies journals such as *World Development, Journal of Development Studies* and the *Journal of Latin American Studies.*

André Averbug worked as an associate to the World Bank, Latin America and Caribbean department. He also worked as a United Nations contactor to the Brazilian Development Bank (BNDES), Economic Research Department, where he published several papers on trade and economic integration. He is currently pursuing further graduate studies at McGill University, Canada.

Ha-Joon Chang teaches, and is Assistant Director of Development Studies, at the Faculty of Economics and Politics, University of Cambridge. He has published widely in the areas of development economics and institutional economics. He is the author of *Kicking Away the Ladder — Development Strategy in Historical Perspective* (Anthem Press, 2002).

Fabio Giambiagi is an economist at IPEA, a Brazilian think tank attached to the Ministry of Planning of Brazil. He worked previously as economist in the Economics Departament of the BNDES, as assistant in the Brazilian Ministry of Planning and in the Inter-American Development Bank (Washington) as country economist for Colombia and Venezuela. He is the author of, *Finanças públicas: teoria e prática no Brasil* and has published widely in Brazilian and international journals, including World *Development* (USA), *Pesquisa e Planejamento Econômico* (Brazil) and *Desarrollo Económico* (Argentina). He writes regularly for *Valor Econômico*, a Brazilian financial newspaper.

Andrea Goldstein is a Senior Economist Investment Officer at the Foreign Investment Advisory Service of the World Bank Group. He was previously at the OECD Development Centre. His current research interests include e-commerce in developing countries, regulatory reform in network industries, the political economy of the global aerospace industry and high-skill migration from Latin America. He is the author of *Globalizzazione e sviluppo* (Bologna, 2003) and has published widely in academic journals.

Louise Haagh is a Lecturer in Politics at the University of York. She is the co-editor of *Market Governance in Latin America* (Basingstoke, 2002). She has written widely on social and ecoonomic policy in Latin America and East Asia.

Tat Yan Kong is Lecturer in Politics at the School of Oriental and African Studies, University of London. A specialist on comparative political economy, he is the author of *The Politics of Reform in South Korea: A Fragile Miracle* (Routledge, 2000).

Jose Ricardo Ramalho is Professor of Sociology in the Graduate Program of Sociology and Anthropology of the Federal University of Rio de Janeiro, Brazil. His main research interests have been related to the sociology of work, trade union and working class movements and development studies.

Ben Ross Schneider is professor and chair of political science at Northwestern University. His recent books include *Business Politics and the State in Twentieth Century Latin America* (Cambridge University Press, forthcoming 2004) and co-edited with Blanca Heredia, *Reinventing Leviathan: The Politics of Administrative Reform in Developing Countries* (North-South Center Press, 2003).

Jang-Sup Shin is Associate Professor in the Department of Economics at the National University of Singapore. He is the author of *The Economics of the Latecomers: Catching-Up, Technology Transfer and Institutions in Germany, Japan and South Korea* (London, 1996) and is a specialist in globalisation and financial crisis, and technology and innovation.

List of Tables

LIST OF FIGURES

CHAPTER 1

Economic Crisis and Restructuring in Brazil and South Korea: Overview

Edmund Amann and Ha-Joon Chang

The 1990s saw lower and middle-income countries throughout the world come under sustained and unprecedented pressure to open up their domestic markets to international trade and investment. In promoting the cause of global economic integration, so it was argued, such countries would in turn serve their own best interests as foreign capital flowed in, industry and commerce restructured and productivity gains drove an acceleration in GDP growth. However, with the emergence and continuing aftermath of the Asian and emerging markets economic crisis of the late 1990s, proponents of trade, investment and market reforms have been given pause for thought. Despite the progressive implementation of market-friendly policies, many emerging market countries both within and outside East and South East Asia have proved distressingly prone to episodes of financial market volatility, exchange rate collapse and slumps in output.

One of the most stunning features of the crisis and its aftermath has been the fact that it embroiled not simply the more obviously fragile, poorer economies, but that it has also profoundly affected two of the world's largest middle income industrialised countries: Brazil and South Korea. The fact that both economies, despite substantial industrial sectors and, by and large, an impressive post-war growth track record should succumb so rapidly to crisis remains a matter of considerable debate. The debate is made especially complex by the fact that, despite superficial similarities, prior to the onset of crisis both countries had employed very different models of industrialisation and had adopted contrasting approaches to trade and market reform. Against this background, the first objective of this book is to examine and clarify the factors underpinning the emergence of crisis in both South Korea and Brazil, pointing out both the areas of similarity and of divergence. The second key focus of this book lies in analysing the alternative paths taken by both economies away from crisis, examining both the role of policy and long existing variations in structural characteristics. The chapters that comprise this volume were originally presented at the Institute of Latin American Studies, University of London, 'Workshop on Brazil and South Korea' held in December 2000.

In the first, Giambiagi and Averbug focus on the development and short-term impact of the 1998–99 economic crisis in Brazil. A particular preoccupation of the chapter is to determine why the depth of crisis in Brazil was considerably less severe than in the case of East and South East Asia. In analysing the evolution of the Brazilian economic crisis the authors point to a number of determining factors, among the most significant of which were the onset of growing fiscal fragility and the widespread perception that the *real* was overvalued. With investors increasingly preoccupied as to the sustainability of policymakers' medium term policy stance and, more especially, the continued viability of the currency peg, the authorities had little choice but to engage in successive rounds of interest rate rises. The latter, of course, speeded the arrival of crisis in that they jeopardised both growth prospects and the authorities' attempts to maintain the fiscal deficit within reasonable bounds. To this extent, the authors argue, it is possible to characterise the events which preceded the forced currency devaluation of January 1999 as containing elements of both a Krugman first generation and an Obstfeld second generation currency crisis. In the case of a 'Krugman style' crisis, of course, speculative attacks against currencies result from the perception that the maintenance of a given currency parity is unsustainable given the deterioration of the fiscal position. For Obstfeld, by contrast, currency crises manifest themselves because the cost of maintaining the high interest rates necessary to defend a given parity becomes excessive.

The central objective of the authors, however, is not so much to explain why the Brazilian crisis of 1998–99 came about so much as to establish why its impact turned out to be far less severe than was the case in East Asian countries faced with similar (though not identical) currency crises. Giambiagi and Averbug argue that a number of factors distinguish events in Brazil from those in East Asian economies such as South Korea and Thailand. In the first place, in the run up to the forced maxi-devaluation of January 1999, there was a general consensus among Brazilian policymakers that additional devaluation of the *real* was inevitable, indeed desirable. Indeed, for a considerable period the authorities had permitted the *real* to gently decline in value against the dollar and other major currencies. The only real source of controversy centred on the rapidity and scale of further devaluation rather than on the need for it per se. Second, careful management of the currency by the Brazilian Central Bank (in particular its marked reluctance to engage in ruinously expensive market interventions) meant that in the run up to, and during, the crisis there was no catastrophic haemorrhaging of international reserves.

In addition, unlike many economies in East and South East Asia, the authors argue that the Brazilian financial system was better prepared to cope with the strains of rapid devaluation. Not only was Brazil characterised by a low level of financial depth — which limited the spill over of crisis into the real economy — but the financial system itself had in recent years benefited from a number of beneficial structural reforms, not least the accelerated participation of foreign capital, the imposition of tougher minimum capital requirements in the banking system, technological upgrading of institutions and greater powers of intervention for the Central Bank. These developments ensured that the integrity of the financial system was maintained during and after devaluation, paving the way for the surprisingly rapid return to positive economic growth experienced in 1999 and 2000. The recovery that took place during these years also benefited, so the authors argue, from the successful implementation of an inflation-targeting framework. Thanks in large part to the coincidence of devaluation with generally depressed levels of economic activity, the inflationary pass-through effects of the *real*'s fall, proved to be both transient and limited.

In their chapter, Goldstein and Schneider adopt a longer-term, structural view of the Brazilian economy in the 1990s, focusing on the critical issue of corporate reorganisation. The authors argue that the decade constituted a period of considerable change for the Brazilian corporate sector. Over this period, quite apart from the signal macroeconomic shifts encapsulated in the launch of the *real* in 1994 and the abandonment of the exchange rate anchor four and a half years later, the Brazilian economy was subject to a series of far-reaching trade and market reforms. More particularly, from 1990 onwards a series of sweeping tariff cuts was put into place while non-tariff barriers were drastically pruned. With the wave of trade reform approaching its conclusion in the mid-1990s, the authorities changed tack and embarked upon an ambitious programme of market liberalisation, embracing accelerated privatisation, the opening up of key sectors to foreign investment and the launch of regulatory agencies. Against this background, enterprises throughout Brazil were faced with acute competitive challenges, the response to which proved to be relatively diverse, but which included technological upgrading and concerted attempts to drive up productivity. However, the authors' concern lies less with these developments than with the impact of trade and market reform on patterns of diversification, ownership and control.

Perhaps the most important single development observed by Goldstein and Schneider revolves around the evolution of ownership patterns within Brazilian industry. Over the course of the decade the authors observe a marked trend away from ownership by traditional family-owned groups, towards ownership by quasi public sector pension funds. The latter, representing the employees of recently privatised state enterprises, embarked on a large programme of corporate acquisition in the 1990s, taking stakes not only in privatised utilities but also in long-established private sector enterprises. At the same time, of course, the rising tide of foreign direct investment activity by multinational corporations also gave rise to a slew of corporate takeovers leading in a number of cases to a transfer of ownership from domestic to foreign investors.

Change in ownership is not the only important phenomenon analysed by the authors. The 1990s, so they argue, also witnessed changes in patterns of diversification and specialisation across and within key industrial sectors. In order to chart this development Goldstein and Schneider focus on the experience of a number of different enterprises including Vicunha, Gerdau, Votorantim, Embraer and Ambev. In undertaking this more disaggregated analysis the authors note highly diverse responses so far as specialisation and diversification are concerned. In the case of Vicunha and Votorantim a tendency towards continued conglomerisation is noted. By contrast Embraer and Gerdau appeared to have been pursuing a strategy of specialisation and capacity expansion. In the case of Brazil's largest brewer, Ambev, the strategy of specialisation has involved a marked increase in sectoral industrial concentration, giving rise to serious consumer welfare concerns. Weighing up the evidence, the authors come to the conclusion that while trade and market liberalisation may have provoked considerable change, the Brazilian industrial sector demonstrates only limited convergence towards Anglo-Saxon patterns of ownership, control and diversification.

In his chapter, Amann focuses less on issues of industrial structure, ownership and control and more on the impact of economic crisis and trade and market reform on the production process. The chapter begins with a summary of changes in the policy environment with which industry has been forced to contend over the past decade. In particular the issues of trade liberalisation and privatisation are highlighted. In terms of trade liberalisation, it is established that, by historical standards, the progressive reduction in tariffs and the abolition of non-tariff barriers that occurred in the 1990s had few, if any, precedents. At the same time, industry also had to contend with market de-regulation, the accelerated entry of foreign capital and the transfer of substantial chunks of industrial capacity from the public to the private sector.

Taken together these seismic shifts presented a severe competitive challenge to Brazilian industry, which had long enjoyed a substantial measure of protection from foreign competition if not an especially stable or buoyant domestic market. Having sketched out the policy background the chapter goes on to analyse firms' responses on the shop floor. A number of widespread responses are identified including the introduction of new capital equipment, the pursuit of Total Quality Management strategies and the physical re-organisation of the shop floor itself. Perhaps the most notable trend Amann highlights is a concerted attempt across industry to reduce working capital requirements through outsourcing and the implementation of Just In Time arrangements with suppliers. The latter development, it is argued, can in large part be traced to the impacts of tightening monetary policy on the cost of capital and, as such, represents a response to the evolving macroeconomic environment.

Having set out the nature of industry's response the chapter then goes on to trace the evolution of firms' competitive performance over the 1990s, focusing especially on the issues of productivity and export performance. While productivity performance may have been favourable by historical standards, growth in industrial exports remained disappointing throughout much of the 1990s. Following the devaluation of the *real* in January 1999, however, industrial export performance has improved somewhat, representing, perhaps, one of the more favourable longer-term consequences of the economic crisis. Unlike their South Korean counterparts, Amann argues, Brazilian firms have to some extent been insulated from some of the less desirable features of the crisis. Most notably, given their tendency to finance investment from retained earnings rather than through accessing (thin) domestic capital markets many Brazilian enterprises have been partially shielded from the effects of interest rate rises and credit crunches. However, the author concedes that Brazilian industrial enterprises in many other respects lag behind their South Korean equivalents in that they have to contend with a legacy of long-term under-investment in training and technology. In addition, despite a loud and sustained lobbying campaign, Brazilian industry continues to incur competitive disadvantage through the incidence of high indirect taxation, thin capital markets and infrastructural deficiencies. Fortunately, Amann argues, policymakers now appear more ready to confront these questions and address them through legislative reform. In particular, it is argued that recent developments such as the Law of S.A.s and the privatisation of some ports are likely to deliver significant competitive benefits over the next few years.

In the final chapter, Ramalho analyses the politically prominent issue of the evolution of the Brazilian labour market in the 1990s. Not unexpectedly, the industrial restructuring and shop floor reorganisation highlighted by Goldstein and Schneider and Amann has had a significant impact upon the structure and operation of the Brazilian labour market. Beginning his chapter, Ramalho draws attention to the unusual historical circumstances under which the Brazilian labour market has developed. With the accession to power of Getúlio Vargas in the 1930s a highly complex and comprehensive system of labour laws was enacted as part of a wider political project to induce what is now termed 'corporatism'. While other elements of corporatism eroded after World War II, the essential elements of Vargas' labour laws remained intact. Partly for this reason, the basic structure of the labour market endured right through into the 1980s. However, according to Ramalho, from the early 1990s onwards the depth and rapidity of trade and market reform was such that long-established patterns could no longer survive. With firms increasingly engaging in a process of outsourcing and de-verticalisation, the relative importance of the formal labour market fell.

In essence, for the author, the process of outsourcing represented a means through which enterprises could realise substantial savings in labour costs. In the new outsourced entities the use of formal labour contracts (governed by laws originating in the Vargas era) was far less prevalent than the use of informal arrangements. As a result, the 1990s saw a marked tendency towards the casualisation of employment. Added to this development, at least in the early 1990s, the Brazilian workforce had to contend with rapidly increasing unemployment and poor job prospects for those made redundant. Unable to find jobs associated with formal labour contracts, many redundant workers found employment in the informal sector, a process that has gained force with growing outsourcing in industry and the relatively rapid expansion of the services sector. The erosion of formal employment, Ramalho argues, has given rise to a concomitant reduction in labour organisation and trade union power.

The casualisation of employment and the declining role of organised labour are not the only defining features of the Brazilian labour market in the 1990s according to the author. For a very long period, large tracts of the Brazilian labour force have been associated with relatively low educational attainment and restricted on-the-job training. These features are argued to represent a significant challenge that will need to be addressed if some of the more undesirable recent features of the labour market are to be remedied. In addition, Ramalho directs attention towards two other ingrained and unwelcome aspects of the market; namely the relatively poor prospects experienced by women and Afro-Brazilians. Perhaps more unexpectedly, the chapter highlights the significant employment difficulties encountered by younger workers and, in particular, the tendency of this group to be especially associated with labour market casualisation. For Ramalho, these challenges are only likely to be effectively faced if the Brazilian economy is able to embark upon a prolonged phase of sustainable, rapid economic growth. In addition, it is argued that far more investment is needed in basic education and skills.

Turning to the South Korean case, Chang offers a rather unconventional interpretation in his chapter overviewing the causes, the management and the consequences of the 1997 financial crisis.

Chang critically examines a variety of conventional explanations that identify as the causes of the crisis some institutions and policies that are allegedly unique to Korea (some, but not all, of which are also found in other crisis-stricken Asian economies). They include: (i) industrial policy, which made corporate management lax by ensuring state rescue for firms in favoured industries; (ii) cronyism, which made possible the survival of inefficient but politically well-connected firms; (iii) (explicit and implicit) deposit insurance, which made the bank managers lax in their lending decisions; (iv) the logic of so-called 'too big to fail', which made large firms lax in their management because they expected to be bailed out of trouble thanks to their large size (and the consequent scale of knock-on effects on the rest of the economy); and (v) the peculiar nature of Korea's corporate sector (low profitability and excessively high financial leverage in particular). Criticising these explanations for their theoretical weaknesses and their lack of empirical supports, Chang argues that the crisis needs to be explained as resulting from the combination of the end to the 'traditional' industrial policy with the premature and ill-thought-out financial liberalisation (especially capital account liberalisation).

Chang then shows how the IMF has mismanaged the crisis through poor publicity campaigns ('crying "fire" in a crowded theatre'), excessively high interest rates (which drove even a lot of viable firms into bankruptcy) and the wrongly-timed introduction of the BIS (Bank for International Settlements) capital adequacy standards (which made banks cut down on loans on a large scale, starving the firms of credit). He also criticises the unwarranted incursion by the International Monetary Fund (IMF) into policy areas where they had neither the political mandate nor the technical expertise, such as corporate governance and labour law.

Acknowledging that the Korean economy recovered from the crisis more quickly than expected, Chang points out that the recovery is not as impressive as it seems. First of all, the apparently large scale of the recovery was due to the unnecessarily large downturn caused by the excessively contractionary macroeconomic policies imposed by the IMF in the early days of the crisis. Secondly, the recovery was accompanied by a much higher rate of unemployment and worse income distribution compared to the recovery from previous crises, especially the one in the early 1980s. It is also noted that the rapid pace of the recovery did not prove sustainable in the medium term.

More worrying than the quality of the recovery from the crisis, Chang argues, however, are the consequences of the post-crisis institutional changes for the long-term dynamism of the economy. According to Chang, despite some retention of the traditional interventionist streak in the process of industrial and financial restructuring (Haagh's chapter makes the same point in relation to labour market policy), the crisis has resulted in a number of important institutional changes. First of all, the link between industry and finance has been weakened through the emphases on reduction in corporate borrowing, on the one hand, and bank profitability and capital adequacy, on the other. Second, a range of 'pro-finance' policies were adopted — such as the introduction of an inflation-focused independent central bank and the granting of greater power to the shareholders in the running of the banks — which made the banks even more reluctant to lend to industrial firms. Finally, changes were made in the corporate governance and financing systems in ways that discourage long-term-oriented investments — for example, pressure to reduce corporate leverage and the policies to strengthen the power of shareholders more interested in financial profitability than long-term growth (also see Shin's chapter). Chang argues that these changes are likely to dampen the dynamism of the Korean economy in the long run by discouraging long-term-oriented investments.

Shin's chapter delves deeper into many of the more general observations made in Chang's chapter in relation to post-crisis industrial restructuring in Korea and comes up with some very sobering conclusions. Shin argues that a proper understanding of the Korean industrial and corporate systems requires an understanding of the 'big pictures' in terms of the country's industrial catching-up strategy and the process of globalisation that has influenced it. He argues that the Korean economic system combined a highly leveraged and diversified corporate sector with an effective developmental state that underwrote the risks involved in large-scale investments through its control of the financial system. This system was highly effective as a catching-up system until the 1980s, when the current phase of globalisation started accelerating.

The critical changes came from the early 1990s, when Korea started a large-scale liberalisation programme. Trade was further liberalised, industrial policy wound down and, most importantly, the financial market was deregulated and opened. Particularly important was the opening of the financial sector, which was partly due to external pressure but was also an attempt to strengthen the sector, which was deemed, rightly or wrongly, too underdeveloped for the country to survive the increasing challenges of globalisation. However, in line with Chang's arguments, Shin argues that this programme was poorly managed. Financial liberalisation led to the mushrooming of weak financial institutions, while an appropriate financial supervisory system was not put into place. Combined with the winding-down of industrial policy, financial liberalisation created a vacuum in the risk management system, as the traditional system of risk-sharing between the state, banks and the *chaebols* (the large conglomerates) broke down. The result was the financial crisis of 1997.

Shin argues that the post-crisis turn-around in the Korean corporate sector was *not* due to 'structural reforms' of the sector, as the popular view holds it, but due to changes in macroeconomic policy along the Keynesian line — the lowering of high interest rates, currency depreciation and an increase in budget deficits. In particular, Shin argues that the reduction in corporate leverage, the alleged proof of the success of Korean corporate reform, was more apparent than real — it was achieved by new stock issues, asset sales and asset revaluation, rather than by reduction in debt itself. This meant, when combined with the pressure on the banks to raise their profitability, a reduction in new investment financing through the banking system. Given the low internal reserves of the Korean corporations due to their short history, this means that Korean firms now have smaller pool of investment financing. According to Shin, the Korean government has tried to find alternative sources of industrial financing in the forms of foreign direct investment and the venture capital market, but there are some obvious limitations to such methods.

Shin concludes his chapter by arguing that what Korea needs is to build a new system for its 'second-stage catching-up', rather than trying to transplant the systems of the advanced, particularly Anglo-American, countries. He argues that the current industrial restructuring strategy puts too much emphasis on corporate financial prudence, no doubt an important matter, at the cost of the investment mobilisation necessary for catching-up. He argues that regaining the balance between financial prudence and high investment requires an adjustment of the old system, rather than its destruction. He argues that the strengths of the *chaebol* system, such as its ability to mobilise large investment resources and to spread risk through diversification and cross-subsidies, need to be preserved, and ways to reduce its negative consequences, such as unfair competition and the suppression of the small and medium-sized enterprises, need to be developed. Another plank in Shin's 'second-stage catching-up' system is the revitalisation of the state's role in managing systemic risk through appropriate industrial and financial sector policies, while adjusting its policies to the new realities of a maturing economy and intensifying globalisation.

Haagh's chapter looks at the other, and less well-known, side of Korea's post-crisis corporate restructuring — namely, the changes in the labour market and, more broadly, the employment system.

The conventional explanation of the post-crisis labour market changes in Korea is that the crisis has finally introduced the long-overdue discipline in the Korean labour market, which had suffered from extreme rigidities before the crisis (created both by government regulation and by private sector arrangements). According to this view, although the increased unemployment and poverty resulting from the crisis may have been painful in the short run, they were the necessary byproduct of the country's shift to a more market-based employment system with increased labour market flexibility. According to Haagh, however, this conventional explanation is correct neither in terms of its characterisation of pre-crisis Korean labour market nor in terms of its understanding of the post-crisis changes.

As for the pre-crisis Korean labour market, Haagh argues, it was in fact very 'flexible' on a number of indicators. True, firing of regular workers was highly restricted, but the country had a very high ratio of irregular (i.e., flexible) employment (one of the highest among the OECD countries) and a high voluntary mobility of workers. Haagh concludes from these observations, and comparisons with other countries like Chile or Denmark, that notions like 'free labour market' and 'labour market flexibility' are highly contentious and therefore need to be used with the utmost care.

As for the post-crisis adjustment, it is certainly true that firing has become a lot easier than before, but there have been a number of changes that do not support the 'greater marketisation' thesis. For example, despite the new labour law introduced just before the crisis that made firing easier, employers still relied mostly on more 'informal' measures to dismiss workers. Also following the crisis state involvement in the labour market became greater, rather than smaller, with the introduction of the Employment Insurance System and the strengthening of social welfare policy. Thus, Haagh argues, while in some important ways the Korean labour market has become 'freer' since the crisis, in other ways it has become less so.

Haagh's greatest concern is with the implications of the recent changes in the labour market for the country's long-term human resource management. She argues that, while increasing the short-term flexibility given to the employers in terms of hiring and firing decisions, the recent changes are likely to diminish the supply of skilled workers. With the reduction in employment commitment to the workers (as manifest in easier firing) and the resulting decline in reciprocal worker loyalty, there is less incentive for the employers to invest in worker skills. This means that there is a greater need for external training institutions like skill certification and transitional welfare support for the workers. Unfortunately, they remain weak at the moment (owing largely to the weakness of the political representation of labour), thus threatening the country's ability to ensure a long-term supply of high quality, skilled labour. Therefore, Haagh argues, if the increased power of dismissal by the Korean employers is not going to harm the long-run supply of skilled labour, institutions that deal with skill certification, retraining and social welfare need to be further strengthened.

Kong's chapter deals with the evolution Korea's government-business relations in the making and in the aftermath of the 1997 Korean crisis.

Kong traces the origins of the collaboration between political elite and business elite in Korea back to the Japanese colonial times (1910–45), but in his view it was the most intense in the 1970s during the period of the so-called Heavy and Chemical Industrialisation (HCI) under the military dictator General Park. However, strain in this relationship began to appear in the early 1980s, when the new military government of General Chun Doo Hwan associated itself with pro-market faction in the bureaucracy and implemented some liberalisation measures that hurt business, while increasing its extortion of political funding from business.

The strain was deepened, Kong argues, with the democratisation period since the late 1980s. During the post-democratisation period, however, it was the increasingly confident business elite, rather than the pro-market faction of the bureaucracy as in the early 1980s, that demanded liberalisation. The post-democratisation governments of General Roh Tae Woo and of Kim Young Sam (the first civilian president in over 30 years), while liberalising other aspects of the economy, actually tried to intensify the regulation over big business, being acutely aware of the problems arising from increasing concentration of economic power and mindful of popular distaste for big business. The result was an uneasy stalemate, where the state's attempt to rein in the big business was met with frequent reversals while the fragmentation of the state-business relationship made it more open to corruption, which in turn led to greater popular demands for reform.

The uneasy balance was broken, according to Kong, by the 1997 crisis and the election of Kim Dae Jung, the centre-left pro-democracy politician, as president just after the outbreak of the crisis. In Kong's view, Kim's policies have obviously been heavily constrained by the IMF conditionalities, but it is not as if he has blindly followed the IMF dictates. Kim's vision of 'democratic market economy', while sharing many aspects of the neo-liberal vision behind the IMF policies, was more complex than the standard neoliberal policies implemented in many other developing countries. For example, when implementing the labour market 'reform' programme demanded by the IMF, Kim's government tried to build political consensus for it through a tripartite commission (the first of the kind in the country's history) on 'burden-sharing' between labour and capital. In this commission it was hoped that the government could broker a deal between labour and capital, where labour unions would agree to accept mass redundancy in exchange for things like enhanced political rights, increased social welfare spending and reform in the corporate sector.

Kong's assessment of the Kim government's attempt at inclusionary politics is not entirely sanguine. He points out that the tripartite commission broke down, largely because the unions felt excluded from key decision-making and because the corporate reform offered in return for labour's sacrifice was considered too little and too slow. However, the very experience with the tripartite commission gave an unprecedented degree of legitimacy to the labour unions and other popular organisations, in a country where such actors had been at worst brutally repressed and at best marginalised from the political mainstream. Kong argues that, thanks to Kim's ideological inclination, pressures for neo-liberal shift in Korea did *not* result in the familiar pattern observed in many developing countries, where the coming to power of populist or leftist political parties has resulted in the atrophy, or even active repression, of labour unions and popular organisations.

CHAPTER 2

The Brazilian Crisis of 1998–99: Origins and Consequences

André Averbug and Fabio Giambiagi[*]

I n December 1994 Mexico devalued its currency by more than 50 per cent. The consequences of this development proved to be disastrous, at least in the following year. Inflation reached over 50 per cent, GDP dropped around five per cent and the country was gripped by a severe financial crisis. When South Korea was forced to devalue in 1997, inflation behaved much better — it stayed below ten per cent — but GDP suffered a contraction similar to that of Mexico. With the financial crisis reaching drastic proportions the need to promote a programme of financial restructuring was underlined as never before. However, such a programme has yet to be completed. Contrasting with these experiences, when Brazil's turn to devalue the *real* (R$) came in 1999, inflation followed a path similar to that of Korea, GDP experienced modest growth, and nothing close to a financial crisis occurred.

Surprisingly or not, these events were not positively viewed by the Brazilian electorate in the first instance. This was in large part due to the fact that the devaluation had been overseen by the recently elected president and by his finance minister who, in the previous years, had been among the greatest supporters of currency stability. By drastically changing the exchange rate, the government's popularity dropped in proportion to the dollar's appreciation. Perhaps this was understandable, given the emblematic character of the exchange rate in Brazilian economic life. Nevertheless, based on what was said, and comparing the Brazilian situation with that of the other countries that abandoned their more or less rigid exchange rate regimes between 1994[1] and 1999, Brazil experienced the most successful change in an exchange rate regime among all emerging countries, with a substantial real devaluation and a relatively modest cost in terms of the level of activity and inflation.

---

[*] The authors thank James Dinsmoor, Mauricio Mesquita Moreira and Armando Castelar Pinheiro for their comments on a preliminary version of this chapter, excluding them, of course, from any responsibility with regards to its final content.

[1] When, with the 'tequila effect', the 'first financial crisis of the twenty-first century took place', according to M. Camdessus.

How did these events unfold? What characterised the deterioration of Brazil's economic situation throughout the first term of President Fernando Henrique Cardoso? How did the country overcome the crisis in 1999? What may be expected of the new situation? These and other related questions are the issues that this chapter seeks to address.

This chapter is divided into seven sections. The next section describes the arguments of the supporters of the fixed exchange rate strategy during the 1997–98 crisis. The central idea was that Brazil was a special case and, therefore, could sustain its exchange rate policy. Next, a chronology of the Brazilian crisis is presented, from the 1997 Asian crisis until the eruption of the currency crisis in January 1999. The fourth section explains what happened during 1999–2000. The final two sections constitute the analytical core of this chapter: first, attention is drawn to the regime change in Brazilian economic policy in 1999, under the 'umbrella' agreement with the International Monetary Fund (IMF). Here, it is stressed that the greatest test of the new regime was to happen in 2002, with the expiry of the accord. Second, the authors explore why Brazil did not have a financial crisis. The chapter ends with a series of concluding observations.

Why Brazil was not Thailand (or was it?)

Even though the Asian crisis of 1997–98 is a recent phenomenon and might therefore have been expected to generate profuse academic debate, most analyses carried out on the episodes that successively shook the economies of Thailand, South Korea, Indonesia and Malaysia concur in pointing out the fragility of the financial system as one of the most important explanatory factors of the crisis. Financial fragility was associated, in turn, with a previous boom, which could thus be characterised as the origin of an 'overlending crisis'.

Notwithstanding the particularities of each country, the common denominator of these processes, in general terms, was the combination of:

a) An investment boom fuelled by the increasing indebtedness of households, firms and countries

b) The high leverage of banks

c) The lack of appropriate bank supervision

d) Mounting short-term external obligations of firms and banks

e) Fixed, or relatively fixed, exchange rates in a context of increasing current account deficits

In such circumstances, as stated by a local analyst regarding South Korea's case (but whose observation could equally apply to the other countries involved), the crisis was the combination of 'a currency crisis and a financial crisis'.[2]

Two sets of figures illustrate the dimension of the problem: a) according to the BIS, in June 1997 the banking system's external debt as a percentage of international reserves was 216 per cent in Korea, 157 per cent in Indonesia and 141 per cent in Thailand;[3] and b) credit to the private sector, in 1996, had reached 170 per cent of GDP in Korea, 130 per cent in Thailand, 120 per cent in Malaysia and 80 per cent in Indonesia.[4] The success of these economies in such circumstances depended on a 'perpetual motion engine', with growth generating revenue flows that would allow for new investment leverage and so on. In such an environment, it was evident that the stagnation of the economy could have major negative effects on the payment capability of different economic agents, generating a series of 'domino-effect' bankruptcies, where the failure of payment of one agent impedes the ability of lenders to pay their own debts to third parties. This situation stands only a step away from a financial crisis.

The deterioration of the Asian countries' terms of trade, caused by price decreases of key export goods, is understood by some analysts as the critical point of the crisis. Exchange rate rigidity, combined with the short maturity of outstanding external debts, were the two ingredients needed to generate a serious crisis. With a relatively fixed currency and difficulties in sustaining its level, the temptation to buy foreign currency given the upcoming (and predictable) crisis was very high. What happened, then, was a succession of 'self-fulfilling prophecies'.

When Thailand triggered the series of crises in 1997 that affected Asia in that year, the Brazilian authorities made an effort to contrast the Brazilian case from that of the Asian countries who, one after another, started to show the same crisis symptoms that Thailand had experienced. A similar effort had been made — with significant success — in 1995 to show that 'Brazil was not Mexico'.

What were the main arguments in pro of the distinct nature of the Brazilian case? In brief, it was argued that:

i)   Thailand's current account deficit in 1996 was, coincidentally, basically the same as Mexico's in 1994 — about eight per cent of GDP — and more than twice, as a percentage of GDP, that of Brazil at that time.

---

2   Shin and Hahm (1998), p. 1.
3   IDEA (1998). For comparative purposes, based on the same table, this proportion in Brazil was 78%.
4   *Ibid.*

ii)　In contrast to what was happening in Mexico (and in Asia), Brazil was initiating a process of gradual real devaluation of its exchange rate, keeping nominal devaluation at around seven to eight per cent per annum, in a context of declining inflation (around two to three per cent per annum).

iii)　In the 1997–99 period, Brazil would be the recipient of large capital inflows as a result of the privatisation of state companies. In May 1997, Bacha and Welch (1997) estimated that Brazil's privatisation potential was US$56 billion for the 1997–99 period. If two thirds of these resources originated from overseas — which was a realistic scenario — it would represent an annual flow of US$12 billion, enough to finance, per se, more than a third of projected of the US$30 billion current account deficit expected for 1997.

iv)　Even without considering privatisation, however, direct investment was already sharply increasing in Brazil: excluding the privatisation inflows but including the portfolio resources, the net inflow of direct investment reached US$5 billion in 1995, US$13 billion in 1996 and US$16 billion in 1997; it seemed reasonable, therefore, to imagine that the sum of 'pure' direct investment plus privatisation would suffice to finance a substantial part of the current account deficit of the following years. This would enable the country 'to gain time' to promote a gradual real devaluation of its currency and stimulate exports through non-exchange rate mechanisms, in a context of unrestricted international finance.

v)　Brazil had the prospect of a stable economic policy. There was no prospect of a change in government in the short run, with the president leading the polls in the run up to the 1998 elections. Moreover, there was unity among the economic policymaking team, a fact which left little space for dissension regarding the implementation of future economic policy.

vi)　Lastly, the indicators of credit expansion in Brazil differed substantially from those shown by Asia, as total amount of credit provided by the public and private financial systems amounted to only 30 per cent of GDP, far less than the numbers previously shown for the East Asian countries (Figure 2.1).

Figure 2.1: Credit (per cent GDP)

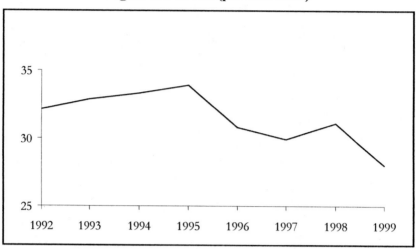

Source: Central Bank

Analysing the arguments retrospectively, it cannot be said that they were wrong. In fact, the Brazilian external deficit never reached the same relative dimension of other countries; the real exchange rate suffered a devaluation of seven to eight per cent in 1998; privatisation was very extensive in 1997 and 1998; external investment kept increasing; the president was re-elected and the finance minister stayed in his job; and domestic credit remained limited.

Why then, contrary to the government's previous policy stance, was Brazil ultimately obliged to devalue its currency? What went wrong? There are two fundamental factors that explain this change. The first was the adverse shock of relative prices: between the months of January 1997 and 1999 — when devaluation took place — the price index of primary and semi-manufacturing goods exported by Brazil fell by 15 per cent and 17 per cent, respectively. The second was the closure of the international markets for credit after the Russian crisis, in August 1998. The Brazilian strategy assumed that the country would have time to make the necessary adjustments, while the rest of the world financed a temporarily elevated deficit on the current account. However, the price shock aggravated this imbalance. The Russian crisis, in turn, meant that the time allowed for this adjustment had expired.[5]

---

5   It is worth noting that these two effects also hit Argentina, which, nevertheless, succeeded in maintaining the parity of its currency. There are a few reasons, however, to explain this difference. First, the Argentine fiscal indicators in 1997 and 1998 were substantially better than Brazil's, generating better 'goodwill' in the market with

Table 2.1: Public Sector Net Debt (per cent GDP)

Composition	1994	1995	1996	1997	1998	1999	2000/p
Domestic debt	**17.6**	**21.8**	**27.0**	**26.7**	**32.6**	**34.5**	**34.5**
Central Government	3.0	6.6	12.0	13.3	17.3	17.7	18.0
Bonds	11.6	15.5	21.4	28.3	36.3	39.9	42.0
Assets	-8.6	-8.9	-9.4	-15.0	-19.0	-22.2	-24.0
States and Municipalities	9.5	10.3	11.1	12.5	14.0	15.6	15.5
State companies	5.1	4.9	3.9	0.9	1.3	1.2	1.0
External debt	**8.4**	**5.5**	**3.9**	**4.3**	**6.4**	**10.5**	**10.5**
Central Government	6.2	3.5	1.6	1.9	4.3	8.0	8.0
States and Municipalities	0.3	0.3	0.4	0.5	0.7	0.9	1.0
State companies	1.9	1.7	1.9	1.9	1.4	1.6	1.5
Total debt /a	**26.0**	**27.3**	**30.9**	**31.0**	**39.0**	**45.0**	**45.0**
Central Government	9.2	10.1	13.6	15.2	21.6	25.7	26.0
States and Municipalities	9.8	10.6	11.5	13.0	14.7	16.5	16.5
State Companies	7.0	6.6	5.8	2.8	2.7	2.8	2.5

a/ Excluding monetary basis.
/p: Preliminar.
Source: Central Bank.

Chronology of the Crisis[6]

After the Asian crisis of 1997, it became clear to everyone, including the government, that Brazil would have to change its economic policy in order to ameliorate its two main sources of macroeconomic imbalance: the budget and current account deficits. The first represented the systematic

---

regard to the country's situation. Second, the perception existed that the country would hesitate before devaluing, which practically eliminated the possibility that it would be an option for the government and decreased the speculative demand for reserves, associated with the fear that the government would change its mind. Third, Argentina maintained parity, but suffered a three% contraction of GDP in 1999, in contrast to modest positive growth in Brazil. Fourth, the strategy of extending the external debt sought in the previous years by the Argentine authorities proved efficient, generating a relative need for amortisation payments smaller than in Brazil in 1998 and 1999. Of course, circumstances were to change dramatically subsequently.

6   For further discussion see Giambiagi (1998) and Franco (1999a).

deterioration of the primary results — that is the nominal deficit excluding interest — of the consolidated public sector, generating an increase in public debt (Table 2.1); and the second the increase — also systematic — of the current account deficit/GDP ratio (Table 2.2). The solution to these imbalances required a combination of expenditure cuts and revenue increases, on one hand, and an increase in the external competitiveness of Brazilian products — fundamentally associated with a lower real exchange rate — on the other.

The chosen path was gradualism. When data from 1998 and 1997 are compared, an improvement of the primary fiscal result, together with a real currency devaluation can be noted. These adjustments, though, fell far short of what was required in light of the developments that actually took place, especially in the second half of 1998. Using an often cited metaphor, it can be said that Brazil changed the course of the *Titanic*, but this change, being slow and delayed, was not enough to avoid collision with the iceberg — in this case, the external crisis. Why gradualism was chosen as opposed to a shock strategy is an open question. However, its answer would certainly involve the combination of three elements: i) a certain amount of confidence by the authorities that they could overcome the effects of the Asian crisis, along the lines of their success in 1995 after the Mexican crisis (an episode promptly forgotten by the international market); ii) the fear that a debacle might result from a more intense devaluation such as occurred in Mexico in 1995, when inflation reached 50 per cent iii) the realisation of general elections in October 1998 in that no government, anywhere in the world, likes to implement a shock treatment in an electoral year.

The events of the first half of 1998 seemed to support the official optimism. The country risk indicators, after the October 1997 deterioration, improved substantially. International reserves began to recover and, in this context, interest rates, which had reached almost 40 per cent at the end of 1997, declined to less than 20 per cent by mid-1998. In July the government successfully conducted the privatisation of Telebrás — one of the 'crown jewels' of the Brazilian public sector — and, with the prospect of President Cardoso's re-election – something the market had already anticipated — there was a favourable expectation in the economic arena that he, once in power again, would do 'something' — still not defined — to improve the fiscal accounts. The country would face a cautiously optimistic scenario of gradual improvement in external accounts beginning in 1999, together with moderate inflation.

Table 2.2: Brazil – Trade Balance and Foreign Direct Investment — US$ billion

	1990	1991	1992	1993	1994	1995	1996	1997	1998	1999	2000/a
1- Trade balance	10752	10579	15239	13117	10843	-3353	-5556	-8365	-6591	-1211	-500
Exports	31414	31620	35793	38597	43544	46506	47747	52989	51140	48011	56000
Imports	20661	21041	20554	25480	32701	49859	53303	61354	57731	49222	56500
2- Services	-15369	-13542	-11539	-15215	-14743	-18600	-21044	-27289	-28799	-25886	-26300
2.1- Interest	-9748	-8621	-7253	-8280	-6337	-8158	-9173	-10390	-11948	-15270	-15500
2.2- Profits and remittances	-1865	-1030	-949	-1931	-2566	-2790	-2821	-5749	-7305	-4099	-4000
2.3- Other services	-3756	-3891	-3337	-5004	-5839	-7652	-9050	-11150	-9546	-6517	-6800
2.3.1- Travel	-121	-211	-319	-799	-1181	-2420	-3594	-4377	-4146	-1460	-2000
2.3.2- Transports	-1644	-1656	-1359	-1700	-2441	-3200	-3480	-4514	-3259	-3096	-3300
2.3.3- Insurance	-68	-133	-58	-65	-132	-122	-64	74	81	-128	0
2.3.4- Government	-328	-370	-166	-345	-327	-339	-275	-350	-385	-498	-500
2.3.5- Other	-1595	-1521	-1436	-2095	-1759	-1572	-1637	-1983	-1837	-1335	-1000
3- Unilateral transfers	834	1556	2243	1653	2588	3974	2899	2216	1778	2032	1800
Current account	-3782	-1407	5943	-444	-1312	-17979	-23701	-33438	-33612	-25065	-25000
Memo: Net FDI /b	169	-43	1443	-380	934	2569	9966	15516	22619	28608	28000

/a Author's forecast.
/b Excluding portfolio.
Source: Central Bank.

This, then, was the context in which Russia defaulted on its debt in August 1998. Contrary to what happened previously to Mexico, or even Asia, this time the international financial markets closed almost completely — and for a long time — to emerging market nations, particularly those seen as having chronic problems. In part, the negative track record of Brazil explains this kind of extreme reaction.

The effects on Brazil were devastating. In the third trimester of 1998 rudimentary calculations showed that the country's external accounts for 1999 simply 'did not close'. This generated speculation in the press that, for this reason, Brazil would need to adopt some form of capital controls. Brazil, however, which had a *flow* problem in 1999 — in the sense that the predicted current account deficit would be larger than the predicted capital inflow — started to face a *portfolio reallocation* problem with economic agents in general. The emergence of this problem was due to the need of agents to recover losses suffered with Russia, the fear of a Brazilian external default or simply the pending likelihood of devaluation. Not surprisingly, this set of circumstances provoked a massive capital flight. In fact, by the first week of August, right after the financial liquidation of the first payment of Telebrás sale, Brazil's international reserves had reached almost US$75 billion. Only 50 days later, however, by the end of September — labelled 'black September' — Brazil lost US$30 billion of its reserves (Figure 2.2).

Figure 2.2: International Reserves — US$ billion — International Liquidity Concept

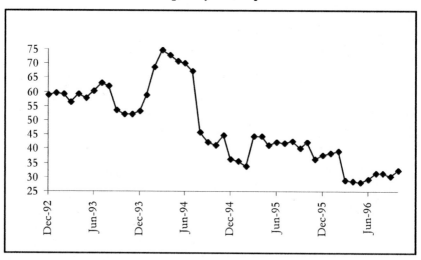

Source: Central Bank

It was in this context that, a few weeks from presidential elections, the government officially announced that it was negotiating with the IMF an agreement to rectify this situation. The agreement was based on four pillars: i) a strong fiscal adjustment; ii) a tight monetary policy — the interest rates increased to approximately 40 per cent again in mid-September; iii) an external rescue package — from the IMF, multilateral organisations and G7 countries — of US$42 billion; and iv) the maintenance of the 'crawling peg' exchange rate policy, a policy issue where change was still considered a 'taboo' by the authorities.

The announcement of external aid — despite the fact that the details had not been released — the launch of the first adjustment measures and the confirmation of President Cardoso's victory in the first round of the elections enabled the government to finally catch its breath. The country-risk levels dropped again and interest rates again declined, falling to around 30 per cent (Figure 2. 3), and the government made preparations to receive the promised external aid. The authorities, despite the loss in credibility due to the successive traumatic and brusque changes in policy, believed that history could be repeated, with interest rates — as after the Mexican and the Asian crises — decreasing and the economy returning to its normal rhythm. However, popular opinion held that this optimistic scenario was unattainable while the view that, ultimately, Brazil would be forced to devalue continued to gain currency. Nevertheless, the government still hoped that the situation would gradually improve.

Figure 2.3: Nominal Interest Rate — Overnight (per cent)

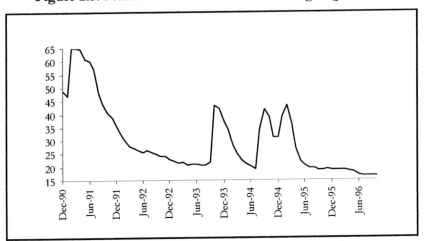

Source: Central Bank

The coup de grâce to the official strategy was delivered by a combination of two events. In December, almost at the same time that the IMF approved the aid package to Brazil, Congress rejected one of its most important adjustment measures. A few weeks later, in early January 1999, the government of the state of Minas Gerais, which had assumed power only a few days earlier, called for a temporary *default* of its domestic debt with the federal government. Even though the fiscal effect of this latter measure was practically nil — because the federal government had mechanisms to compensate this through the reduction of the legal transfers it regularly made to the State — the combined impact of both measures was dramatic. On one hand, the possibility that Brazil would start receiving resources from the IMF and fail to reach the fiscal targets, revived old prejudices against the country in the international financial markets: the seven letters of intention signed and not honoured in the 1980s were insistently quoted. On the other hand, the spectre of a 'default' was reintroduced in a context where the transfer of resources from one place to another occurred with extreme facility, agility and on a much more intense scale than in the 1980s.

Almost as soon as this happened, the government reacted to these events with the habitual renewal of the promises of monetary and fiscal austerity. At that point, though, scepticism had become rampant. Additionally, strict adherence to monetary austerity itself created two additional problems. First, operating with interest rates of over 30 per cent with no inflation, implied an increase in the public debt by almost one-third in one year, something unimaginable considering it had already increased from 26 per cent to 38 per cent of GDP between 1994 and 1998. Second, since the fiscal targets of the IMF agreement were expressed in terms of the expected behaviour of the Public Sector Borrowing Requirements (PSBR), either the additional interest rates would have to be offset by equivalent primary adjustments — something virtually impossible given the dimension of the rates — or, alternatively, the fiscal targets of the agreement would not be honoured in the first quarter of the year.

In mid-January, then, Brazilian credibility reached very low levels. Economic agents were convinced, day after day, that devaluation was inevitable. Drazen and Masson described the uselessness of certain 'tough messages' when the market simply did not believe them to be viable:

> Our results may be illustrated by a simple story. One afternoon, a colleague announces to you that he is serious about losing weight and plans to skip dinner. He adds that he has not eaten for two days. Does this information make it more or less credible that he really will skip dinner? [Some models imply] that with each meal he skips, the 'tough policy' of skipping the next meal becomes more credible, as each

observation of playing tough raises the probability we assign to his being a fanatic dieter. Once we realise that his skipping one meal makes him hungrier at the next mealtime (i.e., that policy has persistent effects), we are led to the opposite conclusion, namely, that it becomes less likely he will stick to his diet the more meals he has skipped.[7]

In the Brazilian case, the idea that the government was losing its autonomy to be able to decide over the maintenance of its currency policy was reinforced by the fact that the original agreement with the IMF, signed when the exchange rate was still controlled, established that 'adjusted net international reserves' — defined as gross reserves minus the gross official obligations — could not be less than US$20 billion. It is worth mentioning that gross reserves were approximately US$40 billion when the IMF agreement was approved. By definition, the resources from external loans did not affect the concept of net reserves because they increased gross reserves but also the obligations. In fact, then, the IMF agreement limited the Central Bank margin of intervention with respect to the defence of the currency policy. Worse, in fact, it may have stimulated the demand for reserves, once it had undermined the manoeuvring space that the authorities had in which to react to what was clearly becoming a speculative attack.

In the first days of January 1999 the reserve loss was dramatic. By the end of the controlled exchange rate regime reserve losses approached US$1 billion a day. On 13 January the government announced the replacement of the Central Bank president and the adoption of a band system, which in fact represented a nine per cent devaluation. This could have been an interesting idea in other circumstances, but it was not viable, given the huge uncertainty that prevailed at that time. Consequently, the loss of reserves continued and, on the first day of the band system, the exchange rate reached its ceiling.

Once again, we saw the same script that had been played out in other currency crises where, after the government 'blinked', nobody believed in its promises that the new limit would be respected. The new system lasted exactly 48 hours. Finally, due to the absolute lack of alternatives, the Central Bank let the currency fluctuate on 15 January.[8] Brazil experienced,

---

7   Drazen and Masson (1994), p. 736.
8   In the words of a Central Bank ex-president, Afonso Celso Pastore, the abandoning of the controlled currency policy followed between 1994 and the beginning of 1999, in the circumstances it occurred, represented an initial relief similar to that of a puncture. Once rid of the 'infection' that was causing the bleeding of reserves, it was necessary to put in place a wide series of measures so that the country could overcome the crisis. However, at that moment the feeling was that either the previous regime was to be abandoned, or the country would be left with no reserves, or even that an external default would become inevitable.

then, a textbook case of overshooting. Before the currency was floated the exchange rate was at R\$/US\$1.21. On 14 January it reached the band's ceiling: 1.32. At the end of January it reached 1.98;[9] and then at the beginning of March — the peak of devaluation — it soared to 2.16.

Krugman's analysis of the Asian crises of 1997–98 has become well known not least for its observation that existing models of crisis had conspicuously failed to explain events.[10] In the 'first generation' models,[11] a government with successive fiscal deficits tries to maintain a certain currency parity that the agents perceive as unsustainable over time, which promotes a speculative attack against the currency. In the 'second generation' models,[12] the propagation mechanism of the crisis is different because, even though the exchange rate is defendable, currency policy has a cost for the government, represented by the interest rate required to win over the confidence of the economic agents regarding the maintenance of the policy. The Brazilian external crisis had a few components of the second-generation models, where self-fulfilling prophecies play an important role. It was, nevertheless, largely a classical textbook crisis — that is, of a first generation crisis — where fiscal and current account imbalances, and a rigid exchange rate regime, led to a successive gradual loss of reserves, speculative attack and devaluation. The Asian crisis may have caught analysts by surprise and left many perplexed. In the Brazilian crisis case, though, it was an outcome expected by many of the — increasingly numerous — critics. Moreover, the government knew perfectly well that such a crisis could happen, given the events in Mexico in 1995 and in Asia in 1997–98.

A few weeks later, with the economy in the process of normalisation, the dollar appreciated to 1.65. In the overshooting phase of the devaluation, however, a situation close to panic emerged with respect to what

---

9   On the last day of January, facing the risk of losing control over the inflationary process, with internal conflicts within the economic staff and in the midst of conflicts between the Central Bank's president and the IMF mission, President Cardoso dismissed the president of the Central Bank, naming Mr Arminio Fraga for the post. For approximately 40 days, though, Brazil, in the midst of a dramatic currency crisis, stood in the bizarre situation of having simultaneously four Central Bank presidents: Gustavo Franco, who left on 13 January but had not formally passed his post onto his successor; Francisco Lopes, approved by the Senate but dismissed before the formal ceremony of job handover; the director of External Affairs, who became the provisional president; and the new president, Arminio Fraga, who could only take over after being approved by the Senate and was only confirmed in March. Thus, with two leadership changes in the supreme monetary authority in 20 days, the lack of a president in post and absence of directors in the Central Bank, it is difficult to think of a worse scenario in which to implement a change in currency regime!

10   Krugman (1998).

11   Krugman (1979).

12   Obstfeld (1994).

could happen with the public debt.[13] The latter closed 1998 at 38 per cent of GDP. Nevertheless, the debt affected by devaluation – that proportion of the external debt and internal debt in bonds, that was indexed as 'dollar linked' to the exchange rate – before it occurred, was of approximately 15 per cent of GDP. With the hike in nominal interest rates during January, the nominal devaluation of 64 per cent that took place between December and January (and even before the nominal drop of the exchange rate),[14] the public debt in January reached 48 per cent of GDP: a ten-point GDP jump in only 30 days.

The analysis that debt was following an explosive path and the threat of a default of the internal debt brought to life old ghosts and the trauma of March 1990, when President Fernando Collor blocked a substantial part of the country's financial savings. Specifically, on the last business day of January, there was a race to the banks all over the country and a generalised rumour — though unfounded, as it later turned out — that the government would declare a bank holiday and President Cardoso would default on the internal debt, in a fashion similar to President Collor previously.[15] In this context, the original agreement with the IMF would have turned into dust only a month after it had been formally approved by that institution's board in December 1998.

The End of Gradualism: What Happened in 1999?

In the light of what had happened at the beginning of the year, the path followed by the various macroeconomic variables in the months following the devaluation was simply unimaginable. Nobody could have guessed that, in the context of the exchange rate overshooting which lasted until March, the year would end with inflation — in terms of consumer prices —below ten per cent and a small increase in GDP.

The turning point was the fact that Arminio Fraga took office at the Central Bank in March and the important decisions that were made during the next few months. The economic staff, after a few weeks of absolute silence, acted vigorously. First, they took the crucial decision, despite criticisms, to raise nominal interest rates again. This was essential to avoid real rates becoming negative. Thus, the same mistake that had doomed previ-

---

13   The public debt concept used in this chapter refers to the net debt of the consolidated public sector, but excludes the monetary base, which is computed as debt in the official statistics. For comparative purposes, it is important to recall that the monetary base in Brazil has been around 3 to 4% of GDP in the last few years.

14   Not to mention that, in fact, the price increase that followed this change inflated GDP.

15   It was on this day, in the face of complete apathy on the part of the Central Bank, which was also paralysed by the impasse of the IMF negotiations, that President Cardoso decided to promote the second change in the Central Bank's presidency.

ous stabilisation plans was avoided. Second, the economic team combined with political leaders promptly to approve the remaining planks of the adjustment programme. Finally, the economic team organised a series of 'road shows' around the world with the objective of reopening credit lines, whose closure was holding back the normalisation of the country's commercial relations. It was this package of initiatives that, even by March, had generated substantial nominal appreciation (see Figure 2.4). At the end of the year, taking as a reference the wholesale price indexes, the real devaluation December–December was limited to 22 per cent. In the case of real exchange rate index, it was substantially higher at 44 per cent (Figure 2.5).

Figure 2.4: Exchange Rate — R$/US$ — End of Period

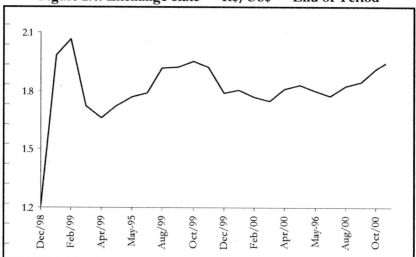

Source: Central Bank

Inflation, if measured by the Consumer Price Index (CPI), followed an amazingly moderate trend, closing the year below 9.0 per cent, which, given the nominal devaluation of 48 per cent, implied a pass-through of just 0.19. This was something that not even the most optimistic defender of the devaluation could have predicted. In only four of the 12 months of the year was the CPI monthly inflation index higher than one per cent (Figure 2.6). This, by the way, was partially due to the hike in the oil prices in the international market —which started the year at approximately US$15/barrel and later reached US$30. The latter generated unbearable pressures, leading the government to implement successive price increases for gasoline and other oil derivatives throughout the year.

Figure 2.5: Real Exchange Rate (June 1994 = 100)

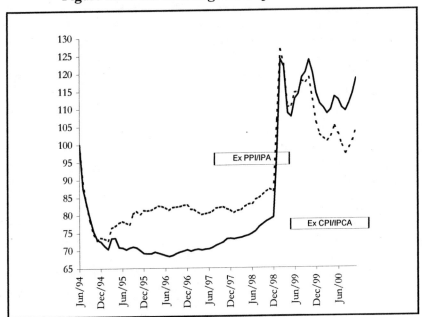

Figure 2.6: Monthly Inflation — CPI (per cent)

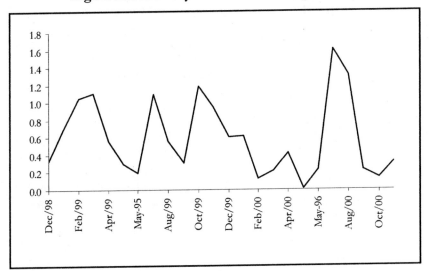

With respect to activity levels, the majority of foreign analysts committed major forecasting mistakes with regard to what could happen to GDP after the devaluation. There were reasons to fear a strong increase in inflation, which ended up not happening, but the predictions of GDP decrease were clearly exaggerated. Some foreign investment banks, in their analysis about Brazil, stated with conviction that the fall in GDP could reach six or seven per cent, similar to levels in Mexico and Korea as a consequence of their respective crises. Three reasons, though, supported the hypothesis that this would be unlikely to occur in Brazil:

i)   Unlike those countries, Brazil had already experienced recession in the previous year, making it difficult to believe in a new and profound decrease in the level of activity given the scenario of already low demand.

ii)   Historically, Brazil had had two very grave crises in the past 50 years: the external debt crisis in the beginning of the 1980s and the contraction caused by the blocking of financial assets in 1990, during the Collor Plan. During the latter, for a whole month many sectors simply ceased production, affecting the annual result. Nevertheless, in neither of these cases was the fall of GDP greater than four per cent.

iii)   In Brazil, nothing close to a financial crisis and its typical 'domino-effect' happened, as had occurred in both Mexico and Korea.

In any event, due to the decrease in real wages and the high real interest rates observed at the beginning of the year, it was reasonable to imagine a drop in GDP. The government, though, out of fear at being considered excessively optimistic — a sin it had already committed in the past and which caused a loss in its credibility — opted to be conservative and officially assumed that GDP would drop between three and four per cent in 1999.

The observed trajectory, though, was completely different. In fact, in seasonally adjusted terms, GDP began to grow in the first quarter of the year compared to the previous quarter (Figure 2.7). The reasons for this have been linked to two factors: i) a movement towards import substitution by industry, with the greatest increases in production occurring in those sectors where the demand for imports fell the most; and ii) the drop in real interest rates.[16] At the same time, the contraction of real wages that

16   To measure real interest rates in a situation of relative price change is always difficult. The fact is, however, that, in the end, the nominal overnight rate stayed at 25.6% in 1999, against a variation of industrial prices in January–December of 28.3%. Therefore, the reality in terms of real interest rates turned out to be significantly different from what was initially feared, when prices had not yet increased and interest rates were stratospherically high. To have an idea of the contrast with the previous situation, in 1998, the nominal overnight rate was 28.8% and industrial prices dropped 0.2%.

was initially predicted did not occur at the level expected due to the moderate inflation. Consequently, a strong contraction of consumption outlays did not happen. For this reason, GDP ended up having a slightly positive growth of around one per cent, due basically to the negative carryover inherited from 1998. If we compare the GDP from the last quarter of 1999 with the same quarter of 1998, however, there was an increase of 3.5 per cent. In this context, unemployment remained remarkably stable at approximately 7.5 per cent because, although employment did not grow, the number of those seeking work fell as discouraged workers temporarily gave up the search for jobs.

Figure 2.7: Quarterly GDP, Seasonally Adjusted (1990 = 100)

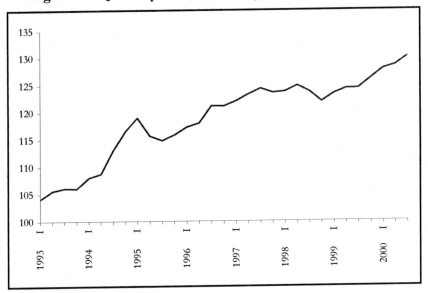

Source: IBGE

In general terms, January 1999 marked the end of the gradualist strategy used to confront the crisis. As stated before, the primary balance of the non-financial public sector had improved in 1998 in respect to 1997 at the same time that the real exchange rate had already been devaluating in real terms. The crisis, though, precipitated the realisation that the government had to be much faster in the external and fiscal adjustment process. Besides letting the exchange rate fluctuate, it adopted extremely ambitious targets for the public accounts in the context of the IMF agreement. In the agreement negotiated at the end of 1998, before the devaluation, the target was to achieve a consolidated primary surplus of 2.6, 2.8 and 3.0 per cent of GDP for the years 1999, 2000 and 2001, respectively. When the agreement was revised, after the devaluation, two important modifications were made on the fiscal side.

The first was the substitution of the Public Sector Borrowing Requirement (PSBR) by the primary surplus as a performance criterion to evaluate the agreement. In the final version of the 1998 accord the primary surplus was included in the calculations that generated the agreement, but the formal target was represented by the PSBR, which left the agreement too vulnerable in the face of an eventual need to tighten monetary policy. Brazil argued — reasonably — that, in the context of uncertainty that surrounded interest rates at the beginning of 1999, it would be dangerous to assume PSBR targets, and it managed to convince the IMF authorities to change the performance criteria.

The second modification was an increase in the primary surplus targets, to 3.10 per cent, 3.25 per cent and 3.35 per cent of GDP in 1999, 2000 and 2001, respectively (Table 2.3).[17] The movement was justified because, with the increase in public debt caused by devaluation, the primary surplus necessary to meet (at the end of the three-year programme) a certain target of the relationship debt/GDP would have to be higher to compensate for the increase in debt. For a country with such a negative fiscal record and with the prospects of a fall in per capita income for the second consecutive year, going from an equilibrium in the primary result to a surplus of 3,1 per cent of GDP in only one year was a major challenge. This challenge was only politically feasible given the 'feeling of being a step away from the precipice', that dominated the country's leadership at the time.[18]

Table 2.3: Primary Surplus — IMF Agreement (per cent GDP)

	1999	2000	2001/a
Central Government	2.50	2.65	2.60
States and municipalities	0.30	0.50	0.65
State companies	0.30	0.10	0.10
Total	3.10	3.25	3.35

/a Total surplus lately revised: 3.00% of GDP.

17   The target for 2001 was reduced to 3.00% of GDP in 2000 within a more favourable scenario.
18   For a description of the historic problems of the Brazilian public sector, see Giambiagi and Além (1999).

Contrary to the expectations of the majority of analysts and the nation's historical record, however, Brazil achieved all the performance criteria — including the 3.1 per cent of GDP primary surplus target — that had been agreed to with the IMF for 1999 (Table 2.4). Contributing to this achievement was the fact that inflation, despite remaining within the limits desired by the government, somehow 'facilitated' the real fall in expenditure.

Table 2.4: Public Sector Borrowing Requirements — PSBR (per cent GDP)

	1998	1999	2000/a
PSBR /b	7.58	5.85	4.10
Central Government /b	5.00	2.74	2.10
States and Municipalities	2.05	3.18	2.40
State companies	0.53	-0.07	-0.40
Primary deficit /c	-0.01	-3.24	-3.30
Central Government /c	-0.56	-2.36	-2.10
Federal Government and BC /c	-1.36	-3.33	· -3.00
INSS /c	0.80	0.97	0.90
States and Municipalities /c	0.19	-0.22	-0.50
State companies /c	0.36	-0.66	-0.70
Interests /b	7.59	9.09	7.40
Central Government /b	5.56	5.10	4.20
States and Municipalities	1.86	3.40	2.90
State companies	0.17	0.59	0.30

a/ Author´s forecast.
b/ Not including effects of devaluation.
c/ (-) = Surplus.
Source: Central Bank.

The combination of i) currency appreciation, following the overshooting at the beginning of the year; ii) the fall in nominal interest rates after March; iii) inflation, which ultimately made real interest rates[19] fall substantially throughout the year with respect to 1998; and iv) real growth of

19   These, of course, determine the dynamics of the debt/GDP relationship

the economy during the year, made the debt/GDP ratio drop from a high of 48 per cent in February to 45 per cent at the end of the year.

On the other hand, the main disappointment in 1999 was in the trade accounts. Specifically, the trade deficit, despite falling significantly, still reached US$ 1.2 billion at year-end. In light of the facts, though, it is not difficult to explain what happened. There are fundamentally four reasons that explain the result and the, by extension, the contrast of the Brazilian experience with those of Mexico and Korea:

a) The collapse of commodity prices in the international market strongly affected Brazil. The average price index of basic products fell by 15 per cent in comparison to 1998 while that for semi-manufactured goods declined by 17 per cent, causing a sharp drop in the total export index (Figure 2.8).

b) An important chunk of Brazilian exports is composed of manufactured goods and, within this product category, there is a certain concentration in sales to Latin American countries. In particular, during 1999, all Latin America — except Mexico, with which Brazilian trade is limited, and Peru, a small country — was in recession. As a result, Brazil's manufactured exports to the region suffered a substantial reduction.

c) Instead of suffering a big fall, as many had initially predicted and as had happened in Mexico and Korea, Brazil's GDP grew by around one per cent in 1999, meaning that a contraction of aggregate demand did not happen in the economy.

d) Oil prices increased in a fashion comparable to the 1973 and 1979 shocks This had an adverse effect on the nation's trade accounts, since Brazil imports around one third of its oil requirement;

In this context, however, it is important to highlight the rise that occurred in the export quantum following devaluation after only a small time lag (Figure 2.9). The still high demand for imports and the fall in prices, however, impeded a more accentuated improvement in the trade balance. In the full-year balance, exports fell six per cent and imports 15 per cent, but the country finished 1999 with a trade deficit of approximately US$1.2 billion — substantially below the US$7 billion in 1998.

Figure 2.8: Export Prices Index — Average 1996 = 100

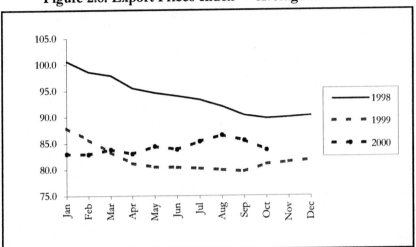

Source: FUNCEX

Figure 2.9: Exports in Manufactured Goods — Quantum Index — Moving Average 12 Months (1996 = 100)

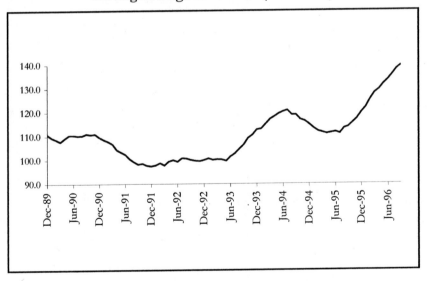

Source: FUNCEX

The current account, in turn, experienced an important improvement. Besides the drop in the trade deficit, the currency devaluation had a positive impact on two other important components of the current account: the transportation account — linked to the trade movement — and especially the travel account — travelling abroad became very expensive. At the same time, after devaluation, the heavy profit and dividend remittances of 1998 — obviously stimulated by the fear of an exchange rate change — did not reoccur. Together, these two factors decreased the current account deficit from US$34 billion in 1998 to US$24 billion in 1999. This did not translate into an improvement of the same magnitude as measured by deficit/GDP ratio, due to the simple fact that the devaluation decreased the GDP value in dollars. However, due to the resumption of GDP growth, the ratio of the current account deficit can be expected to decline over the short-term even if the exchange rate remains unchanged.

Following the fiscal improvement and the perception that the change in the external situation, despite its tardiness, was beginning to occur, investors were gaining more confidence in the future perspectives of the economy. Then the country-risk, measured by the spread of the of the 30-year Par Bonds, in basis points, over the US treasury bond of similar characteristics, which had passed the 2300 points in the most critical moments in January 1999, started to descend (Figure 2.10).

Figure 2.10: Country Risk (Basis Points)

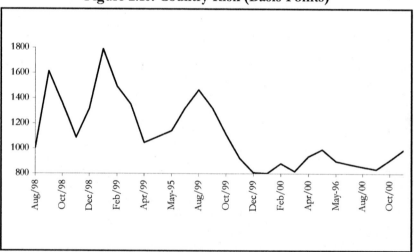

Source: JP Morgan. Par bond: basis points over USA T-Bonds (30 years)

From the Deficit of Targets to the Deficit Targets: a New Economic Policy Regime (Temporary or Permanent?)

In the years of fiscal deterioration, a proposal was frequently put forth in debates on economic policy that the government should commit itself to fiscal targets; i.e. 'Maastricht style ceilings', that would limit governmental action and control the evolution of public debt. In fact, though, such proposals were made in vain since the government did not adopt them. Instead of deficit targets, Brazil experienced a 'deficit of targets'.

In 1999, in the context of the IMF agreement, this situation changed dramatically as the government was led to adopt a fiscal rule corresponding to a behavioural principle, in the form of a variant of the Kopits and Symansky definition: 'A fiscal policy rule may consist of a limit on, or a target for, the stock of public debt as a proportion of GDP'.[20] Even though the difficulty of accurately projecting the behaviour of interest rates had led Brazil to adopt a primary surplus target instead of a nominal deficit target,[21] in fact the objective was to redirect the trajectory of public debt. Specifically, the idea was to 'substantially reduce the ratio of public debt to GDP' throughout 1999 — after the jump that resulted from the devaluation — and continue with this declining trend in 2000 and 2001. These objectives were stated in the memorandum of economic policy approved by the IMF board in March 1999, after the revision of the original 1998 accord.

The economic policy regime adopted in 1999 was based on four pillars:

a) Fiscal austerity, in the form of strict targets of primary results for the three-year period 1999–2001.

b) Approval of the so-called 'reforms'.

c) Adoption of inflation targets.[22]

d) Free-floating exchange rate.

The targets established in the IMF agreement have been mentioned earlier. Nevertheless, it is valid to compare these targets with the surplus that would be required, ceteris paribus, to maintain debt stable at 45 per cent of GDP, with a seignorage of 0.2 per cent of GDP. In a situation of relative normality — inflation at two per cent, nominal interest rates at ten to 12 per cent and real economic growth of four to five per cent — the public sector would need to generate a primary surplus of 1.0 per cent to 2.3 per

---

20 Kopits and Symansky (1998), p. 26.
21 At least as long as the interest rate did not exceed the premises of the exercise that served as basis for the calculation of the primary surplus requirement.
22 See Mishkin (1999) for the logic of adopting an inflation target regime.

cent of GDP (Table 2.5). It is important to recall that, in the 1999–2001 period, interest rates stood above these figures and growth below them. This is why primary surplus has to be so substantial. In the future, provided lower interest rates could be implemented and growth prospects improved, the required primary surplus could be lowered to the levels mentioned above.

Table 2.5: Primary Surplus Required to Stabilise Debt at 45 per cent of GDP (per cent GDP)

Nominal gross interest rate (%)	GDP Real Growth Rate (%)			
	3.0	4.0	5.0	6.0
8.0	1.06	0.61	0.18	-0.25
10.0	1.92	1.46	1.02	0.58
12.0	2.77	2.31	1.86	1.41
14.0	3.63	3.16	2.70	2.25
16.0	4.49	4.01	3.54	3.08

Seignorage = 0.2% GDP
Inflation = 2%

Focusing on the remaining elements, in 1999, the government tried to create the basis for a permanent change in the country's fiscal situation. Two measures were relevant in this respect. The first was the approval of new rules for retirement, limiting the income of those who retire too early. Even though early retirements are still possible, whoever has an early retirement will have a low pension ceiling. Conversely, those individuals who postpone retirement will receive higher pensions. This development has improved the outlook of the Social Security account over the next few years. The second measure was the proposal of a constitutional amendment that would free until 2006 part of the earmarked budgetary resources, widening the government's room for manoeuvre for cutting public expenditure.

Also, in 1999, Brazil adopted inflation targeting, along with a group of approximately ten countries, including New Zealand, England and Canada. The authorities defined an inflation target of eight per cent for 1999, six per cent for 2000 and four per cent for 2001, with a two-percentage point margin of tolerance. In the first year, inflation (CPI) rose at 8.9 per cent, within the accorded interval, and for 2000 the expectations were around six or seven per cent. With this, the government committed itself, formally and explicitly, to the goal of attaining price stability, something that represents a new experience for Brazil. If these targets are met, bringing national inflation to international levels (2.0 to 2.5 per cent) in 2003 or 2004, their achievement would certainly shape the behaviour of future governments. Such a development would represent a true cultural revolution in the Brazilian context, where some politicians in the past were always willing to allow 'a little more' inflation in exchange for growth.

The free exchange rate regime, finally, completes the array of the policy tools available. In the controlled exchange rate regime, the nominal devaluation of seven to eight per cent a year, in a context of practically no inflation, represented a source of pressure on domestic interest rates, which, despite not being particularly attractive when measured in dollars, were extremely high when adjusted by a domestic price index. With the devaluation and the floating exchange rate, the monetary authority gained degrees of freedom. Therefore, interest rates, fell significantly in real terms during 1999, reflecting these new circumstances.

The remaining doubts regarding the Brazilian economic policy regime were in relation to its sustainability over time. Even though the adjustment effort is evident, a substantial part of the surplus has been obtained through temporary and emergency measures to raise revenue and/or cost cuts (Table 2.6). The most notorious example is the Temporary Tax on Financial Transactions (Contribuição Provisória sobre Movimentações Financeiras — CPMF), which was only renewed in 2002 after considerable political pressure on Congress.

Table 2.6: Extraordinary Factors of Fiscal Adjustment (per cent GDP)

Composition	1998	1999	2000
CPM	0.9	0.9	1.3
Concession	1.0	1.0	0.5
Additional income	0.1	0.1	0.1
Income tax: financial	0.3	0.0	0.0
Elimination of deductions	0.0	0.3	0.3
Fiscal stabilisation	0.3	0.3	0.0
Debt	0.0	0.6	0.2
Total	**2.6**	**3.2**	**2.4**

The government's challenge from now on is to continue the adjustment effort, even if with a less ambitious primary target. However, this will have to take place i) without the aid of these temporary sources of adjustment; and ii) without the 'umbrella' of the IMF, now taking on the role of a convenient scapegoat for the authorities.

Why did Brazil not have a Financial Crisis?[23]

Up to this point we have analysed the Brazilian crisis and compared it with some of the other crises that occurred in the second half of the 1990s. As mentioned, even though Brazil suffered a traumatic currency devaluation in 1999, unlike some Asian countries it did not experience a financial crisis per se. But why did a financial crisis not happen in Brazil? What differentiated Brazil's financial system from Asia's?

An important characteristic of the Brazilian financial system, which differentiates it from the Asian case, is its low level of financial depth. In 1996, for instance, private sector total credit in Brazil accounted for 31 per cent of GDP, much lower than in the case of several Asian countries where the equivalent figures sometimes exceeded 100 per cent. These numbers indicate that Brazil, when compared to the Asian countries, had a much less vulnerable financial system. This in turn provided more stability and confidence to the market and lessened the chances of a 'domino effect' breakdown in the system due to a possible series of defaults, such as occurred in Asia due to the high leverage levels.

After the Real Plan (1994), many changes took place in the Brazilian financial system due, most importantly, to the banks' significant loss in revenue linked to the end of inflationary transfers, i.e., the so-called *float*. At the time, many financial institutions significantly expanded their credit lines — favoured by the economic growth that followed stabilisation — increased their leverage and exposure. Later, with the impact of the Mexican crisis in 1995, there was a significant increase in non-performing loans. This was in part due to interest rate increases — which also had a direct negative impact on the banks' profits — and the drop in the level of activity. Many banks could not survive and went bankrupt.

This financial crisis took place in 1995 and forced the Brazilian government to take action in order to overcome the turmoil and strengthen the financial system, under the Basle standards. In 1999, these changes assumed vital importance in keeping the currency crisis from expanding

---

23   Most data presented in this section — unless otherwise stated — were extracted from Puga (1999) and the Central Bank of Brazil.

into a financial crisis as well. The adjustment was made mainly through a series of legislative changes, such as:

- The establishment of minimal capital requirements for banks.

- The establishment of a minimum level for the financial institutions' adjusted net worth at 11 per cent of their risk weighted assets (it started at eight per cent and jumped to ten per cent before reaching the final level).[24]

- Fiscal incentives for the incorporation of financial institutions.

- More power granted to the Central Bank in order to allow it to take preventive actions to strengthen the financial system.

- The obligation of banks which depend on, or have, the ownership participation of international financial institutions to operate within accorded operational limits.

- The enabling of financial institutions to charge for a series of services (many of which had been free of charge in times of high inflation).

- The obligation of financial institutions to identify and inform the Central Bank about all clients who were granted credit of above R$50,000.

- The obligation of financial institutions to present the Central Bank with a programme of internal system control, again in line with Basle Committee standards.

- The creation of the Proer programme, whose goal was to secure the liquidity and solvency of the system.

- The creation of the Proes programme whose goal was the strengthening of the public financial system at the state level.

One of the most important steps taken by the Brazilian government in restructuring its financial system was the effort to encourage mergers, acquisitions, incorporations and transference of ownership control. This process intensified with the Proer programme, instituted in November 1995. The programme consisted of the creation of a special line of financial assistance for the administrative, operational and ownership reorganisation of financial institutions. This process deepened in subsequent years and concentration in the bank industry increased as a consequence. In

---

24 The 11% ratio is even more conservative than the Basle requirements.

December 1994 the ten largest banks in the country accounted for 63 per cent of the system's total assets and the 20 largest for 76 per cent, while in December 1998, these figures rose to 68 per cent and 81 per cent, respectively. Another tendency was the increase in participation of privately owned institutions in the banking system, which grew from 49 per cent in December 1994 to 54 per cent in December 1998. These two trends have played an important role in making the system more solid and reliable.

Another major development that contributed towards transforming Brazil's financial system was the implementation of the Proes programme in August 1996. The plan consisted in either privatising, liquidating or changing the role of public state-level banks. At the beginning of the programme, the public state financial system was composed of 35 institutions and, when completed, it is expected that around nine state level banks will remain. So far, of the 26 institutions that have entered the programme, ten have been privatised, five abolished and 11 have become development agencies. The highlight of the programme was probably the acquisition of the Banerj (the Bank of Rio de Janeiro) by the Banco Itaú, the second largest private bank in the country. The Proes played a major role in making the system more solid and healthy, decreasing the leverage ratio of multiple and commercial state-level banks (credits/net assets) — from 15 per cent in June to nine per cent in December 1996 — and increasing loan loss provisions for delayed credits and credits in liquidation.

The increasing participation of foreign banks has also contributed to the improvement of Brazil's financial system. From June 1995 to December 1998 the number of foreign banks in Brazil increased from 37 to 52 (the number of foreign controlled national banks growing from 20 to 36), increasing the participation of foreign banks in the total number of universal and commercial banks from 15 per cent to 26 per cent over that period. If one takes into account the subsidiaries of foreign banks and banks with foreign control, international institutions owned 21 per cent of multiple and commercial banks' total assets by the end of 1998 compared to 12 per cent in June 1994, and banks with foreign shares increased from six per cent to ten per cent over the same period. In this context, an important step was taken when the Banco Real joined forces with the ABN Amro Bank, becoming Brazil's fourth largest private financial group.[25] The importance of foreign participation in the financial system is especially related to improvements in the quality of services, technology transfer, *spread* reduction (even though better results are still expected on this matter), operational efficiency, their improved capacity

25   Some of the other major international players in the Brazilian financial system are the BankBoston, HSBC Bank, Citibank, Creditanstalt, Santander, Bilbao Vizcaya, Lloyds, Chase Manhattan and JP Morgan.

to absorb macroeconomic turbulence and greater facility to protect the system from exchange rate volatility (*hedge*).[26]

The technological upgrading of the Brazilian Bank Industry came with the constant need for change and adjustment linked to the turbulent macroeconomic conditions of the past, with the reforms mentioned above and the input of foreign know-how strengthening the financial system even further. As stated by Standard & Poor's (1999) 'the need to process transactions in different local currency denominations ... and/or refer to a diverse set of multiple indexes, including inflation rates during the hyper-inflationary era, forced banks to constantly upgrade their systems'.[27] Financial institutions in Brazil have strongly invested in technology, not only to improve the processing, payments and telecommunications areas, but also to develop alternative distribution channels. Technology in the Brazilian financial system has reached the highest international standards as indicated by the highly successful Y2K transition, the advanced services provided by banks and brokers on-line (through the internet) and the sophisticated automation of the São Paulo stock exchange.

All of the factors mentioned above helped to prevent Brazil from sinking into a financial crisis after the devaluation of 1999. Brazil's financial system is probably the most solid in Latin America because of its diversification, the presence of strong international players, its good automation, capitalisation level and its fairly low leverage ratios; all of this is backed up by the relatively stable economic environment established by the Real Plan. To sum up, the main reasons for the system's current good shape are:

- The corrective action taken after the 1995 crisis, including the Proer and Proes programmes.

- The increase of foreign participation in the national financial system.

- The low levels of financial depth and non-performing loans.

- The increase in efficiency brought about by, among other things, technology improvements and competition.

---

26 By the end of 1998 the banking system's external obligations for multiple and commercial banks reached US$50.3 billion. Nevertheless, only 28.7% corresponded to national private banks obligations while 40.3% belonged to foreign banks, which have more facility to honour these debts because they can always count on their headquarters overseas, therefore lessening their vulnerability to volatility.

27 Standard & Poor's (1999), p. 8.

Conclusions

Unlike Argentina, where the defence of a nominal peso/dollar parity has been the common denominator among the immense majority of economists, in the Brazilian case the consensus among economists after the Asian crisis was that the exchange rate should be devalued. The controversy regarded the speed of the process. The government — and those who support its policy — argued that as long as the rate of nominal devaluation remained constant or even declined gradually, in a context of virtually no inflation, currency appreciation would disappear. The critics, on the other hand, were in favour of a discontinuity.

The official line of argument before the devaluation can be summarised by the following words of one of the authors of this chapter: 'Brazil … in contrast with England in 1992, is not committed to a fixed exchange rate but to a policy of gradual — yet intense — real devaluation of its exchange rate, which has been depreciating at a rate of seven to eight per cent a year in a context of inflation close to zero. [Then], as time passes by, [the] exchange rate will become closer to [the] "ideal" point'.[28]

This strategy had two drawbacks. First, it was based on the premise that the rest of the world would continue to finance the country, which proved to be incorrect. Second, the internal cost of this policy, represented by the effect that the announced gradual real devaluation implied for the interest rates, pressured public debt and limited the growth potential of the country. On the other hand, the benefit from the maintenance of the policy was obvious: the preservation of price stabilisation, which the government thought might be threatened by modifying exchange rate policy.

It is worth noting that, rhetoric aside, fear concerning the inflationary effects of an eventual devaluation was not limited to the defenders of the policy. As sincerely stated by one of the most outspoken critics of the policy followed until January 1999 — in light of the amazingly low inflation of 1999 — 'even the economists who were more optimistic regarding the realisation of a currency devaluation without the destruction of the stabilisation programme, among them myself, none could have predicted such a combination of nominal exchange rate and inflation for 1999'.[29]

To understand why, one should reflect on the fact that after devaluation, annual inflation (CPI) was over 50 per cent in Mexico and less than ten per cent in Brazil, despite the fact that GDP in Mexico suffered a historic fall while in Brazil a modest rise. This contrast in fortunes will certainly be a theme for research in the Brazilian academic community for the next few years. A few factors may, however, provide some pointers regarding what may turn out to be the correct interpretation of events.

28   Giambiagi (1999).
29   Batista (1999).

Firstly, Brazil did not suffer a complete erosion in its international reserves. Full currency flotation in Mexico was decided when it was clear that there was no alternative and the Central Bank had no more room for manoeuvring. In Brazil, flotation was also the only way out, but at that time the country still had around US$40 billion in reserves, which created a certain facility to switch directions in the case of an overshooting. This facility was actually employed, not to excess, but undoubtedly with favourable results, at certain critical junctures.

Secondly, even though GDP had grown in Brazil in 1999, devaluation found the country in the middle of a 'valley' in terms of its level of activity.[30] As a result, at the time of devaluation, the conditions were hardly amenable for Brazilian companies practising a generalised exchange rate passthrough. By contrast, in the case of Mexico and Korea economic crisis and devaluation burst onto the scene hot on the heels of a cyclical upswing.

Thirdly, monetary policy played a preponderant role in disarming inflationary expectations after devaluation. Although it had revealed itself useless in avoiding external crisis, the opportunity cost of continuing with speculation became too high once devaluation had occurred, and the fact that the Central Bank hiked nominal interest rates to 45 per cent when all political pressures pushed in the opposite direction, represented a clear indication that the 'anti-inflationary philosophy' that had marked Central Bank's behaviour since 1999 still stood.

Fourthly, despite all fears to the contrary that existed before devaluation, the 'de-indexation' of the economy proved to be more deep-rooted in Brazil than in Mexico. The decision to announce a nominal adjustment of the minimum wage of less than five per cent in April (still in the period of relative price turmoil associated with devaluation) was also a decisive issue in the maintenance of stability — in this case, represented by sustainability of annual inflation below one digit. Lastly, even though promulgated once the panic had abated, the announcement of the inflation-targeting regime in June was another sign in favour of agents adopting a relatively benign inflationary outlook.

The fact, though, is that devaluation seems to have been relatively 'cheap' for Brazil. In other words, the government firmly resisted pressure to devalue for many years because of the assumption that the inflationary

---

30   In December 1998, immediately before devaluation, seasonably adjusted monthly industrial production reached the minimum of the 1997–98 period, staying eight% below the maximum level before the Asian crisis of 1997 and 6% below the maximum level registered after the recovery from the Asian crisis and before the Russian crisis. In order to have an idea of the intensity of the recessive process that preceded devaluation in Brazil, it is worth recalling that this same level in December 1998 was 9% below the 'peak' of December 1994 — four years previously — at the very peak of the Real Plan, and was not reached again until the year 2000.

impact of changing monetary policy would be too great. More than one year after the devaluation, however, with the country resuming growth and inflation staying below two digits, it seems reasonable to assert that the cost of devaluation was actually low in Brazil.

It seems that there is no way to conduct a balanced assessment of the role that the IMF played in the success of the economic policy without concluding that, in general terms, the IMF agreement and the economic policy that followed it were actually good for Brazil. The 'liquidity mattress' represented by the US$42 billion loan permitted Brazil to overcome dramatic circumstances; interest rates were elevated at the right moment and reduced at the right speed and intensity during 1999; the fiscal austerity policy radically changed the economic context of the country — traditionally seen as reckless in fiscal matters; inflation did not increase substantially; and the country resumed growth, in seasonably adjusted terms, right after devaluation — even though the negative carryover inherited from 1998 prevented this growth from being better in 1999.

On the other hand, the IMF seems to have committed some mistakes of perception in the case of Brazil. Three of them were important at the time. The first was the clause with the reserve requirement established in the first agreement, which, as stressed in this chapter, limited the room for manoeuvre of the authorities in defence of the original parity. Even recognising that it was difficult to lend US$42 billion to a country with such a negative background as Brazil, objectively this limitation ended up contributing to the speculation against the continuity of the currency policy practised until January 1999.

The IMF's second mistake was to have contributed to the paralysis that overcame the authorities in the first weeks of the crisis after devaluation. Regardless of the eventual divergences that may have existed between the former Central Bank president and the finance minister, and the difficulty of implementing a stabilisation programme without having voted the fiscal measures of the adjustment, it seems that having passively watched the daily advance of the dollar (on average, of more than 4.5 per cent *per business day* between 14 and 29 January) was a mistake, to which the Miffs delay in re-establishing negotiations country contributed partially.

Having let the dollar reach R$2.00 again in the second half of the year — without revising the allowance to spend part of the reserves in the currency market — after having dropped to R$1.65 following the initial overshooting was the third problem, which explains in part the spasmodic inflation increase at the end of 1999. At the time, the authorities hid themselves behind the old saying that 'with a fluctuating exchange rate regime, the exchange rate fluctuates', when actually, as aptly stated by professor Ilan Goldfajn from Pontifícia Universidade Católica do Rio de Janeiro (PUC/RJ), for a country like Brazil, 'a fluctuating exchange rate is good when it does not fluctuate'. It was obvious that a new round of dollar appreciation would detonate a new series of price increases and that the economic authorities would like to avoid this. However, they found themselves with their hands tied because the terms of the intervention margin in the currency market had not yet been negotiated with the IMF. A better acceptance by the IMF of these rule changes — giving more manoeuvring power to the Central Bank — would have been desirable. Proof of this is the fact that the mere announcement of the terms of this new agreement helped to 'break' the dollar's rise.[31]

Aside from these specific reflections, one additional issue that forms part of the future agenda of the country concerns whether the exchange rate regime should be made 'permanent' in Brazil. The experience of a controlled exchange rate regime in some senses traumatised the country. On the other hand, as Paul Volcker reminded the Brazilians in one of his visits to the country in 1999, 'pure free exchange rates are something for just two or three countries in the world' and, as already stated in this chapter, this 'purity' led to high inflation in the second half of 1999 for not having halted the merely speculative demand pressure for dollars.

If the Brazilian experience with an (almost) fixed exchange rate regime was negative and if pure fluctuation also brought problems, what type of regime should be targeted for the future as a means of minimising the drawbacks associated with these two types of extreme regimes? This is an incipient debate in Brazil but one which will probably intensify in the coming months or years and could lead to the adoption of some type of regime similar to Mexico's, with daily forms of intervention by the authorities directed at the goal of reducing volatility.

Finally, it is worth reflecting on the potentialities of the Brazilian economy and the long-term effects of the modernisation that Brazilian enterprises have undergone in the past ten years.[32] Despite the different economic policies applied in the period, there is a common denominator in the evolution of the Brazilian economy since 1990: the adoption of policies vaguely denominated 'market friendly' and, in an associated development, the modernisation of Brazilian companies. In the first half of the decade these phenomena were masked, however, by truly impressive levels of inflation — the price variation rate in 12 months, measured by the General Price Index of the Fundação Getúlio Vargas, was 5,154 per cent, when the Real Plan was adopted in June 1994. In the following years, inflation dropped drastically but public debt increased and the external deficit — which practically did not exist in 1994 — became a major problem. In 1999, measures were taken in order to correct these two imbalances but inflation increased and income per capita dropped once again.

---

31   The US currency closed at R$1.79 at the end of the year.
32   Franco (1999b); Moreira (1999).

From 2000 on, though, Brazil has conditions favourable for initiating a new growth cycle such as it has not had since the 1970s, even though circumstances point to lower growth rates. The two imbalances — fiscal and external — mentioned above are starting to fade away, inflation is falling again and, in the official scenario, the combination of a lower country-risk and decreasing domestic interest rates will stimulate growth, improve revenues, deepen the fiscal adjustment, provide new drops in the risk indicators and generate a virtuous cycle of growth and reduction in the risk premium.

In these circumstances, the permanence of a significant inflow of foreign direct investment (FDI) could gradually reduce the external vulnerability of the country. The evolution of FDI is one of the most impressive transformations observed in the Brazilian economy in the last five years. Even discounting the portfolio inflows and the Brazilian investment outflows, net FDI inflow in the country, which had been on average around US$1 billion a year for the 1980–94 period, jumped to US$3 billion in 1995, US$10 billion in 1996, US$16 billion in 1997, US$23 billion in 1998 and US$28 billion in 1999. The prospects are favourable for the continuity of a net inflow of external long-term resources of around three per cent of GDP; this would be sufficient to finance most of the current account deficit and, also, would allow for a drop in the ratios of Net External Debt to Exports and Net External Debt to GDP. Even though the amplified external debt (i.e. debt taking into account the foreign capital stock in the country) may not vary substantially, its composition is likely to change, with an increasing proportion taking on the form of external debt for long-term investment. This, in turn, would make the country less vulnerable to sudden fluctuations in the international financial scenario. In conclusion, over the next few years if inflation recedes to international levels as the authorities hope, if the public debt continues to decline in real terms, if the current account stabilises at around three per cent of GDP and further crises can be averted in world financial markets, Brazil's economic performance should improve substantially compared to other emerging market nations.

Appendix

Table A2.1: Brazil: Economic Indicators

	1993	1994	1995	1996	1997	1998	1999	2000/a
GDP (US$ billion) /b	429.7	543.1	705.5	775.8	807.7	787.7	529.7	620.0
GDP growth (%)	4.9	5.9	4.2	2.7	3.3	-0.2	0.8	4.0
GDP deflator (%)	1996.2	2240.2	77.6	17.4	8.3	4.7	4.3	10.0
Real interest rate (%) /c	7.1	24.4	33.1	16.6	16.4	26.5	4.7	7.0
Unemployment - IBGE (%)	5.3	5.06	4.64	5.42	5.66	7.6	7.6	7.2
Current account deficit (% GDP)	0.1	0.2	2.5	3.1	4.2	4.3	4.5	4.0
National accounts (% GDP, current prices)								
Final consumption	77.75	77.5	79.48	80.99	80.87	80.85	80.67	n.a
Private	60.08	59.64	59.88	62.50	62.67	62.05	61.81	n.a
Government	17.66	17.87	19.6	18.49	18.20	18.80	18.85	n.a
Gross capital formation	20.85	22.15	22.29	20.92	21.50	21.17	20.45	n.a
Investment	19.28	20.75	20.54	19.26	19.86	19.64	18.93	n.a
Change of inventories	1.56	1.4	1.74	1.66	1.64	1.53	1.52	n.a
Goods and non-factors services	1.41	0.35	-1.76	-1.91	-2.37	-2.02	-1.12	n.a
Exports	10.5	9.51	7.72	6.99	7.51	7.63	10.60	n.a
Imports	9.10	9.16	9.49	8.90	9.88	9.65	11.72	n.a
Total	100.0	100.0	100.0	100.0	100.0	100.0	100.0	n.a

Big Business in Brazil: States and Markets in the Corporate Reorganisation of the 1990s[*]

Andrea Goldstein and Ben Ross Schneider

> Name some Brazilian multinationals.
> Even harder than 'famous Belgians', isn't it?
> *The Economist*, 23 September 2000.

Introduction

In 1999 President Fernando Henrique Cardoso endorsed the fusion of Brahma and Antarctica, Brazil's two largest brewers, in AmBev with the general idea of creating huge Brazilian corporations capable of competing internationally.[1] This support was consistent with Cardoso's past work as a prominent sociologist of business. As early as the 1960s Cardoso was already arguing that Latin American development, political and economic, was hampered by the stunted growth of its business or bourgeoisie. Cardoso's statements also reflected a more pervasive attitude among his economic team that the structure of private business should not to be left exclusively to the newly invigorated play of market forces in Brazil. However, it is still unclear empirically how various government policies have influenced business restructuring, nor what to make of this impact theoretically.

In this chapter, we tell the story of how Brazilian big business reorganised in the last decade against the background of macroeconomic stabilisation, trade liberalisation, privatisation and regulatory reform. The 1990s witnessed a flurry of mergers and acquisitions. There were several main features of the reorganisation. In terms of ownership of the largest firms in Brazil, the state and traditional family-held firms have been displaced by multinationals (MNCs) and some new domestic corporations, where control is (at least partly) separated from ownership. In terms of

[*] We thank Joaquim Oliveira Martins, Charles Oman, Laurence Whitehead, workshop participants at the Institute of Latin American Studies at the University of London and seminar participants at the University of Kobe for comments and suggestions on an earlier draft. The opinions expressed are the authors' own and do not reflect the position of the institutions to which they are affiliated.
1   *Isto E*, 14 July 1999.

large conglomerates, some have specialised while others have diversified.[2] A core puzzle we seek to explain in this chapter is why there has been no convergence to a single corporate strategy modelled around the so-called Anglo-Saxon model of business organisation. In particular, why do some major Brazilian conglomerates continue to diversify when the business literature is increasingly sceptical about diversification?

The next section takes a brief theoretical and comparative look at factors that contribute to conglomeration. This is followed by an analysis of privatisation in Brazil and complementary regulatory policies. The subsequent section delves deeper into several case studies of leading corporations: Vicunha, Gerdau, Votorantim, AmBev, Metal Leve and Cofap and Embraer. In the conclusion we derive some tentative lessons from the experience of Brazil for scholars interested in the dynamics of state–business interactions in countries of very late industrialisation, the so-called emerging markets.

Where do Big Diversified Conglomerates Come from?

Since the demise of dependency theory in the early 1980s there has been little theorising by Latin Americanists on what factors were driving the evolution of big business.[3] Moreover, existing theories of the emergence of big business elsewhere are not generally useful. Alfred Chandler, for example, pioneered the study of the multidivisional corporation in the United States and argued that this form was superior for managing larger business units. The argument for the rise of big business is largely endogenous; firms grow big by exploiting technological and managerial economies of scale.[4] McCraw highlights the 'transcendental fact [that,] in the absence of very strong and specifically targeted government policy, industry structure in every country is determined largely by basic industry

2   See especially Carvalho and Bernardes (1998). Ruiz (1997) found a similar dispersion of corporate strategies in his study of 18 groups in the 1980s and early 1990s.
3   See Cardoso (1964 and 1978), Evans (1979), and Gereffi (1990).
4   The benefits of bigness, primarily in undiversified firms, is one of the repeated conclusions of the chapters in Chandler et al. (1998). For Chandler and Hikino, for example, large industrial enterprises made four types of contribution to economic growth. Big business: 1) exploited economies of scale; 2) became the 'locus of learning for the initial development and continued enhancement of their product-specific intangible organisational assets'; 3) was the core of a 'network of suppliers, equipment makers, retailers, advertisers, designers ...' and 4) was the 'primary driver of technological advancement through their heavy investment in research and development activities' (Chandler, Amatori and Hikino, 1998, p. 26). For Dosi, 'there are size thresholds for the ability of firms to internalise the capabilities of mastering the activities of innovation, production, and marketing in complex products, so that, other things being equal, "bigness" confers a differential advantage' (Dosi, 1998, p. 466). See Schneider (1998) for a fuller review.

conditions – that is, by the underlying technology and demand conditions of the industry'.[5] Market size is probably the most important variable that explains the early emergence of big business in the United States and its slow development in most other smaller countries. Chandler et al. (1998b) offer a number of other factors, on a case-by-case basis, that retarded the development of big business, ranging from inappropriate training for managers in France to macroeconomic mismanagement in Argentina. However, these and other insights are less helpful in explaining variations among still developing countries where big business has taken fundamentally different forms.

At first glance, late industrialisation appears everywhere to generate large diversified conglomerates comprised of many technologically unrelated subsidiaries.[6] Several major factors have contributed to greater diversification in large firms in developing countries. First, small, protected domestic markets, usually combined with highly unequal income and wealth distribution, made expansion in unrelated areas a more promising strategy for business than expanding a core business. As the scope of import substitution widened, industrial policy increased the return on investing in new import-substituting industries. Expanding firms had few options but to enter new sectors as their original product lines saturated small domestic markets. Second, in the absence of well-developed markets for capital, risk and managerial labour, diversification was seen as the best hedging strategy.[7]

Third, as industrialisation in the late twentieth century depended on the rapid absorption of foreign technology, some diversified business groups developed a generic expertise in project execution that could be applied across technologically diverse sectors (economies of scope).[8] Specifically, through a learning process associated with internalising the elements of foreign technology acquisition, especially related to establishing or expanding a

---

5   McCraw (1998), p. 526.
6   Amsden (1989), p. 125. While the existing literature acknowledges some variation among developing countries, the usual intent is to provide a general explanation for convergence in the organisation of business in late industrialisation. What is lacking is a general argument on variation in the organisation of big business and the consequential role of the state in producing the variation, considering how consistent and substantial state intervention has been in late industrialising countries. Even Leff (1978, p. 674), who argued that the business group was nearly universal, concludes with the question of 'why groups or a similar pattern of industrial organisation has not emerged with equal frequency in all development contexts, both contemporary and historical'.
7   Leff (1978); see Ruiz (1997).
8   Amsden and Hikino (1994). In the Korean case Amsden concluded that, 'one may venture to guess that the group's ability to enter new industries rapidly and cost effectively became a major economy of scope' (1989, p. 129). Amsden uses a modified notion of 'economies of scope' to describe increasing returns to management assets across multiple sectors (see Chandler 1990).

plant facility (attainment of basic and detailed engineering, equipment procurement, supervision, construction and start-up), the business group could acquire a generic asset that enabled it to diversify into start-up industries relatively quickly and at low cost.[9] Fourth, unstable, arbitrary, or highly interventionist states, coupled with chronic macroeconomic volatility, exacerbate political uncertainty which in turn encourages conglomeration in order to diversify risk. Capitalists may create huge conglomerates in order to maximise political influence, as in Mexico where one of the two major motivations for conglomeration was 'the general enhancement of bargaining power vis-à-vis the government'.[10] In Brazil, big national businesses could exploit its advantage in relational capital and knowledge of the local political scene to forge deals with foreign multinationals in unrelated sectors, liaising between the state and international capital.[11]

Fifth, and much more recently, privatisation plans, such as those implemented in Argentina, Chile and Mexico in the 1980s and '90s, modified the structure of corporate control, displacing traditional big business, creating huge new conglomerates and leading sometimes to the emergence of management-controlled firms.[12] Silva (1996) provides a detailed history of government-fomented conglomeration in Chile, where privatisation and financial deregulation created in the space of a few years several giant conglomerates that dominated the economy.[13] After the Pinochet government was forced to bail out privatised groups by massive nationalisation in the aftermath of the 1982 debt crisis (the 'Chicago road to socialism'), in the rest of the 1980s it opted for popular capitalism, giving rise to an ownership structure dominated by private pension funds and, at a later stage, international institutional investors. But two large groups — controlled by the Luksic and Anacleto Angelini families[14] — continue to out-

---

9   *Ibid.*, p. 141.
10   Vernon (1963), p. 21.
11   Evans (1979).
12   See Garrido (2000) on the expansion of conglomerates in Mexico in the 1980s and 1990s.
13   From 1974 to 1977 the BHC conglomerate grew from 18 to 62 companies and the Cruzat-Larraín group exploded from 11 to 85 companies. By the end of 1977 'these two conglomerates alone controlled 37% of the assets of Chile's largest 250 companies [and] 40% of private sector banking' (Silva, 1996, p. 113).
14   The Luksics, in particular, have two main quoted holding companies, Antofagasta in London and Quiñenco in New York. Their own stakes in subsidiaries that are themselves listed in New York, in Santiago, or are private. The group's assets range from Chile's biggest bank to hotels, mining, beer and pasta. In Argentina and Mexico, governments have not even attempted to pursue different ownership structures (Goldstein, 1998; Schamis, 1999). Privatisation, combined with very timid market liberalisation, preserved rents for firms that had provided political support to, and often colluded with, policy-makers.

strip other Chilean companies in size as well as diversity. Privatisation, as discussed later, was a big part of corporate restructuring in Brazil.[15]

The conventional expectation is that cross-national patterns of corporate governance will converge toward the Anglo-Saxon, capital-market driven model characterised by a separation between ownership and control and progressive 'deconglomerisation'. Conglomeration, especially, has not fared well in the popular press. After the wave of conglomeration in the 1960s and 1970s, business leaders and corporate raiders in the 1980s woke up to what one observer called 'the biggest collective error ever made by American business'.[16] More recently Paul Krugman reminisced: 'I am (just) old enough to remember the conglomerate-building era of the 1960s, an era that ended so badly that many thought the word "synergy" would be permanently banned from the business lexicon'.[17]

The literature on the comparative evolution of corporate governance — and, more in general, capitalist systems[18] — suggests a note of caution. On indicators as diverse as corporate ownership, the degree to which firms own each other, forms of executive remuneration, or the working of the market for corporate control, most scholars argue that the degree of convergence is rather limited.[19] In their comparative review Fligstein and Freeland conclude, 'that there is no evidence of convergence across societies toward a single form of governance'. We now turn to an examination of the lack of convergence in Brazil and the reasons behind it.[20]

Privatisation, Regulation and Liberalisation in Brazil

The evolution of big business during the course of the twentieth century has been influenced in Brazil by the structure of the economy, public poli-

---

15   Competition policy may become an additional factor affecting diversification. As developing countries institutionalise more effective anti-trust policies and enforcement agencies, evidence from earlier developers suggests that this policy might have more impact on corporate strategies generally. In the United States, for example, 'the major impetus to this new strategy [diversification into unrelated products] was unintentionally provided by the federal government' (Fligstein, 1991, p. 321). By 1950 half of the one hundred largest firms were facing antitrust suits and thereafter 'all vertical and horizontal mergers became problematic' (*ibid.*). The informal subcontracting arrangements and keiretsu groups in Japan would be illegal or highly suspicious in the United States (Gerlach 1992, p. 28). So, US corporations acquired firms in unrelated markets.
16   *Economist*, 27 April 1991, p. 44, cited in Davis et al. (1994), p. 548.
17   'Media Mania', *The New York Times*, 12 January 2000. In Brazil, the dramatic collapse of the historic, and highly diversified, Matarrazzo group in the late 1980s confirmed negative views on conglomeration and the risks of diversification (see Ruiz, 1997).
18   See, for example, 'ways of producing and organising economic life', Berger (1996), p. 1
19   Guillén (1999), Pauly and Reich (1997).
20   Fligstein and Freeland (1995), p. 21.

cies, international factors and the size and regional configuration of the domestic market. In the model introduced in the 1940s and strongly consolidated in the 1950s and 1960s, the state promoted three kinds of business — state-owned, MNCs and local private — and synergies among them.[21] The auto industry provides a good example of early collaboration among the three. The government attracted MNC assemblers who were looking to invest abroad in larger, protected markets like Brazil. The state created and financed infrastructure and inputs, especially steel, and the state reserved the auto parts sector for domestic Brazilian capital.[22] In other, later ventures such as petrochemicals in the 1970s, the state coaxed MNCs and local private capital into joint ventures with state enterprises, a common model called the 'triple alliance' or *tripé*.[23]

For many MNCs indiscriminate protection encouraged an excessive diversification of product lines — the result of restrictions on specialisation imposed by the limits of the domestic market, together with the opportunities offered by the lack of international competition — as well as a high degree of vertical integration, as a counterpart to demands for a high level of national components.[24] These factors prevented firms from benefiting from gains due to specialisation. In this framework, private domestic capital also developed rent-seeking characteristics, with a low degree of genuine international competitiveness. Ownership and control mostly remained in the hands of the founding family: in the absence of strong pressures to improve production efficiency and expand into the world market, cash flows were sufficient to finance internally the limited investment needs of Brazilian groups. Moreover, opacity in accounting and related fields discouraged outside investors from acquiring equity. Brazilian firms hence tended to raise external capital through bank loans or issues of debt securities (such as debentures and bonds), rather than by issuing shares.[25] Maturities were usually short, with the exception of Banco Nacional de Desenvolvimento Econômico e Social

21 First, public ownership has been dominant, when not exclusive, in the provision of public services, i.e. telecommunications, gas and electricity, water and sanitation, railways and urban transport. Second, the state has owned exclusive rights for the exploitation of non-renewable natural resources such as petroleum and iron ore, where strategic reasons made private, most often foreign, ownership undesirable. Third, governments have chosen to intervene directly in some manufacturing industries where private entrepreneurship was not forthcoming: steel in the 1940s, petrochemicals in the 1960s, aeronautics, aluminium and electronics in the 1970s.

22 Addis (1998).

23 Evans (1979).

24 Mesquita Morreira (1999).

25 Singh (1995), in a sample of listed companies in ten developing countries, found that Brazilian ones tend to rely relatively less on equity finance and show lower gearing ratios.

(BNDES) long-term credit.[26] Family control was further entrenched by a network of interlocking directorates.

As in most countries of Latin America, domestic firms also diversified into related and unrelated sectors. Often the state, especially through the BNDES and state enterprises promoting joint ventures, made it hard for firms to resist creating subsidiaries to enter into new sectors. Even firms like Votorantim that sought to maintain their autonomy from the state (and avoid joint ventures with state partners) diversified.[27] Nonetheless, in contrast to much of Latin America, and especially Chile and Mexico, finance was relatively isolated from industry and big conglomerates did not form around a banking pole, at least until the 1980s.[28] Then the two largest private banks, Itaú and Bradesco, acquired significant participations in non-financial enterprises, including electronics where, to be fair, they were among the world's earliest credit institutions to recognise the importance of extensively using information technology.[29] The large construction companies (*empreiteiras*), such as Andrade Gutierrez, Camargo Corrêa and Odebrecht, also invested heavily in unconnected activities, as well as in foreign markets.

Since 1990 the macro context has changed dramatically. Brazil made deep cuts in tariff rates, eliminated most non-tariff trade barriers and dramatically reduced the inflation rate following the initiation of the Real Plan in mid-1994. Low inflation spurred a consumer boom, as the income of poorer Brazilians was no longer eroded by inflation and the middle class gained accessed to credit for the purchase of consumer durables such as cars and dishwashers. The formation in 1991 of Mercosur with Argentina, Paraguay and Uruguay made this large market even bigger. In general, trade liberalisation and Mercosur encouraged specialisation; privatisation however offered new opportunities for diversification.

Privatisation

Privatisation and regulatory reform have had a more direct impact on ownership and corporate strategies among large firms.[30] The Collor government launched a large-scale privatisation programme in April 1990. The Programa Nacional de Desestatização (PND) clearly spelled out the objectives of privatisation:

26   Founded in 1952, following recommendations by the Brazil-United States Mixed Commission, to provide long-term finance, the BNDES has traditionally been the centre of structuralism economics in Brazil, assisting the overall strategy of import-substitution industrialisation by successively concentrating lending in railroad, electrical energy, steel, automobile, and information technology projects.
27   Schneider (1991).
28   Barker (1990).
29   This need is of course particularly large in high-inflation countries where overnight cash management is probably the most important determinant of corporate results.
30   Goldstein (1999).

- To allow the state to modify the nature of its intervention, focusing actions and resources on social policy

- To reduce the public debt

- To increase investment

- To stimulate competition, contributing to the qualitative improvement of goods and services

- To strengthen the stock market, through widespread shareownership (*pulverização*)

The PND established a clear and transparent legal and regulatory framework for state retrenchment. Legal state monopolies existed in a number of sectors, making it necessary to introduce constitutional amendments to liberalise ownership and access in telecommunications, electricity and oil. Responsibilities have been tightly concentrated in a single agency, the BNDES, which responds to the government but is functionally independent. In most other countries, both in Europe and in developing economies, responsibilities are more evenly spread across different bodies,[31] but in Brazil the predictable opposition to privatisation made it preferable to insulate technical decisions from political pressures. The BNDES is indeed a quintessential example of the *bolsões de eficiencia*, parts of the bureaucracy where reformists reinforced the merit system while continuing to use other parts of the state apparatus for political patronage.[32] Despite its pro-intervention imprinting, the BNDES was chosen because it had accumulated an unsurpassed expertise and had started to recognise the opportunities which privatisation opened to Brazil well before a consensus in this sense emerged in the rest of the elite.[33] Moreover, BNDESPAR, its fully owned investment bank, had been accumulating direct shareholdings in a number of important companies as a result of the conversion of non-performing loans.

In 1991–92 managing the sell-offs proved more difficult than expected, reflecting the shaky financial situation in some state-owned enterprises (SOEs) earmarked for immediate sale, the presence of minority shareholders (often entrusted with a priority right to acquire other shareholders'

31   See Goldstein and Nicoletti (1996, table 1, p. 432), for a comparison of institutional arrangements in privatisation. A similar *problematique* has emerged in other countries. In Chile, the Corporación de Fomento de Chile (CORFO) has been the government's agency devoted to privatisations, whereas Italy's Istituto di Ricerca Internazionale (IRI) has often laid obstacles in the way of the government's plans to divest of the former's subsidiaries.

32   Sikkink (1991), p. 176.

33   Velasco (1997).

stocks) and the decreasing credibility of the Collor administration. Despite such problems, however, total receipts realised during Collor's presidency, slightly less than US$4 billion, mainly in the petrochemical and steel sectors, far outweighed those obtained in the previous decade. Following Collor's resignation, the new administration, headed by his vice-president Itamar Franco, initially froze the PND, but was then obliged to resume the programme in the face of mounting fiscal concerns, finally leading to the almost complete exit of the state from manufacturing.

During the Cardoso presidency moving on to public utilities and banks was a key element of economic policy. Privatisation also reached the state level, as governments entered into agreements with the Finance Ministry to restructure decentralised debt on condition that they increase the primary surplus and sell public enterprises owned by state governments. A milestone was passed in May 1997 when the 'strategic block' of Companhia Vale do Rio Doce (CVRD), the world's largest producer of iron ore, was sold to a consortium led by Companhia Siderúrgica Nacional (CSN), despite a heated legal controversy. With consolidated sales of US$5 billion in 1996, CVRD also owned large subsidiaries in aluminium, railroads, ports, shipping and pulp and paper, as well as stakes in four Brazilian steel firms, including CSN. Another important advance was the beginning, in 1997, of the privatisation of the telecommunications sector. Three concessions to operate cellular telephone services were sold at auction for US$4 billion. In July 1998, the federal government sold 12 holding companies created by the spin-off of the Telebrás System, transferring to the private sector all the wire-line and long-distance operators, as well as the 'A' Band cellular operators. Total proceeds from the sale of the 12 companies totalled R$22 billion, an average premium of more than 50 per cent over the minimum set auction price (Table 3.1). Privatisation in telecoms accelerated several of the major trends noted at the outset, especially the massive inflow of foreign direct investment, expansion of the role of institutional investors such as insurance and pension funds, and diversification of banks and *empreiteiras* into communications.[34]

---

34   The privatisation programme attracted a lot of foreign investment and, as discussed later, increased the share of MNC control of the largest firms in Brazil. However, other features of the privatisation programme, especially the *moedas podres* ('rotten monies',various discounted public liabilities that were accepted at face value in privatisation sales), gave domestic firms some advantages and helped increase their participation. See Montero (1997).

Table 3.1: Telecoms Privatisation 1998

Company	Value (US$ b)	Acquirers (Share per cent)	Countries (Share per cent)
Telesp	4.97	Telefónica: 56.6 Telecom de Portugal: 23 Iberdrola: 7 Banco Bilbao Vizcaya: 7 RBS: 6.4	Spain: 70.6 Portugal: 23 Brazil: 6.4
Tele Centro-Sul	1.77	Timepart: 62 Telecom Italia: 19 Techold (Opportunity, Previ, Sistel): 19	Brazil: 81 Italy: 19
Tele Norte-Leste	2.94	Andrade Gutierrez: 21.20 Inepar: 20 Macal: 20 Fiago (Funcef): 18.70 Brasilseg: 10.05 Cia. de Seguros Aliança: 10.05	Brazil: 100
Embratel	2.27	MCI International: 100	United States: 100
Telesp Celular	3.08	Portugal Telecom: 100	Portugal: 100
Tele Sudeste Celular	1.16	Telefónica Internacional (Tisa): 92.98 Iberdrola: 6.98 NTT Mobile Communications: 0.02 Itochu: 0.02	Spain: 99.96 Japan: 0.04
Telemig Celular	0.65	Telesystem International Wireless: 48 Opportunity: 21 Pension funds (Previ, Sistel): 18 Others: 13	Canada: 48 Brazil: 52
Tele Celular Sul	0.60	UGB Participações (Globopar and Bradesco) Bitel Participações (Telecom Italia)	Brazil: 50 Italy: 50
Tele Nordeste Celular	0.57	UGB (Globopar/Bradesco): 50 Bitel (Stet Mobile Holding N.V.): 50	Brazil: 50 Italy: 50
Tele Leste Celular	0.37	Iberdrola + Telefónica Internacional (Tisa)	Spain: 100
Tele Centro-Oeste	0.38	Splice	Brazil: 100
Tele Norte Celular	0.16	Telesystem International Wireless: 48 Opportunity: 21 Pension funds (Sistel and Previ): 18 Others: 13	Canada: 48 Brazil: 52

Source: BNDES.

Within the PND, at the end of October 2000, 66 companies and minority holdings in companies owned by the federal government (the majority in the steel, chemicals, petrochemicals, fertiliser and electricity sectors) had been transferred to the private sector. Also considering state and telecoms privatisation, total receipts amounted to US$96.57 billion, of which roughly 80 per cent represented cash revenues with the rest being debt transferred to the private sector (Table 3.2).

Table 3.2: Privatisation Proceeds 1991–99 (US$ million)

Programme	Sale Proceeds	Debt Transferred	Total Proceeds
Federal Privatisations	50,762	11,326	62,089
Telecommunications	26,978	2,125	29,103
PND	23,785	9,201	32,986
State Privatisations	27,734	6,750	34,485
Total	78,497	18,077	96,573

Source: BNDES

The most recent, highly symbolic partial privatisation concerned Petrobrás. In 1997 the new petroleum law broke up Petrobrás monopoly in production and drilling and eliminated cross subsidies over a three-year transition period. An estimated seven per cent of national reserves were made available to the private sector, although it is important to note that Petrobrás, acting alone or in alliance with private companies, bid aggressively in the first auction of oil exploration licences. While the government was obliged, by law, to hold a controlling majority in the company, in August 2000 some 250,000 Brazilians bought Petrobrás's share in the first sale of a state-owned company specifically targeted at retail investors. The government raised US$4 billion and reduced its stake from 81.7 per cent to 55 per cent of the voting capital.

Regulatory Policies

Although Brazil has had laws regulating competition policy since 1945 (and an entity since 1962), their impact was limited at best.[35] During the

---

35 Brazilian antitrust legislation makes reference to three different entities. CADE (Administrative Council for Economic Defence, an autonomous agency composed of six commissioners and a president appointed by the President of Republic and confirmed by the Senate for a fixed term), SDE (Secretariat for Economic Law, of the Ministry of Justice) and SEAE (Secretariat for Economic Monitoring, of the Ministry of Finance). Their responsibilities, according to the law, are as follows: SDE is in charge of starting and conducting investigations related to antitrust cases, as well as monitoring the market for anticompetitive practices. SEAE is responsible for preparing

1990s the overall focus of competition shifted from basically direct intervention in the market for the purpose of protecting the so-called 'popular economy' (essentially, controlling prices) to the analysis of mergers, abuse of dominant position and other topics more in line with the international trends in antitrust regulation. CADE was given more autonomy from the central administration and its members gained a fixed two-year term renewable once. Congress also approved legislation creating regulatory agencies in the areas of telecommunications (Anatel), electricity (Aneel) and oil (ANP) (Table A3.1). In parallel, Congress approved, also in 1995, a law (the concessions law) governing the central aspects of the provision of public utilities under licence agreements.

Anti-trust agencies and sectoral regulatory bodies are still in flux and so far have not established a single coherent government policy on sectoral concentration. Anatel, for example, has forced telecom firms to sell off shares to ensure competition across regions and subsectors. CADE has blocked some mergers,[36] but approved AmBev, its largest case to date (see below). The lack of coherence is compounded by overlapping responsibilities and competing jurisdictions among several general and sectoral agencies.

Changes in Big Business

In 1984, the last year before the return of democracy, the federal government owned 12, and states four more, of the 20 largest non-financial firms in Brazil (Table 3.3). Nonetheless, excluding utilities and Petrobrás, only four of the 20 largest manufacturing firms were public-owned, although admittedly the biggest four.

Trade opening, price stability and the downsizing of government demand exposed the poor technology and management in family firms. No longer able to set prices at will, companies suddenly had to scrutinise costs. Moreover, many Brazilian family businesses founded in the 1950s were also facing succession problems. According to Siffert Filho and Souza e Silva (1999), the total volume of mergers and acquisitions that took place in Brazil during the 1991–98 period was equal to US$142 billion, including privatisa-

---

non-binding economic opinions on merger cases and may issue opinions in the case of anticompetitive practices. CADE is an autonomous agency that enforces the competition law in adjudicating cases, deciding on what constitutes a violation of the law and applying penalties when needed. CADE can also conduct additional investigation when necessary. In recent years there have been several proposals to combine these functions into a single agency. See Clark (2000) for a recent review.

36 Following Colgate's acquisition of Kolynos, a toothpaste company, giving the combined group 80% of the Brazilian market, the CADE ordered the sale of part of the stock and banned the Kolynos brand for four years in order to give competitors a chance to establish themselves. In 1997 two separate joint ventures between US and Brazilian breweries (Miller and Brahma, and Anheuser-Busch and Antarctica, respectively) were both blocked.

tion that accounted for half of the total. In 1998 alone, these transactions represented a volume estimated at between US$35–40 billion.

Table 3.3: The Largest Non-Financial Corporations in Brazil in 1984 and 1998

	1984	Owner	Sector	1998	Owner	Sector
1	Petrobrás	CG	RM	Petrobrás	CG	RM
2	CVRD	CG	RM	Furnas	CG	U
3	CESP	SG	U	TELESP	PF	U
4	TELESP	CG	U	CESP	SG	U
5	Furnas	CG	U	SABESP	SG	U
6	CHESF	CG	U	EMBRATEL	PF	U
7	RFFSA	CG	U	CVRD	PN	RM
8	Copene	PN	IC	Fiat	PF	CD
9	EMBRATEL	CG	U	Eletropaulo	PF	U
10	CEMIG	SG	U	RFFSA	CG	U
11	Usiminas	CG	IC	CEMIG	SG	U
12	SABESP	SG	U	CSN	PN	IC
13	Eletronorte	CG	U	Light	PN	U
14	Light	CG	U	CBD	PN	CND
15	Petroquimica União	CG	IC	CHESF	CG	U
16	Mercedes Benz	PF	CD	Usiminas	PN	IC
17	COPEL	SG	U	Brahma	PN	CND
18	Camargo Correa	PN	C	Petrobrás Distribudora	CG	RM
19	Mendes Junior	PN	C	Mercedes Benz	PF	CD
20	VARIG	PN	U	COPEL	SG	U
21	TELERJ	CG	U	CPFL	PF	U
22	Suzano	PN	IC	TELERJ	PF	U
23	Belgo Mineira	PN	IC	TELESP Celular	PF	U
24	Volkswagen	PF	CD	VARIG	PN	U
25	Petrobrás Distribuidora	CG	CND	Eletronorte	CG	U
26	Mannesmann	PF	IC	COSIPA	PN	IC
27	Rhodia	PF	IC	Ceval	PN	IC
28	Klabin	PN	IC	Gerdau	PN	IC
29	Aracruz	PN	IC	CST	PN	IC
30	Brasileira Aluminio	PN	IC	Shell	PF	RM
31	Votorantim	PN	IC	Bandeirante	PF	U
32	Andrade Gutierrez	PN	C	Credicard	PN	CND
33	Dow Quimica	PF	IC	Ericsson	PF	CD
34	Eletrosul	CG	U	Souza Cruz	PF	CND
35	Pirelli	PF	CD	Copene	PN	IC
36	Nestlé	PF	CND	TELEMIG	PF	U
37	ESSO	PF	RM	VASP	PN	U
38	White Martins	PF	IC	CEDAE	SG	U
39	Docenave	CG	U	CRT	PF	U
40	Ford	PF	CD	Ipiranga	PN	RM

Ownership: CG=central government; SG=state government; PF=private foreign; PN=private national

Sectors: C=construction and engineering; CD=consumer durables; CND=consumer non-durables and distribution; D=diversified; HT=high-technology; IC=industrial commodities; RM=raw materials; U=utilities

Sources: *Conjuntura Econômica*, September 1985 and September 1999.

There have been four main consequences (Table 3.4). First, the decrease of the role of the state as owner of non-financial assets — although semi-public pension funds representing employees in (formerly) state-owned enterprises dramatically increased the size of industrial holdings they control. Second, shared control between a multiplicity of investors —domestic and foreign, industrial and financial, none of them having a majority in isolation — has become a key instrument of corporate control. Roughly a quarter of the largest companies have this form of control, where management depends on an agreement between the controlling stockholders covering key variables such as the extent of areas of operation, funding mechanisms, degree of exposure to risks, technology and marketing policies and the parameters that define the behaviour of managers. In privatisation, the coalition model of control allowed to associate employees as investors, usually with a seat on the board and to appease nationalistic fringes through the participation of public-sector banks, foundations and pension funds. Moreover, in the early phase when inflation control was far from assured, authorities shied from the temptation of practising 'corporate re-engineering' as the risks of picking winners (or, more correctly, of creating losers) outweighed the possible benefits.

Table 3.4: Ownership of the 100 Largest Non-Financial Brazilian Companies (percentage share of total revenues for the 100 largest companies)

	Dispersed Ownership	Shared Control	Family Ownership	Government Ownership	Foreign Ownership	Cooperatives
1990	1	5	27	38	27	2
	(1)	(4)	(23)	(44)	(26)	(2)
1995	3	15	26	23	31	2
	(2)	(11)	(17)	(30)	(38)	(2)
1997	3	19	23	21	33	1
	(2)	(12)	(16)	(32)	(37)	(0)
1998	4	23	26	12	34	1
	(3)	(19)	(17)	(21)	(40)	(0)

Source: Siffert Filho and Souza e Silva (1999).

Third, foreign corporations from all OECD countries (and some non-OECD ones, notably Chile and Argentina) have enlarged their investment in corporate Brazil, from 27 to 34 companies. Companies controlled by MNCs have also become larger, so that their share of total sales by Brazil's 100 largest companies has increased from 26 per cent to 40 per cent. Finally, public companies, where ownership is dispersed and management exercises control, remain limited phenomena — although it is also clear that this corporate form is gaining ground.

Case Studies in Corporate Reinvention

How has Brazilian big business reacted to such changes? And what has government done to mould these processes of corporate reinvention? In this section we explore these issues on the basis of six case studies.[37]

The Rise of a New Conglomerate through Privatisation: Vicunha[38]

In the space of a very few years Benjamin Steinbruch, whose family owns half of Grupo Vicunha, Brazil's largest textile firm has become one of the most powerful businessmen in the country. In 1993, with the help of local banks, pension funds and some foreign investors, Vicunha bought CSN, in which it holds a 14 per cent stake (Table 3.6). In addition to being Latin America's biggest integrated steel maker, CSN is the world's largest single-mill producer of tin plate. Although it was already well run by the state, since 1995 CSN has thrived, cutting operating costs by 30 per cent by the end of 1998 and recording rising profits since 1997. In May 1998 Steinbruch and a group of investors (four Brazilian pension funds, NationsBank of the USA and São Paulo's Opportunity Asset Management) outbid a more powerful consortium — that included Votorantim, a traditional Brazilian family business (see below) — for a controlling stake in CVRD. With Telecom Italia, Vicunha later won a mobile-phone licence for Bahia. The third largest electricity consumer in Brazil, CSN is investing in the construction of a co-generation thermoelectric plant at its Volta Redonda steel mill, is part of the consortia responsible for the construction and operation of two hydroelectric power plants, and owns a 7.25 per cent shareholding in Light, Rio de Janeiro's electricity utility. And finally, to ensure efficient transportation of its raw materials and products, CSN is active in the control of railroads in the centre-east, southeastern and northeastern regions and it has acquired the concession rights to the coal and containers terminals at the Port of Sepetiba.

37   Our selection of cases is not designed to be strictly representative, but the cases do illustrate well the wide range of different corporate strategies among major firms as well as the variable impact of government policies.

38   This section partly draws on Ruiz (1997); 'The Iron Chancellor,' *The Economist*, 17 January 1998; 'Shaping up for the Struggle of the Titans,' *Financial Times*, 8 July 1999. See also www.vicunha.com.br.

Behind most of such deals was the idea that privatisation was a unique opportunity to gain control of assets that would otherwise take generations to assemble. To do this, Steinbruch took a few risks. In general, Brazil's family entrepreneurs avoid debt and insist on control in any venture. Steinbruch was prepared to borrow to win CVRD — most of CSN's 39 per cent stake was covered by a US$1.1 billion loan — and to accept shared control in all its ventures. His empire, however, soon faced the conglomerate dangers of management overstretch and lack of focus. Moreover, CVRD's complex shareholder structure and a jumble of non-core business interests dragged the share price down by nearly half since privatisation. Steinbruch was therefore obliged to reshuffle his impressive industrial portfolio. In 1999 CSN sold its Riberão Grande cement firm to Votorantim and its struggling alumina refinery subsidiary to Norway's Norsk Hydro. CVRD's various pulp and paper holdings were also consolidated, and Steinbruch is apparently negotiating with potential buyers. Most importantly, the cross-ownership between CSN and CVRD is being severed (*descruzamento*), leaving Steinbruch in control of the mining group while transferring his shares in CSN to other investors.

The BNDES promoted this *descruzamento* in part because the BNDES was worried that the complicated financial web could impede the consolidation of the Brazilian steel industry. In commodity steels, Brazilian firms are already among the world's lowest-cost producers, partly as a result of mergers completed in recent years.[39]

Gerdau: Specialisation and International Expansion[40]

One firm that has performed remarkably well is Gerdau, and its recent past shows a rather different history. Gerdau is highly focused — it specialises in long steels, used mostly in construction and heavy machinery industry, has a transparent ownership structure and, once it reached a dominant position in the domestic market, found it expedient to invest abroad. It initially expanded through privatisation (Table 3.5), has mills in Chile, Argentina, Uruguay and Canada and bought control of AmeriSteel, a US maker of steel bars, in 1999. Gerdau owes its success abroad — where it cannot count on the low cost of raw materials and power in

---

39　In 1998, Usinor, the French steel group, acquired a 40% controlling stake in Acesita, that since its privatisation in 1993 had taken over Aços Villares and CST. The entry of Usinor into the Brazilian market was motivated by the possibility of expansion in the international market, taking advantage of the synergies between a stainless steel producer and the access to CST's slab production, a strategic raw material for Usinor itself.

40　This section partly draws on 'Gerdau lifts Overseas Production Capacity,' *Financial Times*, 9 August 1999, 'Who Dares Wins,' *The Economist*, 23 September 2000 and Ruiz (1997). See www.gerdau.com.br.

Brazil, nor on the fact that Gerdau used its market power to impose its standards in the Brazilian construction industry — on its ability to export its logistics-based organisational approach and management style.

Table 3.5: Steel Privatisations in the National Privatisation Programme

Company	Auction Date	Minimum price (US$ Millions)	Final price (US$ Millions)	Premium (per cent)	Main Investors
Usiminas	10-24-91	974.1	1,112.4	14.2	Bozano
Cosinor	11-14-91	12.0	13.6	13.8	Gerdau
Piratini	02/14/92	42.0	106.3	153.0	Gerdau
CST 1	07-16-92	294.8	295.4	0.2	Bozano, CVRD and Unibanco
CST 2	07-23-92	36.9	36.9	-	Bozano and Unibanco
Acesita	10-23-92	347.6	450.2	29.5	Previ, Sistel and Safra
CSN	04-02-93	1,056.6	1,056.6	-	Bamerindus, Vicunha, Docenave, Bradesco and Itaú
Cosipa	08-20-93	166.3	330.6	98.8	Anquila and Brastubo
Açominas	09-10-93	296.4	554.2	87.0	Cia. Min. Part. Industrial

Source: *Gazeta Mercantil*, Panorama Setorial, quoted in Andrade Silva Cunha and Tavares Gandra (1999).

What is peculiar about Gerdau is that the founding Johannpeter family still retains control — top management is made up of four brothers well into their sixties who hold equal shares of the family's 70 per cent stake — and decided to finance its recent foreign take-over with debt and cash instead of opening up its share capital. Paradoxically, while Jorge Gerdau Johannpeter leads an industrialists' group that lobbies politicians for modernising company law, he also believes that his family's controlling share is vital for Gerdau's stability.[41]

---

41   On Gerdau's political activities, see Schneider (1997–98).

The Transformation of an Established Business Group: Votorantim[42]

Founded in 1917 as a textile firm, Votorantim is Brazil's largest and most diversified industrial group. The group's patriarch, Antônio Ermírio de Moraes, is well known in Brazil as a man of austere habits and a social conscience. Votorantim is Brazil's largest cement producer, its third-largest pulp and paper maker and its citrus-juice subsidiary claims to have the world's largest orange grove (in which it has planted 3.5 million trees). It also has aluminium, zinc, nickel, steel, chemical and packaging businesses, as well as a small investment bank. Though small stakes in the cement and paper businesses are publicly traded, the de Moraes family retains firm control over the group. Antônio Ermírio and his three siblings each have 25 per cent of Hejoassu, the holding company. All the important decisions are taken by these four and must be approved unanimously. Their children, who number 23, occupy senior management positions and sit on the holding company's advisory board. Votorantim's big asset is a strong balance sheet: despite operating in capital-intensive industries, as it pertains to a group that epitomised Brazil's import-substitution, total debt is less than cash holdings.

Stability was the aim at Votorantim, which has avoided entanglements abroad. Yet, an open economy creates threats as well as opportunities. The cement business has proved vulnerable to cheap Asian imports, because its main markets are close to Brazil's coastal ports, and the paper industry, while it has low costs, thanks to its fast-growing eucalyptus trees, competes with countries like Indonesia. Already the country's largest private electricity generator, Votorantim has become an important investor in energy privatisation, where it has formed VBC, a joint venture with Camargo Corrêa and Bradesco. In 1998, for the first time, Votorantim tapped international capital markets, raising US$400m in bonds. The group says it may take on more debt and sell minority stakes in some operating companies. But experience of economic volatility makes Votorantim congenitally conservative: according to Ermírio de Moraes, a more leveraged capital structure would be 'premature' while Brazil's stabilisation is incomplete and world markets are so uncertain. While Votorantim has pursued a strategy of diversification into sectors with few technological or commercial connections to its other subsidiaries, the strategy seems to take advantage of some economies of scope. Industries like aluminium, pulp and paper, cement, steel and orange juice are similar in that they use established technologies and require sophisticated logistical management in processing and transporting high bulk goods.

---

42   This section draws on Bonelli (1998); 'Votorantim Task is to Keep Pot Boiling,' *Financial Times*, 13 February 1997; 'Sou nacionalista, mais não sou burro,' *Veja*, 3 June 1998; and 'Easy Now,' *The Economist*, 20 June 1998.

Consumer Goods: the Restructuring of the Beer Industry[43]

The consumer goods sector, and in particular the food and beverage industry, has shown high growth rates since 1994 and high return margins. Brazil already had powerful local brands, many of them founded in the 1950s by European immigrants, but its food industry was highly fragmented. Given the huge costs of building consumer loyalty and extensive distribution networks, MNCs have hence grown through purchase of existing brands. Since 1993, for example, Parmalat, an Italian food firm, has bought ten local firms, mainly producers of dairy products, and its Brazilian sales are now bigger than those at home. The retail sector has also seen the arrival of the world's largest super- and hypermarket chains. One of the consequences of this is that of the 20 largest companies in the sector in 1991, only two were foreign, while in 1998 the number of foreign companies among the 20 largest had increased to 13.[44] It is only in the meat and grain processing segments that local companies still dominate.

The brewing industry is a good example of this transformation. Beer is largely a matter of local taste; not much is traded internationally. At the same time, local breweries import 100 per cent of hops, colupolin and other primary inputs, so that trade opening and exchange rate appreciation led to a 146 per cent increase in imports between 1992 and 1996. The fast growth of the market, as well as its oligopolistic structure (the four largest breweries account for 98.5 per cent of sales), allowed cost reductions to be translated into mark-up and profits increases.[45] The issue of market dominance by the two largest breweries, Brahma and Antarctica, came to the fore in the mid-1990s as they reached preliminary agreements with Miller and Anheuser-Busch, respectively, to import the US brands. Competition authorities ordered both joint ventures to be dissolved on the ground that the Brazilian companies were using the tie-ups to limit competition from the American competitors, which could have entered the market independently.

In June 1999 Brahma announced it was taking over Antarctica, its smaller rival, in a friendly deal to create American Beverage Company (AmBev), which would give them 71.3 per cent of the domestic beer market. The two companies had combined revenues of R$10.3b in 1998, making AmBev the world's third brewer after Anheuser-Busch and Heineken.

---

43   This section partly draws on 'Brazilian Takeovers: the Buying and Selling of Brazil Inc,' *The Economist*, 9 November 1996 and 'Flag of Convenience,' *ibid.*, 7 August 1999; 'O superbebê das loiras,' *Época*, 5 July 1999; 'Brazilian Beer Giant plays the Politics,' *Financial Times*, 12 July 1999; 'Giant Thirsts after Global Expansion,' *ibid.*, 10 April 2000; and 'Coca-Cola marque un point dans la guerre l'opposant à AmBev,' *Le Temps*, 16 November 1999.

44   Siffert Filho and Souza e Silva (1999).

45   For beverages, mark ups rose by 38% between 1990 and 1995 (Moreira and Correa 1996).

Management has been trying to get clearance for their planned merger by arguing that only by joining forces can Brazil boast a national champion mighty enough to take on the world's drinks giants and occupy spaces globally. AmBev, however, relies on neighbouring markets for less than ten per cent of its sales, and the merger is more about the domestic market. Antarctica has large debts and has been losing market share. Brahma, though stronger, lacks a premium-brand soft drink, which its former arch-enemy has in the form of Guaranà Antarctica, a type of fruit soda. The government pondered cuts in import duties to tempt more foreign drinks firms into the domestic market. But customers' loyalty to existing brands is so strong that new entrants would be attracted only if Brahma-Antarctica raised beer prices.

AmBev mounted a shrewd political and public relations campaign to ensure the swift approval of the merger by competition authorities. Nonetheless, in view of the developments outlined in Section 2, government approval of the merger without requiring significant divestments could signal an important change in Brazilian industrial policy. In its inquiry, made public in November 1999, the Secretaria de Acompanhamento Econômico (SEAE) argued that such a concentration should not be approved. It suggested that AmBev should get rid of Skol, which represents 27 per cent of the market.[46] In March 2000 CADE imposed less harsh conditions for the deal, ruling that Ambev be forced to sell the Bavaria brand (whose market share is only five per cent) as well as five factories. In a country with few internationally known companies, the national champion argument seemed to drown out potential threats to competition in the domestic market.

Investment Goods: Foreign Acquisitions in Autoparts[47]

The Brazilian auto industry has been a symbol of industrialisation not only in that country but in Latin America in general. Autoparts suppliers, working with state officials, were instrumental in shaping legislation, policies and industrial practices from the 1950s to the present and this alliance resulted in protectionist policies and legislation that helped form cooperative relationships between assembly operations and suppliers.[48] The hybrid form of organisation that combines features of mass production and flexible production helped suppliers to adapt to changing political and eco-

---

46 The most likely buyer would have been Kaiser, Brazil's second largest brewery. Coca Cola — which controls 40% of Brazil's soft drinks market and owns a 10% stake in Kaiser — has not shied from advertising against the government's approval of the AmBev deal. For its part, the latter has accused Coca Cola of threatening not to sell its flagship soft drink to retailers that were not willing to buy Kaiser also.

47 This section partly draws on 'Mais uma que vai embora,' *Veja*, 7 May 1997.

48 Addis (1998).

nomic conditions and the most successful suppliers were able to organise into cartels to maintain leverage over assemblers.

When, in June 1996, Metal Leve, a maker of pistons and ball bearings in Sao Paulo, was sold, many Brazilians therefore saw the deal as a landmark of sorts. The firm had long been held up as an example of Brazilian industry at its best. Founded in 1950, Metal Leve grew to have sales of US$350 million a year, employ 7,000 people and enjoy a return on equity of over 20 per cent. It had been exporting to the United States since the 1960s and in 1989 had invested more than US$25 million in building a factory in South Carolina to be able to supply their customers 'just-in-time'. They had experimented with joint ventures with German partners to gain technology. And they had cut costs, shedding half the workforce. But, as Brazil's car industry has begun to modernise, scouring the world for components, the company could no longer compete in its home market. Sales halved from their peak, to just US$303 million in 1995, as Metal Leve needed to invest US$100 million a year to compete, well beyond its owners' resources. Faced with mounting losses, the six families who owned the firm sold it for US$300 million to a group of investors including Mahle, a big German car-parts firm, Cofap (Cia. Fabricadora de Peças), another Brazilian car-parts firm and the largest in Latin America; and Bradesco, owning 50, 33 and 15 per cent respectively.

Cofap itself was hit hard by the 1995–96 appreciation of the currency, and Bradesco swapped its credits vis-à-vis Cofap with its ageing owner against a 40 per cent equity stake. In 1997 Magneti Marelli, the parts division of Fiat, the Italian carmaker, took over Cofap and its nine plants. As part of a wider and more powerful international group, Cofap has remained the market leader in Brazil and exports to 98 countries. Sales abroad in 1998 amounted to US$152.5 million on total turnover of US$563.9 million.

Embraer: The Ugly Duckling of High Technology Exports[49]

Created in 1969 for reasons of national security, Embraer (Empresa Brasileira de Aeronautica) had become by the early 1980s an important aircraft manufacturer, designing and producing fuselages and final assembly. The company's strong focus on the export market was crucial in offsetting development costs. It permitted longer production runs, stimulated customers to bring new ideas for technical change and demanded exacting performance standards. Since the mid-1980s, however, Brazil's macroeconomic crisis, combined with an excessive attention to engineering — as opposed to marketing — requirements and the abrupt closure of the

---

49   This section draws on Goldstein (2001).

Middle East weapons market hit Embraer. Delays mounted, orders were cancelled and some of Embraer's specialised suppliers went bankrupt

In December 1994 a consortium bought a controlling 45 per cent stake for US$89m. The syndicate included a New York investment boutique; Bozano Simonsen, one of Brazil's greatest financial conglomerates, and Previ and Sistel, respectively Banco do Brasil's and Telebras's pension funds.[50] The government assumed the debt and retained 6.8 per cent of the company's shares. The new owners hired an outside executive to chair the firm and adopted a new organisational chart, structured around single projects to enhance flexibility, interaction and autonomy. The number of managerial levels was cut and the payroll fell from a peak of 12,700 in 1990 to 3,600 in 1995.

In the mid-1990s Embraer broke into what was then a niche market for civilian regional jets with the EMB–145, a 50-seater in which it invested US$ 300m; several European and American component-suppliers aerospace firms chipped in as 'risk-sharing partners'. In 1998 the company rolled out the first prototype of the EMB–135, a smaller version of the EMB–145 with 90 per cent commonality. Embraer first became profitable in 1998 and exports, which made up 95 per cent of total sales, were greatly boosted by the 1999 devaluation of the *real*, despite the concurrent increase in the financial costs of raising new debt as well as servicing outstanding dollar-denominated liabilities. The company now claims to lead unit sales in the world market for regional aircraft and by 2000 it has grown into the world's second-ranking regional jet maker after Bombardier (and the fourth-biggest overall), reporting 1999 sales of US$1.8 billion and net income of US$238 million. Employment increased to over 7,000 people. Although Embraer still imports a substantial portion of its inputs, it has also become Brazil's biggest exporter, accounting for 3.5 per cent of total Brazilian sales abroad in 1999. In November 1999, a French consortium acquired a 20 per cent stake, valuing Embraer at around US$1 billion. In July 2000 Embraer's American Depository Receipts started trading on the New York Stock Exchange.

While better management was certainly an important element in this reversal of fortunes, on top of its considerable internal know-how Embraer benefited from its location and from various forms of government support. São José dos Campos stands in the very heart of the Paraíba Valley, where Volkswagen, Ford and General Motors have also established some of their largest plants worldwide, attracting other huge investments in the component and electronics industries that Embraer could tap into. Public sector institutions such as BNDES and the Financiadora de

---

50 In June 1995, after Wasserstein Perella's failure to pay the money it had pledged, Bozano Simonsen bought it out.

Estudos e Projetos (FINEP — part of the Ministry for Science and Technology) have actively supported R&D activities. Another important feature has been the extension of export subsidies to Embraer by BNDES (through Finamex) and Banco do Brasil (through the Proex 'equalisation interest rate programme'). The rationale of this mechanism, which provides up to a 3.5 per cent cut in interest rates on loans to purchasers of exported Brazilian aircraft, is to offset the so-called *Custo Brasil*, i.e. the higher risk of doing business in the country due to a number of structural factors. A heated controversy arose between Brazil and Canada, which requested the establishment of a panel to investigate whether export subsidies granted under the Proex are inconsistent with the WTO Subsidies Agreement. Following various findings, in July 2000 a WTO appellate panel ruled that Canada has complied with an earlier ruling to end illegal subsidies to Bombardier, but that Proex still violates international standards.

Conclusions

Mergers and acquisitions boomed in Brazil in the 1990s, driven by privatisation, new opportunities for foreign investors and changing strategies by domestic firms, some of which shed subsidiaries to specialise while others bought up firms to diversify or expand market share. In terms of corporate structure, among the largest firms the share of state ownership fell, foreign ownership rose, family ownership fell (but not by as much as might have been expected) and a new category of mixed or dispersed ownership rose.

While most large firms in Brazil have sought out foreign partners and foreign markets, these case studies demonstrate the heterogeneity of responses to the changing climate of the 1990s (Table 3.6). On the one hand stand groups that chose to pursue conglomerisation, although their strategies have been different. Vicunha/Steinbruch was aggressive in taking advantage of the privatisation programme to diversify into many unrelated areas. However, insofar as it had to renounce to exert complete managerial and financial control, it then found it difficult to combine conglomerisation with the need to deliver rates of return on capital in line with those required by financial markets. Votorantim approached the privatisation process cautiously. Despite the opportunities to buy state firms in sectors in which Votorantim was already producing, it continued to diversify into unrelated sectors, most notably paper and cellulose, in the 1990s. While there is little apparent relationship among aluminium, cellulose, cement and orange juice, there is however a common thread in the low value-added, primary processing of bulk goods. In Votorantim there is a presumptive strategy designed to exploit economies of scope. In contrast firms like AmBev, Embraer and Gerdau consolidated, merged, specialised and expanded operations (trade and sometimes investment) abroad, sometimes benefiting from government support.

Table 3.6: A Synthesis of the Evidence on the Transformation of Big Brazilian Business

Firm/group/ sector	AmBev	Embraer	Gerdau	Vicunha	Votorantim	Car parts industry
Main market	Domestic	International	International	Domestic for utilities, international for commodities	Domestic for utilities, international for commodities	Domestic
Diversification	Low	Low	Low	High	High	Low
Ownership/ control separation	High	High	Low	Low	Low	Low
Impact of policies						
Trade opening	Low	Low	High	High	High	High
Privatisation	Low	High	High	High	Low	Low
Other significant government interventions	Regulatory[b]	Incentives and subsidies		Financial[a]		Incentives and subsidies[c]

Notes: a. Following privatisation BNDES remained as a shareholder in CSN and helped finance the *descruzamento*.
b. The AmBev merger is easier following CADE's overhaul of initial recommendations on the Antarctica/Brahma merger.
c. In addition to earlier efforts to guide industrial restructuring throughout the *câmaras setoriais*

The Brazilian state has maintained an active role in shaping big business in Brazil. Since its creation in the 1950s the BNDES has consistently influenced the shape of big business in Brazil: by promoting state enterprises in steel and electricity in the 1960s; petrochemicals and *tripés* in 1970s; privatisation in 1980s and 1990s; and most recently mergers and conglomeration. Many, perhaps most, people in big business accept this influence and some argue the case for a common public-private strategy to reinforce Brazilian groups in view of 'realizing national objectives that are larger and stronger than simple corporate goals'.[51] The election of Horacio Lafer to head FIESP also gave new impetus to a revival of a more statist *desenvolvimentismo*. These pressures led to the reinforcement of the Ministry for Development, Industry and Foreign Trade, although this proved an ill-fated attempt surpassed by events. The conditionality clauses imposed by the IMF both before and after the January 1999 crisis gave the upper hand

51   Steinbruch (1998).

to those in government who were sceptical about the desirability of such renewed interventionism. The debate on corporate ownership and the role of domestic capital resurfaced in 2000 around the potential sale of Banespa, formally known as Banco do Estado de São Paulo.[52] Private domestic business suggested that some form of government support should be introduced to prop up the bids by Brazilian banks and to limit the growth of foreign competitors. The government, however, authorised foreign banks to bid for Banespa and maintained its stance in the face of opposition from a broad alliance ranging from the left to officials in previous military governments. In the end, a Spanish bank bought Banespa in November 2000, but the prior debate revealed widespread support for the idea that the state should promote big domestic firms.

A full explanation for differences in business organisation has to incorporate political factors: what state actors do, deliberately and unintentionally, to forge industrial organisation. For McCraw (1998), recounting the history of big business without reference to government 'is a story of Hamlet without the prince, or at the very least without the queen',[53] especially, we would add, for developing countries. The big difference with the past is that in most cases government policies have tried to create markets rather than centralise the allocation of scarce resources. It was only where government perceived that Brazilian business was suffering from the fact that some markets, such as that for export credit, still do not exist in the country that it took a more active role, not shying away from confronting foreign trading partners in the defence of its economic interests.

While the strength of the factors noted in the first part of this chapter that previously served to increase incentives for conglomeration, such as protection, industrial policy, small markets and macroeconomic volatility, mostly receded, conglomerates have far from disappeared.[54] The picture that emerges is thus one of limited convergence towards an 'Anglo-Saxon' model of corporate organisation, confirming the importance of history, politics and institutions in this area. Far from returning to the protectionist policies of the past, the experience of Brazil seems to confirm that WTO membership is not necessarily inconsistent with some forms of industrial policy.[55]

What are, then, the consequences of this restructuring for economic policy and growth? Contrary to what seems the conventional wisdom in the United States, and possibly in other OECD countries, Khanna (2000) finds that group affiliation appears to be profitable in most emerging markets, though the underlying reasons for this effect are unclear. There is

52   See the series of op-ed articles in the *Folha de São Paulo*, 17–24 January 2000.
53   McCraw (1998), p. 544.
54   Garrido (2000) reaches a similar conclusion for Mexico.
55   Bora et al. (2000).

substantial evidence that part of the positive performance effect is due to welfare-enhancing functions originating in the idea that groups substitute for missing outside institutions. What is discomforting for policy-makers, however, is that part of the performance effect is due to welfare-reducing minority shareholder exploitation.[56]

Some policy implications are straightforward. Emerging economies should not follow Western corporate restructuring models that advocate dismantling inefficient, diversified business groups, because it could do more harm than good. Conglomerates may be providing the kinds of services in emerging markets that institutions such as investment banks, accounting firms and business schools provide in advanced markets.[57] At the same time, to ensure that business groups do not exploit other stakeholders — namely consumers, employees and minority shareholders — no effort should be spared to develop effective market institutions by instituting a fair and enforceable system of law and order. In particular, if Brazilian authorities wish to see an increase in the number of large companies in which there is a clear separation between ownership and management, practices and an institutional model that make this relationship efficient must be developed.[58] It remains to be seen, moreover, whether policymakers are able to equally defend producers and customers: in other words, whether a 'national beer' will cater as much for the needs of Brazilians as the limited requirements imposed on AmBev have done for the latter's shareholders. The fact that mergers and acquisitions have mostly served to increase market shares and exclude competitors, rather than seek efficiency and profitability,[59] is somewhat disquieting in this context.

---

56 Khanna and Palepu (1998) show that in Chile the net benefits of unrelated diversification are positive if group diversification exceeds a threshold level, though this threshold increases with time. They conjecture that the evolution of institutional context may alter the value creating potential of business groups, though it does so slowly. For Brazil, Villarim de Siqueira (1999) finds that concentration of ownership does not have a statistically significant effect on the financial performance of companies. He does not control, however, for group membership.

57 Khanna and Palepu (1997).

58 But the difficult advance of a bill that would strengthen the protection of minority investors, outlaw insider trading and pave the way for the introduction of international accounting standards confirms the hypothesis advanced in the literature that there are powerful interests defending the status quo in corporate governance.

59 Ferraz et al. (2000).

Table A3.1: The Regulatory Agencies in Brazil

	ANEEL (electricity)	ANATEL (telecommunications)	ANP (oil)
a. Characteristics of the regulated sector			
Type	Markets	Markets	State-sector enterprise sector and market
Presence of monopolies	In transmission and distribution	Competitive	Vertically-integrated state monopoly
Competition	Generation and distribution	Regulatory asymmetry to favour entrants	Restricted to prospecting concessions; most competition is in wholesale and distribution.
b. Agency oversight			
Governance contract	Yes	No	No
Interface with society	Ombudsman in the board of directors; council of consumers	Independent ombudsman; advisory council in the agency	Ombudsman
Counterpart ministry	Ministry of Mines and Energy	Ministry of Communications	Ministry of Mines and Energy
c. Agency structure			
Law	No. 9427, 26 December 1996	No. 9472, 16 July 1997	No. 9478, 6 August 1997
Creation	6 October 1997	7 October 1997	14 January 1998
Regime	Autarchy under special regime	Autarchy under special regime	Autarchy under special regime
Objectives	Regulate the electricity sector according to the directives of the federal government	Regulate the telecommunications sector and implement the General Telecommunications Law	Regulate the petroleum sector and implement the national petroleum policy
Board	Director general and four directors		
Super-intendencies	25 regional	5 regional	Functional
Degree of insulation	Prohibition of links to business; staggered 4-year terms; no exoneration without motives, except in the first four months; quarantine of 12 months.	Prohibition of links to business; 5-year terms, no re-election; no exoneration without motives; quarantine of 12 months, except for academics.	Prohibition of links to business, including in the year before appointment; staggered 4-year terms; quarantine of 12 months.
Appointment	President after Senate approval	President after Senate approval	President after Senate approval
Budget	Budget law, fees and fines	Budget law, fees and fines, FISTEL	Budget law, fees and fines, FISTEL

Source: OECD

CHAPTER 4

Trade Reform, Market Liberalisation and Industrial Performance in Brazil

Edmund Amann

Introduction

With the inception of trade reform and market liberalisation in the late 1980s and early 1990s, the Brazilian economy appeared to have made a decisive break with the past. Eschewing the interventionism and protectionism that had characterised much of the post-war period, policymakers embarked on a programme of rapid liberalisation under which the Brazilian industrial sector would be opened up as never before to the forces of international competition and foreign direct investment. Underpinning this sea change in the policy environment lay a belief that the years of quasi-autarchy under import substituting industrialisation (ISI) had, whatever their initial achievements, ultimately resulted in chronic uncompetitiveness, technological inertia and a declining capacity to generate employment. Given the exposure of Brazilian industry to global market forces, it was believed, a process of profound restructuring would commence. This would not only restore the vitality of the sector but would also in turn contribute to the overarching goal of macroeconomic stabilisation.

From the perspective of the opening years of the twenty-first century the liberalising zeal that accompanied the inception of Brazilian trade and market reform seems redolent of another era. Since the Asian financial crisis erupted in 1997, less developed economies throughout the world have been coming to terms with a new reality in which cost-effective access to international capital markets can no longer be assured, regardless of the pace and depth of market liberalisation at home. In the case of Brazil and its neighbours, the past few years have proved a period of considerable economic and political turbulence. Across the region, growth has stagnated or collapsed, inflation has mounted and currencies have entered freefall. Against this background, it is hardly surprising that the nostrums of trade and market reform, so readily accepted in the 1990s have come under considerable scrutiny. Within Brazil, this phenomenon has manifested itself in the guise of a slowdown in the privatisation programme and a marked reluctance to embark on further rounds of trade reform. As a more general indicator of the change in the ideological climate, the political fortunes of the interventionist left have recovered significantly, while even within the mainstream centrist parties, talk of rolling back the frontiers of the state has become distinctly passé.

While the ebbing of the tide of neo-liberalism has become evident, it is by no means clear what shape the guiding principles of future economic policy may take. As industrialists and politicians attempt to grapple with possible alternatives to the liberalising creeds of the 1990s, a re-energised debate has surfaced concerning the role of the state in fostering industrial development. Such a debate, however, can only be productive if it is partly grounded on an assessment of the achievements and shortcomings of the neo-liberal period. It is with that issue that this chapter is concerned. Beginning with an overview of the policies of trade and market reform that emerged at the beginning of the last decade, the discussion then turns its attention to the impact of these policies on the performance of the industrial sector. A particular emphasis is placed on the role of market opening on changes in productivity. However, attention is also focused on the issues of export performance and technological dynamism. In the concluding section, some brief comparisons and contrasts are drawn with the case of South Korea, another major industrial economy strongly affected by the emerging markets crisis of the late 1990s.

The Trajectory of Trade and Market Reform in Brazil

The genesis of trade and market reform in Brazil can be traced to the late 1980s when the government of José Sarney, anxious to boost industrial competitiveness launched a programme of limited tariff reductions.[1] In what turned out to be a precursor to the launch of the Mercosul customs union a few years later, Mr. Sarney's administration also negotiated a limited free trade agreement on capital goods with the government of Argentina. Simultaneously, the Brazilian authorities signalled the start of the privatisation programme with the sale of selected enterprises in the steel and petrochemicals sectors.

Although the significance of these policy initiatives was substantial (in that they indicated a new, more liberal approach to industrial policy formation), the actual scale of trade and market reform was extremely limited. This, however was to change dramatically following the election of President Fernando Collor de Melo in October 1989.[2] In tune with the resurgent orthodoxy of neo-liberalism, commonly otherwise referred to in the region as the 'Washington Consensus', on election Mr de Melo pronounced his commitment to a far-reaching programme of trade reform, privatisation and domestic market liberalisation, the scale of which far outstripped that of the restricted efforts of Mr. Sarney, or indeed that of the

1   The abolition of tariffs was also viewed more distantly as a means of reining in inflation.
2   Suzigan and Villela (1997).

military regime during the 'miracle years' of 1967–73. At the core of Mr. de Melo's new blueprint for economic management lay swingeing across-the-board cuts in tariffs together with the virtual abolition of non-tariff barriers (NTBs).[3] Of course, it should be emphasised at this point that the reductions in protection put into train were not only the consequence of Brazil's entry to Mercosul but were also the product of unilateral attempts to open up the domestic market to extra-regional competition. As the table below indicates, the average reduction of tariffs brought about as a consequence of these two imperatives stood in the region of 50 per cent, the cuts being instituted over a four-year period.

Table 4.1: Tariff Rates (All Products) 1990–94

Tariff	1990	1991	1992	1993	1994
Average	32.2 per cent	25.3 per cent	21.2 per cent	17.7 per cent	14.2 per cent
Mode	40.0 per cent	20.0 per cent	20.0 per cent	20.0 per cent	20.0 per cent
Standard Deviation	19.6 per cent	17.4 per cent	14.2 per cent	10.7 per cent	7.9 per cent

Source: Fritsch and Franco (1991), p. 20

Of perhaps even greater significance than these reductions was the almost total abandonment of NTBs ,which up until the early 1990s had de facto provided the real bulwark of protection for most Brazilian industrial products. Very importantly, as the table below also suggests, the combined effects of tariff and NTB reduction were to bring about a substantial shrinkage in the scope of effective rates of protection (ERP)

As will be noted later on, the dramatic reduction in the protection of the Brazilian industrial sector instituted over the first half of the 1990s had profound consequences for its competitiveness. Not surprisingly, however, given the scope of these reforms, they soon began to exercise an influence on the course of macroeconomic events. Following the adoption of the *real* in mid-1994, the new currency began to appreciate substantially against the US dollar, the yen and the deutschmark. With domestic

---

3   Pinheiro and Almeida (1994).

demand buoyant and the local currency cost of imports declining substantially, the trade surplus rapidly eroded, transforming itself into a
deficit. Among the major contributing factors to this deficit was a surge of
motor vehicle imports. Responding to industry lobbying as well as macroeconomic expediency, the new government of Fernando Henrique
Cardoso effectively doubled tariffs on non-Mercosul assembled vehicle
imports in mid-1995.

The hike in vehicle import tariffs under Mr. Cardoso, while subsequently partially reversed, represented a watershed in the approach of policymakers to trade reform. Whereas, between 1988 and mid-1995, the process
of trade reform had been vigorously pursued, subsequently the pace and
scale of reforms have fallen off dramatically. In the case of unilateral trade
liberalisation, in particular, the post-1995 period has witnessed barely any
progress. At the same time, the integrity of Mercosul has been sorely test-
ed as a crisis-ridden Argentina has sought temporary exemptions from
some of its internal free market provisions. More generally, efforts to promote broader hemispheric integration under the aegis of the Free Trade
Area of the Americas (FTAA) have also come to very little so far.

Although the experience of trade reform in the period since 1995
might indicate a slackening in official commitment to the neo-liberal agenda, in actual fact, the policy record in other areas rather suggests the
reverse. The most significant aspect of the authorities' continuing adherence to the process of economic liberalisation lay in the privatisation programme which got under way in earnest only once President Cardoso
gained power in 1995. As the table below demonstrates, the acceleration in
the pace of privatisation during the second half of the 1990s was little
short of remarkable. Between 1994 and the end of the decade some
US$73.9 billion worth of public assets were transferred to the private sec-
tor. The most striking feature of the privatisation programme during this
period lay less in its scale (which was impressive enough) but in the fact
that it embraced sectors once exclusively the domain of the state and/or
domestic capital. This noteworthy aspect of Brazilian privatisation applied
especially to the telecommunication and electrical utility sectors, the sale of
which to the private sector involved the passage of constitutional amendments relinquishing the exclusive preserve of the public sector and per-
mitting the participation of foreign capital.[4]

4   Pires and Piccinni (1999).

Table 4.2: Brazilian Privatisation Receipts, 1991–2002 (US$bn)

1991	1992	1993	1994	1995	1996	1997	1998	1999	2000	2001	2002*
1.9	3.2	4.0	2.2	1.5	6.2	26.3	35.7	4.2	10.2	2.8	2.0

* To June
Source: BNDES

Figure 4.1: Net Foreign Direct Investment Inflows, 1990–2001

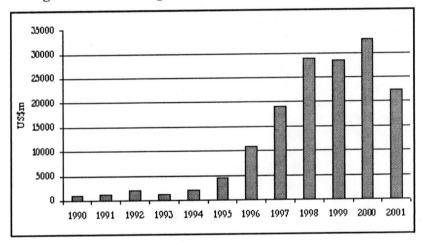

Source: Banco Central do Brasil

Accompanying the wave of privatisation in the 1990s, the pace of foreign direct investment inflows picked up considerably as Figure 4.1 indicates. By 2000, net FDI inflows had surpassed US$30bn, a level more than sufficient to finance the current account deficit. Although expanded privatisation receipts played an important role in the growth in FDI inflows, they were by no means the only factor at work. Thanks to the advent of price stability and the progressive liberalisation and de-regulation of the energy, transportation and telecommunications markets, much foreign investment arriving in Brazil since the mid-1990s has been non-privatisation related. In particular, the second half of the 1990s witnessed a substantial upturn in greenfield investments by transnational corporations (TNCs) as well as increased participation by foreign capital in the Brazilian mergers and acquisition market.

At the beginning of 1998, policymakers could have been forgiven for supposing that year-on-year rises in net FDI inflows were on the verge of becoming an established feature of the economic landscape. Certainly, the increasingly embedded character of price stability and the impressive pace of market reform lent support to the view that the Brazilian economy would remain an attractive destination for foreign investment into the foreseeable future. However, as is now clear, 1998 marked something of a watershed in Brazil's relationship with international capital markets. To the consternation of Brazilian policymakers and businesspeople alike, the years that followed would only reveal how quickly the mood of foreign investors could turn for the worse. Having peaked in 1998, privatisation receipts fell off vertiginously the following year, remaining at a low ebb into the next decade. In the case of net inward FDI, the effects of renewed economic instability have taken longer to make themselves felt. As Figure 4.1 shows clearly, though, there was a sharp drop in FDI between 2000 and 2001.

The declines in privatisation and FDI activity, while not entirely inter-related, nevertheless have at least one common origin. Since 1998, when the privatisation programme reached the high water mark occasioned by the sale of Telebras, the authorities have encountered growing domestic political opposition to the proposed transfer of further state-owned enterprises to the private sector. In particular, attempts to privatise the remainder of the electricity-generating sector (having been met with popular protests, congressional foot-dragging and legal injunctions) have been abandoned for the time being.

Of equal concern have been repeated difficulties in successfully auctioning off mobile telecommunication licences. Recent auctions have ended in failure with foreign and domestic investors baulking at the terms of the operating licence conditions and downgrading their forecasts of market growth. In another example of the changing climate, sales of further equity stakes in the majority state-owned Banco do Brasil have been given the go-ahead by the authorities, but only on condition that the purchasers be domestic (rather than foreign) investors. Thus, after more than a decade of trade and market reform the signs have become all too clear that the tide of liberalisation, if not actually in retreat, has certainly ceased to advance.

Trade and Market Liberalisation: a Force for Industrial Change?

Since the end of the 1990s, as has been made clear, the policy objectives of trade and market liberalisation have come under tight scrutiny. Despite concerted attempts to roll back the frontiers of the state and expose the domestic market to international competition, so it is suggested, Brazil has proven unable to escape its historical external vulnerability. Succumbing once more to the vicissitudes of international financial markets so the argument runs, Brazil has once again failed to embark upon a path of sustainable, equitable growth. Underpinning these arguments is the suggestion that the transformative power wielded by economic liberalisation may have been less than originally anticipated. This view, articulated in varying forms by an influential section of academics and politicians, has already begun to shape policy in a number of areas, not least in regard to the privatisation programme. Given the ascendancy of this view, what, then, is its empirical basis? As will be shown, at least so far as industry is concerned, the track record of trade and market reform is by no means disastrous.

In examining the impacts of trade and market liberalisation on industrial performance, one obvious starting point is the evolution of productivity. According to the theoretical literature supportive of both trade and market reform, the exposure of previously protected enterprises to enhanced levels of domestic and international competition might be expected to bring about significant productivity increases.[5] Such increases result as enterprises are forced to drive down unit costs through improving the utilisation of available labour and capital inputs. As productivity rises are generated, not only does the international competitiveness of the industrial sector rise — with beneficial implications for export performance — but GDP growth also accelerates as more intensive use is made of existing factors of production. Hence, not only may trade and market liberalisation be good for removing industrial inefficiency, by implication, it may also be good for propelling economic growth. These arguments, central to the proponents of trade and market reform were, of course, integral to the profound policy shifts advocated by successive administrations after 1990.

Not surprisingly, given the high profile of the issues concerned, a number of studies have emerged, all of which have attempted to gauge the impact of policy shifts, most particularly trade liberalisation, on productivity growth.[6] Most studies agree that trade liberalisation has, by and large helped to stimulate productivity growth within industry. However, there is a considerable divergence of views as to the precise nature of the linkages involved and the extent to which trade liberalisation rather than some other variable is primarily responsible for improving productivity performance.[7] In addition, as most studies attest, the productivity gains within industry (captured by Figure 4.2 below) conceal wide sub-sectoral variations. Significantly, the latter are far from wholly explained by any observed sub-sectoral divergence in the evolution of the protective regime.

---

5   Little, Scitovsky and Scott (1970).
6   For a concise review of this literature see Markwald (2001), Hay (2001) or Feijó and Carvalho (1997)
7   For instance, exogenous technological change or output growth.

Figure 4.2: Evolution of Labour Productivity in Manufacturing (1991 = 100)

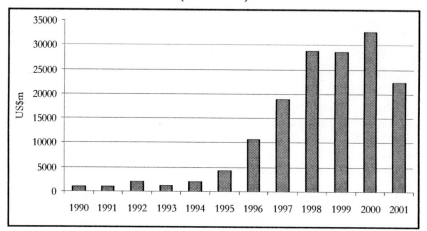

Source: IPEA

Still, as Figure 4.2 reveals, it would be hard to assert that trade and market liberalisation since its inception in 1990 has *not* been associated with a sharp upturn in industrial productivity. Between 1990 and 2001, average output per employee in manufacturing rose by no less than 64 per cent. This impressive increase stands in marked contrast to the largely reform-free 1980s when productivity growth remained anaemic. The suggestion that trade and market liberalisation played an active role in stimulating productivity receives additional support when one examines some of the numerous industry case studies which have been conducted over the past five years or so.

Examining changes in employment patterns, alterations in management strategy and the evolution of technological strategy on the shop floor, Amann (2000), ECIB (1993) and Ferraz et al. (1997) all emphasise the role of trade and market liberalisation in forcing change in once heavily protected sectors. As firms moved beyond simply slashing capacity in attempting to drive down costs the evidence suggests they embarked on thoughtfully elaborated competitive strategies.[8] The latter have had as their specific aim the objective of driving up productivity and quality levels in order to confront head-on the challenges implicit in ever more keenly contested domestic and international markets. Such strategies comprise a number of discrete elements:

8   Dantas (1990) and Ferraz et al. (1997).

- **Re-organisation of the shop floor.** Given the increasing movement towards flexible specialisation, a number of enterprises have reconfigured the layout of the shop floor with the objective of facilitating smoother production flows and the substitution of production cells for assembly lines.

- **Investment in computer numerically controlled machine tools and other current generation capital equipment.** With a more liberal import regime now in place, enterprises have invested growing quantities of resources in new capital equipment. This new equipment is often characterised by a substantial electronic/automated component and is strongly associated with the move towards flexible specialisation.

- **The pursuit of Total Quality Management (TQM).** This strategy has proved virtually universal within the Brazilian manufacturing sector with growing numbers of enterprises now achieving ISO 9000/9002 certification or its equivalents.

- **The outsourcing of activities where appropriate or possible.** In a development that has become endemic throughout Brazilian industry, increasingly both core and non-core activities are outsourced to sub-contractors. In an extreme development of this manufacturing philosophy, production at the new VW factory at Resende in Rio de Janeiro state is entirely carried out by sub-contractors. VW itself just retains responsibility for product design, marketing and quality control.

- **The pursuit of Just In Time (JIT) inventory management strategies.** With the cost of holding inventory (and financing it) increasingly on the minds of companies, the deployment of JIT strategies has increased enormously over the past few years. Since the implementation of the Real Plan in 1994, high real interest rates have pushed working capital costs upward, encouraging the lower inventory holdings which JIT strategies are designed to deliver.[9]

Although the improvement in productivity performance depicted in Figure 4.2 is substantial, its implications for the evolution of Brazilian industrial competitiveness can only be fully assessed once regard is paid to productivity gains in other major industrial economies. Unfortunately from a Brazilian perspective, the period since 1990 has been one in which productivity growth has accelerated markedly elsewhere, notably (at least up to 2001) in the United States. Thus, to coin a phrase, in trying to boost its own productivity performance through trade and market liberalisation, Brazil has been chasing a moving train. As a result, despite all the efforts

9   Adapted from Amann (2002).

of policymakers, the evidence to hand suggests that Brazil has continued to encounter difficulties in closing the productivity gap.[10]

Figure 4.3: The Evolution of Brazilian Industrial Exports, 1990–2001

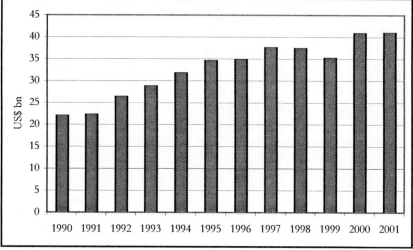

Source: IPEA/SECEX.

Partly as a result of the growing international competitive challenge, the expansion of Brazilian industrial exports for much of the 1990s proved less explosive than policymakers had anticipated. Nevertheless, between 1990 and 1999 annual industrial exports rose by some 60 per cent while, between 1999 and 2001 they experienced a further sharp rise, boosted by the accelerated depreciation of the *real*. Perhaps less impressive, however, has been the evolution of the structure of industrial exports. With the notable exception of aircraft, the period since 1990 has witnessed a tendency towards greater concentration on exports of resource intensive semi-finished industrial products rather than higher value-added goods such as electronics or machinery.[11] In accounting for the relatively modest expansion of industrial exports a number of explanations present themselves beyond those relating to the internal efficiency of the Brazilian industrial sector. In particular, it is commonly accepted that exporters

10   For a comprehensive study of the Brazilian productivity gap see McKinsey Global Institute (1999). For a case study of the productivity gap in the steel industry see Amann and Nixson (1999)
11   Pinheiro and Moreira (2000).

throughout Brazil suffer a serious international competitive disadvantage as a result of the incidence of cascading indirect taxes.[12] Unlike their counterparts elsewhere, Brazilian industrial enterprises do not benefit from an extensive series of exemptions on such taxes. Of additional concern to the exporting sector, despite some restructuring and investment, Brazil's creaking highway and port systems impose considerable costs on exporters, especially those located well inland.[13]

The final area of industrial performance to be reviewed relates to levels of technological dynamism and self-reliance within Brazilian industrial enterprises. Despite the quasi-autarchic model of industrialisation adopted prior to the 1990s, enterprises remained heavily reliant on imports of technology as they sought to introduce new products and processes.[14] As a result, Brazil tended to run a substantial deficit in the technological balance of trade, purchasing from overseas a far greater number of foreign technology licences than it was ever able to sell abroad.[15] At the same time, despite an extensive programme of import substitution, Brazil continued to be heavily reliant on imports of technologically advanced capital goods such as mainframe computers, telecommunications equipment and even aircraft.

Figure 4.4: Brazil's Technology Balance of Trade, 1990–99

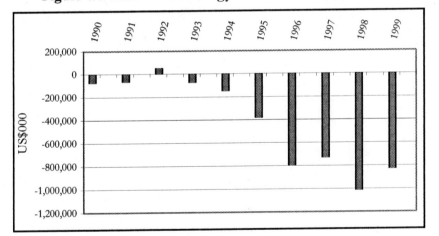

Note: The technology balance of trade includes 'imports' and 'exports' of the following items: patents, licences, technical assistance, trademarks.
Source: Ministério de Ciênca e Tecnológia.

12   Teixeira Lima and Carvalho (2000).
13   *Ibid.*
14   Schwartzman (1995).
15   Amann (2002).

Following the advent of trade and market liberalisation, if anything, the deficit on the technology balance of trade has tended to increase (see Figure 4.4). However, this growing imbalance is not necessarily indicative of declining domestic technological effort. In fact, when one examines data on domestic corporate spending on research and development, clear evidence emerges of an increase in technological activity, at least up until 1999 — the latest year for which data are available (see Table 4.3b). Equally, up until the same year there are also encouraging signs of an upturn in total national spending on research and development. Having hovered at around 0.7 per cent of GDP in the early 1990s, by the end of the decade expenditure on R&D had reached 0.88 per cent of GDP. Moreover, in selected areas Brazilian corporations have continued to operate at the frontiers of technology, gaining significant export market share in the process. By far the most important example in this regard lies in the field of the aerospace sector where Embraer has become a leading player in the passenger jet market.[16]

Table 4.3a : Spending on R&D as a Percentage of GDP, 1999

Public Sector:	0.55 per cent
Private Sector:	0.33 per cent
Total:	**0.88 per cent**

Source: Ministério de Ciênca e Tecnológia.

Table 4.3b: Evolution of Corporate Spending on R&D, 1993–99 (Constant 1999 R$M)

1993	1994	1995	1996	1997	1998	1999
1166.0	999.5	1215.5	1528.6	2011.8	1724.3	2394.9

Source: Associação Nacional de Pesquisa, Desenvolvimento e Engenharia das Empresas Inovadoras (Anpei) Ministério de Ciênca e Tecnológia.

16   Da Silva (1999).

In sum then, the available evidence appears to suggest that the pursuit of trade and market liberalisation has been associated with an increased emphasis upon technological expenditures, whether directed at imports or domestic R&D programmes. However, it is important to bear in mind that the data in question do not encompass the turbulent years of 2000 and 2001. Given the uncertainties and higher interest rates associated with these years, it seems possible that R&D data, when finally released, may indicate a reversal of the trend experienced up until 1999.

Conclusions and Some Reflections on the South Korean Experience

More than a decade on from its inception, Brazil's experiment with trade and market liberalisation remains a matter of great controversy. Recounting events following the eruption of the Asian financial crisis in 1997, it is hard not to share some sympathy with the view that, whatever their theoretical justification, market opening and the retreat of the state have failed to extract Brazil from its ancestral mire of macroeconomic instability and external vulnerability. However, as this chapter has shown, at least so far as the industrial sector is concerned, some of the current pessimism may be overdone. Faced with accelerated entry of foreign capital and unprecedented exposure to international competition, the sector has been busy reformulating itself. In the process, productivity has picked up, spending on technology has increased while growth in industrial exports — though certainly below expectations — has occurred.

Of course, it can certainly be argued that more needs to be done, especially given the pace of technological change and productivity growth elsewhere in the world. However, what appears to be beyond dispute is that the Brazilian industrial sector has at least begun to move in the right direction after several years of stagnation. Looking ahead, the major challenge facing the sector will be to enhance its competitive standing in the face of uncertain domestic and international market conditions. In this respect, the state will have a crucial role to play. Having largely abandoned its role as a producer, the state will need to continue to refocus industrial policy, concentrating on the promotion of competitive change. This is as likely to involve the provision of positive incentives (such as training and R&D grants) as the removal of obstacles (such as cascading indirect taxes). Thus far, there are signs that such a reformulation of policy is afoot. In particular the passage of the Law of S.A.s in 2001 has facilitated easier access by small and medium enterprises to domestic equity markets. The privatisation and de-regulation of the ports sector has also continued to proceed, lowering the transportation costs faced by exporters in the process. These achievements aside, the central responsibility of policymakers will continue to be to ensure as stable a macroeconomic environment as is possible.

In this endeavour, the future evolution of international financial markets will exercise a fundamental influence.

Brazil's transition to greater economic openness has coincided with a period of fundamental policy re-orientation in another newly industrialised economy, South Korea. What useful parallels, if any, can be drawn between the two countries' experiences? Superficially, the parallels would appear quite striking. Both economies are characterised by substantial, integrated industrial sectors built up largely over the past 50 years as a result of heavy protection and substantial government intervention.[17] In both cases, the policy developments of the past few years can be seen as an attempt to address serious structural problems whose origins can be traced to this legacy. However, the character of these problems in both economies contrasts strikingly.

In the case of South Korea, while the industrial sector emerged under a protective regime, the export-orientated character of its development helped ensure that productive inefficiencies of the Brazilian kind could not multiply. Instead, in South Korea, as industrialisation proceeded too little care was taken to match capacity to eventual demand. This inevitably resulted in chronic over-investment and excessive corporate indebtedness. Such a strategy may have been viable so long as corporate debt could be cost-effectively financed. Once this no longer became possible, following the financial crisis of 1997, little option was left but to begin a long and painful process of corporate restructuring and rationalisation of capacity. By contrast, in Brazil, whatever the productive inefficiencies of enterprises at world prices, levels of corporate debt have always been remarkably low. Given the legacy of years of high interest rates and periodic credit crunches, the Brazilian corporate sector has always tended to finance investment out of retained earnings. While this has arguably resulted in under investment and missed market opportunities, it has none the less placed Brazilian industry on a far sounder financial footing than its South Korean counterpart.

Curiously, therefore, the industrial sectors of Brazil and South Korea now find themselves having to mimic each other's strengths while avoiding each other's weaknesses. In the case of Brazil, the challenge is to follow South Korea's undoubted lead in productivity, training and R&D expenditures while avoiding the pitfalls of unsustainable growth in corporate indebtedness. From a South Korean perspective, there is clearly much to learn from the generally sound financial state of the Brazilian industrial sector. However, at least as regards export growth, the *chaebol* would find rather less to emulate among their Brazilian counterparts.

---

17   Baer (2001) and Amsden (1989).

Statistical Sources:

Associação Nacional de Pesquisa, Desenvolvimento e Engenharia das Empresas Inovadoras (Anpei)

Banco Central do Brasil

IPEA Data

Ministério de Ciênca e Tecnológia

Secretária de Comércio Exterior (SECEX)

CHAPTER 5

The Brazilian Labour Market in the 1990s: Restructuring, Unemployment and Informality

José Ricardo Ramalho

Rated as one of the emerging nations of the global economy during the 1990s, Brazil has seen sweeping changes in its economic and political structures over the past ten years, prompted by the need to become more competitive in the global market and to attract international investment. This set of changes may be viewed as a major departure for an economy once much more closed to international trade and capital and where the state historically played a leading role as a producer of goods and services. Accompanying this break with the past, the Brazilian economy has been thrust into the competitive globalisation process in the wake of lighter trade protection measures and the deregulation of capital flows. At the same time, efforts have been made to shrink the sphere of action of the state through a broad-ranging privatisation programme.[1] This process of international insertion also ushered in a shake-up of the domestic macro economy in order to address the inflation that soared during the 1980s, while complying with the global parameters established by the international regulatory organisations. Although all these changes directly affected the pace and structure of Brazil's economic growth, by the end of the decade, the absolute level of the nation's GDP remained disappointing.

Whatever its lack of success in boosting GDP, the macroeconomic policy regime adopted strongly affected the performance of the labour market. Shrinking industrial employment with growth spurts in real income for workers and employment in the trade and services sectors accompanied relatively high unemployment rates, especially towards the end of the decade. This situation extended and confirmed Brazil's reputation for economic and social contrasts. At the same time as its GDP (US$777.1 billion in 1998) placed it in the group of the richest nations, Brazil also posted one of the world's worst disparities in income distribution.

The purpose of this chapter is to offer a brief overview of the Brazilian development process and its effects on the labour market over the past ten years. Based on recent data and analyses, the chapter will attempt to show how this process took place, and the alternatives that have

---

1   Ministério do Trabalho (1998), p. 5 and Neri et al (2000), p. 1.

been presented for dealing with the problems of unemployment, informal work and poorly skilled workers in the labour market.

Table 5.1: Income Distribution among the Economically Active Population, Brazil — 1960–95

Year	Poorest 50 per cent	Richer 10 per cent	Poorest 10 per cent
1960	17.7	39.7	1.2
1970	15.0	46.5	1.2
1980	14.1	47.9	1.2
1990	11.9	48.7	0.8
1995	13.3	47.1	1.0

Source: Gonçalves (1999); IBGE/PNAD (1995).

Table 5.2: Distribution of Workers by Wage Level, Brazil — 1997 (minimum wage-around US$100)

	Occupied (number)	Occupied (per cent)
Total	69,331,507	100.0
Up to ½ minimum wage	4,343,918	6.3
More than ½ m.w. to 1 m. w.	10,352,181	14.9
More than 1 m.w. to 2 m. w.	12,.938,053	18.7
More than 2 m.w. to 3 m. w.	9,360,382	13.9
More than 3 m.w. to 5 m. w.	9,818,182	14.2
More than 5 m.w. to 10 m. w.	6,959,214	10.0
More than 10 m.w. to 20 m. w.	3,105,557	4.5
More than 20 m. w.	1,857,294	2.7
No income *	9,479,979	13.7

Source: Desep/ CUT (1999).

Various Phases in the Development Process

The State has played a key role in Brazil's development process, acting as a direct investor and facilitator for private investment. The strategy of creating a structure for the build-up of industrial capital began with the 1930 Revolution when President Getúlio Vargas strong-armed his way into power, imposing a new political and economic order. This was sustained by the might of a centralised interventionist State based on the ideas of nationalism, corporatism and progress. Confident of the populist relationship between Vargas and the masses, this new regime introduced labour legislation and trade union regulations that protected workers' rights, binding class conflicts in rigorous legal constraints. According to Cardoso (1999), in order to achieve this objective, 'on the one hand, labour legislation was progressively fine-tuned through top-level acts based on the social and labour legislation of the Western capitalist countries; on the other, the details of worker and capitalist associationism were regulated, making this heavily dependent on State bureaucracy and independent of its members'.[2] This meant that the conflict between capital and labour was transferred to State structures. The State was assigned the task of keeping the peace between the two sides through the coercion and repression of labour movements, annulling them through the absorption of conflicts by the state apparatus.

Brazil's *Estado Novo* under President Vargas ended in 1945. During the wave of democratisation (1945–64) that followed World War II, new political parties appeared. The shift in economic hegemony during the 1950s 'with the concentration and centralisation of capital under the influence of a wave of international investment' reshaped the situation of Brazil.[3] This industrialising boom ushered in rapid expansion of the various types of paid labour and the organisation of production on a capitalist basis, when a modern working class began to form 'as well as an appreciable contingent of non-industrial urban wage-earners employed in activities that were increasingly more massified in terms of public and private services'.

Lasting 20 years, Brazil's military dictatorship (1964–84) consolidated a highly concentrated capital accumulation model based on foreign capital and an internationalised fraction of Brazil's capitalist class. These features confirmed the incompatibility between this model and the political domination mode.[4] The 1970s was a time of marked industrial expansion for Brazil, reflected not only in appreciable growth in industrial output and employment, but also in the development of an integrated industrial structure based on the heavy industrialisation process that began from 1956 onwards. This process took place within the framework of a type of competition basically

2   Cardoso (1999), pp. 28–9.
3   Munck (1984), p. 221.
4   *Ibid.*, pp. 221, 222.

focused on an expanding domestic market, protected by an importation control policy. The capital goods sector developed in order to meet public sector demands on the one side (huge government projects in various fields) and, on the other, the consumer durables sector also expanded.[5]

During the 1980s, the appearance of new standards for technology and production was accompanied by a period of high inflation and economic stagnation. But according to Mattoso (1995), Brazil had its own specific characteristics in this process, and despite economic crises, de-industrialisation or industrial restructuring did not take place.[6] The same industrial structure was maintained basically intact. Although modernised in some sectors, the preservation of the industrial structure is an important factor in understanding the apparent contradictions of the Brazilian economy, the labour market and the trade unions during this period. This explains why, despite the Lost Decade of the 1980s, Brazil posted the highest GDP growth in Latin America and remained the leading industrial producer in the Third World.

The stagnation of its productive sector during the 1980s halted the process of formalising wage and labour relationships in Brazil, extending poverty, exclusion and the heterogeneity of the labour market structure. But, paradoxically, difficulties in implementing the restructuring processes for the production sector and preserving Brazil's industrial structure kept the grassroots bases of the trade unions alive. This context made room for the struggle for trade union rights, establishing trade union confederations, expanding membership and legitimising the role of trade union negotiators.[7]

The 1990s — Economic Deregulation, Restructuring the Production Sector

In contrast to the previous decade, the 1990s saw great changes in the Brazilian economy and its labour market. These were related to the deregulation of Brazilian markets, opening them up to international competition and forcing companies to restructure their operations, seeking greater efficiency and better quality products and services. This spurt in industrial output contrasts with the latter part of the 1980s. However, some industries were better able to introduce the changes needed to achieve fast gains in productivity.[8] Companies began to focus their efforts on organisational strategies, while also introducing new ways of managing their labourforces that were more compatible with the need for increased flexibility and worker commitment to quality and productivity. In contrast to earlier

5   Leite (1994), pp. 563–4.
6   Mattoso (1995), pp. 136–7.
7   *Ibid.*, p.126.
8   Amann (1995), p.4.

days, when many companies saw innovation as buying new equipment and/or introducing organisational or motivation packages and programmes that were implemented in their various sectors (often by some department or another with patchy results), from the late 1980s onwards, an increasingly large number of companies began to introduce deep-rooted restructuring processes based on decisions taken by their boards that introduced an entire set of interlinked innovations. These better-integrated restructuring drives were often reflected in the introduction of some type of Total Quality Programme.[9]

It should be noted that although even the multinationals were protected from international competition in Brazil, they nevertheless had to act fast in order to avoid losing market share. For Brazilian-owned companies the situation was more difficult, and dealing with the globalised economy resulted in an upsurge in bankruptcies in many productive sectors, together with mergers or take-overs by foreign groups.

The strategy of setting up a South American Common Market as a way of dealing with globalisation was also attempted, through the introduction of the Mercosur Southern Cone Common Market linking Argentina, Brazil, Paraguay and Uruguay. Discussions over bringing it into full operation were relatively successful until Brazil's foreign exchange crisis in early 1999. However, up to then, trade flows among these countries had risen steadily during the 1990s, making these activities vital to their respective economies.

Backed by the economic stabilisation policies implemented from the middle of the decade onward, the deregulation of the economies of South America and its huge potential market for new products attracted a steady inflow of international capital, some invested in stock markets, but some also channelled to the productive sector. Other than investments associated with the privatisation process implemented as part of Brazil's economic policy (which injected huge amounts of funding into the telecommunications, steel, transportation and mining sectors), well-established industries in Brazil also experienced an increase in investment levels. This was the case of the automotive sector, for instance. Although established in Brazil since the 1950s, it underwent a great transformation process underpinned by fresh investments during the 1990s, to some extent making it symptomatic of the effects of opening up the Brazilian economy to international competition.

The auto-assembly industry has played a leading role in Brazil, not only due to its strategic position in the economy, but also as its labour-force is extremely assertive and influential in labour disputes. In economic terms, this sector accounts for a hefty 12 per cent of Brazil's industrial GDP, but the characteristics of the production chain extend these effects strongly to other areas. During the 1990s, the restructuring of this sector altered its

9   Gitahy, Leite and Rabelo (1993), p. 15; Leite (1994), pp. 573–4.

parameters in a number of ways.[10] Initially, it virtually wiped out Brazil's auto-spares industry through a process of sell-outs and mergers that radically reshaped the profile of this sector: today it consists of fewer companies and is increasingly dominated by multinationals and linkages with global auto-assembly projects.[11] In second place, fresh investments demanded the decentralisation of new ventures, blocking the trade union clout built up in the older plants, and taking full advantage of the tax laws that pitted Brazilian states against each other as they fought for fresh investments. Third, new experiments are under way in the production management process, making good use of low wages, skilled labour and somewhat inexperienced trade unions. Fourth, the intensive down-sizing process and the quest for productivity that pumped up automobile output to over two million vehicles in 1997 while employing only half the number of workers in registered jobs during the early 1980s finally forced the trade union movement not only to negotiate alternatives in order to preserve jobs, but also to reorganise its thinking, drawing up more general lists of demands for workers scattered throughout a number of new plant locations.

Figure 5.1: Evolution of Employment in Brazilian Car Assemblers since 1970

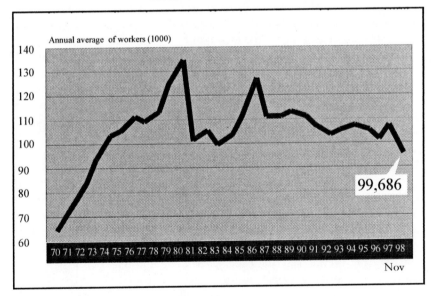

Source: Anfavea (1999).

10 Abreu, Gitahy, Ramalho and Ruas (1999).
11 Posthuma (1997), Addis (1997) and Arbix (1997).

The Brazilian Labour Market during the 1990s

Despite different diagnostic approaches to the Brazilian labour market during the 1990s, some points are common to the leading experts. A shift in direction or even a fresh course is widely acknowledged from the early 1980s onward, dividing the development of the labour market into two separate periods. A structuring drive took place during the industrialisation process with the institutionalisation of labour relations and working conditions (1940–80), with the expansion of wage-paying jobs and positions in the organised segments of the economy. For Pochmann there was an about-turn in the general employment process after 1980, with marked signs of a steady collapse of the labour market structure. The loss of wage-paying jobs by a rising proportion of the Economically Active Population (EAP) and the expansion of work in non-organised segments, in parallel to rising unemployment, all took place as Brazil's national industrialisation project was abandoned, replaced by the adoption of macroeconomic policies fostering reinsertion into the global economy, as labour laws became less effective. 'Out of every ten jobs generated from 1989 through 1995, only two were wage-paying, compared to eight that did not pay wages, of which almost five consisted of self-employment and three were non-remunerated. While the non-remunerated jobs showed an average annual variation rate of around five per cent, self-employed workers reached three per cent, employers 0.8 per cent and wage earners 0.48 per cent. This resulted in a widespread trend towards the loss of wage-earning employment during the 1990s, triggered mainly by the elimination of jobs registered in work-books.'[12]

The data presented in a recent diagnosis by the Brazilian Ministry of Labour (1998) also show that the quality of the Brazilian labour force is poor by international standards, despite improvements over the past few years: 'estimates of the average schooling levels of the EAP (ten years or more) indicate that it rose from under four to 6.4 years during this decade: six years for men and seven years for women, according to the 1996 National Household Sampling Survey (PNAD — Pesquisa Nacional por Amostragem de Domicílios) (...). However, 63.3 per cent of this EAP had less than eight years schooling in 1996, meaning that these workers failed to complete their elementary education.'[13] This aspect is certainly among the primary disadvantages of Brazil in a competitive world that demands knowledge-intensive participation to an increasing extent.

In a more detailed analysis of the Brazilian labour market covering the entire decade, Neri et al. (2000) suggested a split into two periods — 1990 through to economic stabilisation in 1994, and from 1994 to the present day. During the first period, the economy became bogged down in a heavy

12   Pochmann (1999), pp. 75–9.
13   Ministério do Trabalho (1998), p. 9.

recession, with an increase in the open unemployment rate ('there was a drop in industrial employment and an increase in jobs in the trade and services sectors that kept pace with the development of activity levels in the economy'),[14] extremely high inflation levels and sweeping structural changes prompted by trade deregulation.

According to Neri et al., during the second period inflation was brought down to relatively low levels and the GDP growth rate moved into the black through to 1997, followed by stagnation from then on. This period is characterised mainly by price stabilisation. 'Due to keener competition in the economy and the adoption of a foreign exchange anchor, the inflation rate — which topped 40 per cent a month by June 1994 — was pruned drastically down to around five per cent a year by 1997. In parallel to rising demand triggered by price stabilisation, one of the main effects of the foreign exchange anchor was an alteration in the behaviour of relative prices in the economy. The prices of non-tradable goods began to rise faster than those of tradable goods, inverting the trend noted during the previous period.'[15] However, industrial employment began to drop from 1995 onward, despite increased output, while jobs in the trade and services sectors expanded rapidly through to late 1996. 'However, during the early days of the stabilisation process, expansion in the trade and services sectors more than offset the drop in industrial employment, which was not the case from 1997 onwards. The result is a clear trend towards rising unemployment rates that year, worsening in 1998 with the drop in employment for these two sectors (trade and services). In the industrial sector, despite tumbling employment levels, the real income of the workers rose through to year-end 1998. The drop in industrial employment levels is the outcome of wider-spread trade deregulation backed by the foreign exchange anchor.'[16]

Although subject to political argument among specialists in the government and the opposition, these economic measures — commercial and financial deregulation, high interest rates, rapid privatisation, pruning the regulatory capacities of the State and over-valuation of the *real* – in practice resulted in the lowest ten-year growth for Brazil's Gross Domestic Product (GDP) during the whole of the twentieth century. Against this backdrop 'in ten years, the *per capita* GDP remained almost unaltered, while real average income dropped eight per cent'.[17] 'The country was unable to return to sustained GDP growth, and was barely managing to cope with sharp swings in activity levels or to deliver growth rates for the economy close to population growth rates'.[18]

14   Neri et al. (2000), p.12.
15   *Ibid.*, p.13.
16   Neri et al. (2000), p. 14
17   Mattoso (2000), p.3.
18   Pochmann (2000c), p. 3.

Additionally, 'in 1999, despite low inflation rates, real average worker incomes were 6.5 per cent lower than in 1995. In contrast, GDP rose 11.8 per cent over the same period. As work income shrank while the national income rose, this leads to the conclusion that the functional income distribution grew worse. This means that the highest increase in national income was found among the proprietary classes (interest, profits and property rentals). There is nothing new in the fact that the share held by earnings on work in the national income reached 44 per cent in 1995, and was estimated at only 40.7 per cent in 1999'.[19]

Employment and Joblessness

The main criticisms of the economic model introduced are focused on the type of employment generated over the past few years. A comparison with the late 1970s is inevitable, with the nation's GDP rising at annual average rate of seven per cent since 1950 as Brazil grew into one of the world's leading industrial economies. 'During this phase, the labour market proved highly dynamic. For every ten jobs created, eight were wage paying while seven were registered in workbooks. Through this, open unemployment was generally curtailed, although the labour market continued to display the characteristics typical of an under-developed nation: low wages, unregistered workers, and a large contingent of self-employed workers with no remuneration'.[20]

Table 5.3: Unemployment Rates. Brazil (1) and São Paulo (2)

Type of unemployment	1989	1990	1991	1992	1993	1994	1995	1996	1997	1998	1999
Open Brazil	3.4	4.3	4.8	5.8	5.3	5.1	4.6	5.4	5.7	7.6	7.8
Total (SP)	8.7	10.3	11.7	15.2	14.6	14.2	13.2	15.1	16.0	18.3	19.5
Open (SP)	6.5	7.4	7.9	9.2	8.6	8.9	9.0	10.0	10.3	11.7	12.3
Concealed	2.2	2.9	3.8	6	6	5.3	4.2	5.1	5.7	6.6	7.2
By precarious work	1.5	2	2.9	4.6	4.7	4.0	3.3	3.8	4.2	4.6	4.9
By discouragement	0.7	0.9	0.9	1.4	1.3	1.3	0.9	1.3	1.5	1.9	2.2

Source: PED/SEADE-DIEESE; PME/IBGE.
(1) Brazil´s metropolitan regions; 1999 = average January-May
(2) São Paulo's Metropolitan Region; 1999 = average January–June

19   Pochmann (2000d), p. 10.
20   Pochmann (2000c), p. 3.

During the 1990s, employment grew more precarious, firming up a trend that became more apparent with market deregulation and a keener emphasis on competitiveness.

The Ministry of Labour (1998) acknowledges that, although the Brazilian economy has generated jobs, mostly outsourced, whether formal or informal, the Brazilian labour market has been settling down more on the side of informal labour. However, open unemployment has also been playing an important role in this process.

According to the Ministry of Labour (1998) 'the unemployment rate is graded by gender and age. It is higher for young people and women. Since 1995, it has been rising for both men and women, as well as for all age groups. (…) The social impact of unemployment is greater when it affects the heads of households. From December 1995 through to January 1998, the unemployment rate for heads of households rose from 2.80 per cent to 4.25 per cent in six metropolitan areas. This indicates that unemployment is also becoming more intensive among a group that extends the social impact of joblessness, due to its links with the labour market and its family responsibilities. Additionally, studies indicate that the unemployment of the head of the family results in an increased search for work by other members of the family, boosting the quest for jobs and consequently the unemployment rate.'[21]

From 1989 through 1997, formal employment dropped 8.4 per cent. Over the same period, the processing industry posted a drop of 19.5 per cent. As assessed by the Ministry of Labour, while industrial employment shrank steadily from March 1991 through December 1997 (down 28.5 per cent), productivity levels in the processing industry measured in man-hours doubled over the period. 'The gains in productivity that are so important for endowing the economy with a keener competitive edge, and consequently reaping the advantages of globalisation, have adverse effects on employment levels. Additionally, this hike in productivity has significant consequences for the quantity and quality of jobs generated by the economy. This means that within the context of the modern sector there is a gap opening up between rising productivity and employment. This out-of-step progress constitutes a major issue for economies involved in the process of competitive insertion: they must increase their productivity in order to ensure a keener competitive edge, but it is also necessary to enhance the levels and quality of jobs generated, ensuring that globalisation ushers in better ways for workers to earn their livelihood.'[22]

Specific Characteristics of the Brazilian Labour Market

Some specific characteristics of the Brazilian labour market should be stressed in order to ensure a more complete understanding of what took place during

21   Ministério do Trabalho (1998), p. 30.
22   *Ibid.*, pp. 12–3.

the 1990s. Starting with the comment that 'although ranked among the world's ten highest GDPs, Brazil has a large number of rural workers' — at around 25 per cent, while in the world's seven largest economies, rural workers do not exceed five per cent of the total number of employees.[23]

The issue of employment levels among young people (aged 15–24) during the 1990s also draws attention, as they remain almost unaltered. 'Although 2.3 million young people have managed to enter the labour market, the number of employed young people in 1998 (16.1 million workposts) was exactly the same as in 1989. This means that unemployment has risen rapidly among young people, up from one million in 1989 to 3.3 million in 1998, accounting for 48 per cent of total unemployment in Brazil. By the end of the decade, almost 20 out of 100 every young people were unemployed, while in the late 1980s only six young people were unemployed out of every 100.'[24]

Additionally, there was also shrinkage in wage-paying jobs, pruning the 6.9 million young people with formal employment in 1989 down to only 4.9 million in 1998. 'In the past, their first job offered young people the possibility of building up a career in the course of their working lives. However, this is no longer the case today. Initially, because the jobs available are often temporary and found in a wide variety of different situations (odd jobs, on-the-job training, internships and others), this makes it hard to build up a career.' Another associated problem is that youngsters and adult workers are starting to compete for the same positions. 'Faced with a large surplus work-force, adult workers will try for any job at all, including those previously accepted by young people. In this position, the employer can hire adults who are better trained, while paying wages more appropriate to youngsters.'[25]

Looking at the rising share held by women in the labour market, the situation does not seem too good within this restructuring context. According to the Lena Lavinas,[26] from 1995 onward, when the restructuring process swept through the services sector and pruned the supply of jobs, working women were the most severely affected, resulting in an increase in female unemployment. 'Overall, from January 1997 through January 1998, the percentage of women looking for jobs rose from 6.69 per cent to 8.07 per cent. Over the same period, the rate for men rose from 4.82 per cent to 5.63 per cent.' Additionally, although women today account for 30 per cent of the market, the profile of jobs held by women, according to Cristina Bruschini remains precarious and has shown no significant alterations over the decade.[27] In 1985, 37 out of every 100

---

23   Pochmann (2000c), p. 3.
24   Pochmann (2000b), p. 3.
25   *Ibid.*
26   *O Globo*, 8 March 1998, p. 46
27   *Ibid.*

Brazilian women worked, rising to 48 out of every 100 in 1995. But, of the thirty million Brazilian women working in 1995, 4.7 million (17 per cent) were in domestic employment (maids, cleaners, daily charwomen, etc), with a further 14 per cent in non-remunerated jobs such as assistants in stores or companies, or in rural occupations.

Table 5.4: Women in the Labour Market: Indicators of Economic Activity

Women

| Years | Economically Active Population (EAP) | | | Occupied | Employed | |
	(millions)	Activity rate	Percentage of women in the EAP	(millions)	(millions)	Percentage of women amongst employees
1976	11.4	28.8	28.8	11.2	7.3	30.3
1981	14.8	32.9	31.3	14.1	9.4	32.2
1983	16.8	35.6	33.0	16.0	10.5	33.4
1985	18.4	36.9	33.5	17.8	11.8	34.4
1990	22.9	39.2	35.5	22.1	14.7	36.7
1993	28	47	39.6	25.9	11.1	31.8
1995	30	48.1	40.4	27.8	11.6	32.6

Source: FIBGE – PNADS – 76, 81, 83, 85, 89, 90, 93, 95.
(Tab. 15/ 4 / 3.1 / 4 / 3.1 / 4.2)

Men

| Years | Economically Active Population | | | Occupied | Employed | |
	(millions)	Activity rates	Percentage of men in the EAP	(millions)	(millions)	Percentage of men amongst employees
1976	28.2	73.6	71.2	27.8	16.7	69.7
1981	32.6	74.6	68.7	31.2	19.8	67.8
1983	34.6	74.8	67.0	32.4	21.0	66.6
1985	36.6	76	66.5	35.4	22.5	65.2
1990	41.6	75.3	64.5	40	25.4	63.3
1993	42.8	76	60.4	40.5	23.8	68.2
1995	47.2	75.3	59.6	41.9	24	67.4

Source: FIBGE– PNADS 76,81,83,85

With regard to the participation of the black population in the labour market, a recent survey carried out by the Departamento Intersindical de Estatística e Estudos Socios Econômicos (DIEESE, 2000) clearly shows the results of a combination of poverty, inequality and discrimination in the fabric of Brazilian society. 'The income of black men and women workers is systematically lower than the income of other races, regardless of their status or attributes. This reflects a set of factors ranging from early entry into the labour market, larger numbers of blacks in less dynamic sectors of the economy, a high proportion of blacks in precarious jobs and unskilled activities, and the difficulties facing black women in the work-place.' This inequality appears quite clearly when comparing 'the income earned by the two races, as blacks earn an average of some 60 per cent less than non-blacks'.[28]

Another characteristic that should be taken into account is child labour (aged 10–14). Here, the figures show that in Brazil 4.8 per cent of its Economically Active Population (EAP) of around 75 million consists of children aged between 10 and 14 (around 3.5 million children). An obvious sign of poverty is that a large proportion of these workers, mostly girls, are involved in domestic labour. From 1985 up to 1995 the percentage of people aged between 10 and 17 involved in domestic work rose from 17.23 per cent to 26.67 per cent, according to the Applied Economic Research Institute (IPEA — Instituto de Pesquisas Econômicas Aplicadas).

Expansion of the Informal Sector

The level of informal employment in the Brazilian labour market has always been one of its most striking characteristics. However, all the analyses confirm marked growth in the informal sector during the 1990s, triggered by changes introduced by the economic restructuring and more intensive participation in the globalised market. According to an analysis carried out by the Ministry of Labour (1998) 'there is a gap between the increase in protected employment (with signed work-books) compared to the expansion of wage-paying jobs with no signed work-books and the self-employed (i.e. between the more modern and socially better-protected core of the labour market and its fringes). The results of this process have been to extend the informal sector, revealing that the Brazilian economy is able to generate jobs, although largely of poor quality.' The survey of the six largest metropolitan areas shows that jobs registered in workbooks for the total labour-force fell from 53.8 per cent during the second quarter of 1991 to 46.9 per cent during the last quarter of 1997. The proportion of jobs not registered in workbooks and self-employed workers within the total employed populace rose respectively from 20.8 per cent to 24.6 per cent and almost 20.0 per cent to 23.3 per cent during the same period. This

28   DIEESE (2000), p. 1.

means that 'the informal sector, consisting of the proportion of workers without signed workbooks and the self-employed in the total employed population rose from 40.8 per cent to 47.7 per cent over the same period'.[29]

Table 5.5: The Evolution of Formal Employment by Sub-Sector of Economic Activity, Brazil — 1989–99 (base 1989 =100)

Subsectors	1990	1991	1992	1993	1994	1995	1996	1997	1998	1999*
Total	99.7	96.1	93.5	93.1	94.2	91.5	90.3	90.2	87.7	87.5
Manufacturing Industry	97.8	91.3	86.5	85.8	87.1	82.0	79.7	77.7	73.1	72.9
Metallurgical Industry	88.3	79.4	72.0	71.2	72.6	67.7	65.8	66.7	61.9	61.0
Mechanical Industry	87.4	77.4	67.3	65.9	68.3	64.1	60.5	59.0	54.4	53.2
Electric Materials and Communicatons Industry	92.8	80.2	68.1	62.7	63.0	60.6	58.8	55.6	50.7	50.2
Transportation Material Industry	93.1	82.2	77.7	76.4	77.2	69.8	66.0	67.8	59.8	58.5
Chemical and Pharmaceutical products Industry	92.9	85.3	81.1	78.5	79.9	74.8	73.9	72.5	69.7	69.4
Textile Industry	95.5	83.3	75.3	76.8	78.5	70.6	68.4	64.1	61.9	62.4
Footwear Industry	89.5	82.4	91.2	95.1	92.9	87.8	86.3	78.9	76.0	80.5
Building Industry	97.0	91.0	90.3	86.3	84.9	83.7	82.9	83.7	79.8	76.8
Commerce	101.8	97.6	93.1	93.9	96.1	93.5	93.3	94.8	93.5	92.4
Financial Institutions	96.9	89.1	85.0	83.1	79.2	75.4	69.8	66.1	62.2	60.6
Transport and Communications Industry	100.6	98.4	97.0	96.4	96.3	95.8	95.2	95.0	91.7	91.3
Lodging, food, repairs and others	102.2	102.7	102.1	103.4	106.7	105.6	107.2	108.9	108.6	108.7

Source: MTE/Caged e RAIS.
* referring to May/1999.

According to Amadeo (1998) there are many factors that explain this phenomenon: '1) new forms of production and labour relations tend to

29   Ministério do Trabalho (1998), p. 15.

increase the number of self-employed workers, mainly through outsourcing processes; 2) the relative increase in employment in the services sector — which traditionally generates informal jobs — tends to increase the level of informal employment; and 3) institutional factors associated with the social security system and labour laws may prompt companies and workers to opt for informal labour relations.'[30]

However, it is stressed that not all informal jobs are of poor quality, and that the portion of the skilled labour-force that has shifted towards self-employment should not be characterised as engaging in poor quality jobs, as it is endowed with human capital and working tools that boost productivity and income.[31] This prompted some analysts to state that there has not been an increase in the precarious nature of jobs on the labour market. 'Taking worker income as the measurement of the precarious nature of employment, the marked increase in the real average income of workers in the informal sector ... indicates that it cannot be categorically stated that the labour market has become more precarious'.[32]

Prospects and Dilemmas

The 1990s presented a set of specific economic problems in Brazil, together with the issues thrown up by globalisation. Shifts in the organisation of the productive sector and efficiency-seeking corporate management ushered in improvements in the competitive levels of Brazilian companies. This had contradictory effects, causing much concern in terms of the labour market, due to substantial increases in informal work and rising joblessness. Although it might be possible to discuss the configuration of the informal labour market, identifying situations where incomes actually increased, the most obvious conclusion for the decade is that jobs became more precarious, with shrinking numbers of posts. It goes without saying that this represented an increase in poverty and social inequality.

However, Brazil is in a dilemma: as a player in a globalised and competitive international economy it must boost the productivity of the labour market in order to upgrade the efficiency of its economic system and enhance its chances of its competing successfully. On the other hand, these imperatives obviously tend to reduce the positive impact of rising output on employment generation.[33] The Ministry itself acknowledges that a structural phenomenon is being noted in the Brazilian economy, reflected in this joblessness. Some of the recent upsurge in unemployment is due to technological restructuring and the introduction of new

30   Amadeo (1998), p. 20.
31   Ministério do Trabalho (1998).
32   Amadeo (1998), p. 20.
33   Ministério do Trabalho (1998), p. 6.

ways of organising labour and management, introduced by Brazilian companies in order to trim costs and hone their competitive edge within the context of a deregulated, globalised economy. This structural phenomenon has had appreciable effects on the Brazilian labour market and should be viewed separately from the short-term effects caused by economic tinkering undertaken by the Brazilian government in order to ensure the success of the Real Stabilisation Plan. Lay-offs in the auto-spares, clothing, footwear and textile sectors are all part of this structural shift. Rising productivity in the Brazilian economy also falls within this context, particularly in the processing industry.

Labour market data for the 1990s reflect gains in productivity and higher-skilled workers in different economic sectors, particularly industrial activities. The data presented by Neri et al. reveal a clear increase in the education levels of the workforce employed in the Brazilian economy from 1989 through 1996.[34] 'The percentage of workers with less than four years' schooling fell from 38 per cent in 1989 to 31 per cent in 1996, while the number of workers with over eight years' education rose from 42 per cent to 49 per cent of the labour-force.' 'The industrial sector posted the highest percentage increase, eight per cent, while the trade and services sectors rose six per cent over these seven years. Consequently, the level of skills among the Brazilian labour-force rose over the period analysed, suggesting gains in productivity in the workplace.[35]

Nevertheless, this seems insufficient to trigger an about-turn in a situation that is edging workers into poverty and social exclusion. There seems to be unanimous agreement on one of the measures suggested by analysts in the government and the opposition: the need for a return to sustainable economic growth. Generating new jobs through economic expansion would do much to resolve the current problems of the Brazilian labour market, particularly among younger workers. However, this depends largely on the nation's macro-economic policy, as well as on the global scenario.

But some dilemmas still remain that do not offer easy solutions. For instance, everyone agrees that it is vital to invest in schooling and training in order to endow workers with better education and skills, particularly youngsters. Although some efforts are under way in this direction, they are still relatively limited in terms of the labour market as a whole. However, policies of this type need to be supported by other social welfare policies attacking the poverty that is endemic within Brazilian society. 'Minimum income' policies introduced in some Brazilian municipal districts have proven fairly effective, at least in terms of keeping children in school. Authors such as Pochmann, for instance, suggest that measures should be introduced that delay the entry of young people to the labour market, in addition to steps

34   Neri et al. (2000), p. 26.
35   *Ibid.*

'directed towards promoting jobs specifically for young people; establishing a nationwide plan of action that builds up closer links between the classroom and the work-place, in addition to subsidised jobs in the private sector and community utility programmes in the public sector'.[36]

With regard to formal employment, the challenge seems to lie in fostering sustainable economic development in a manner that will make the labour market more dynamic, despite lower employment requirements by the productive sector. Even in a labour market that is increasingly more informal, macroeconomic pressures remain, urging more flexible labour relations. This has been one of the most controversial issues in this discussion. Why should labour protection be lifted in a labour market that has already become so much more flexible? What would be the economic efficacy of this, other than weakening workers and their trade union representatives?

Finally, there is the issue of income distribution. It is well known already that 'liberalised trading regimes for the countries of Latin America have so far been associated with the reduction of workers' rights and the concentration of wealth'.[37] Everyone agrees that this is a structural problem in Brazil, and despite improvements in some human development indexes over the past few years Brazil is still rated shamefully low compared to other developed or even emerging countries. The solutions under discussion are always long-term. However, the situation in the Brazilian labour market today indicates that these inequalities will worsen as widespread poverty grows even more severe.

36   Pochmann (2000b), p. 3.
37   Weeks (1999), p. 166.

CHAPTER 6

The 1997 Korean Crisis:
Causes and Consequences

Ha-Joon Chang

Introduction

Since the outbreak of the financial crisis in Korea in November 1997, the country's economy and society has been on a roller-coaster ride. In a country where five per cent growth was considered a 'recession', the economy contracted by 5.7 per cent in 1998, which was the biggest and only the second fall in output since the end of the Korean War (1950–53) (a 2.7 per cent fall was recorded in 1980).

However, the following year the economy experienced an upsurge beyond anyone's expectation (10.7 per cent) and continued with a strong growth momentum for most of 2000, with nine per cent growth for the year. In another turn of events, the economy has been showing signs of marked slowdown since the autumn of 2000, following the end of stock market deflation, some major corporate bankruptcies (the Daewoo Group and Hyundai Engineering and Construction), rising oil prices and the slowing-down of the US economy. Experts are divided as to whether this slowdown will be relatively short-lived or is the beginning of longer period of trouble, but there can be no denying that the Korean recovery of 1999–2000 was as short-lived as it was spectacular.

In this chapter, in an attempt to make sense of the recent evolution of the Korean economy, I discuss four groups of issues relating to the recent Korean crisis — the causes of the crisis (Section 2), the management of the crisis (Section 3), the recovery (Section 4) and future prospects (Section 5).

The Causes of the Crisis: Institutional Deficiencies?

The causes of the Asian crisis have been widely and intensely debated, although perhaps not with as much intellectual care as there should have been. On one side of the debate are those who emphasise the political and institutional deficiencies of the Asian economies, summarised in terms like 'crony capitalism' and 'moral hazard'.[1] This view was initially dominant and unquestioned, but it has been increasingly criticised by authors who

---

1   This camp includes the IMF and the World Bank, as well as academics like Krugman (1998a, 1998b), McKinnon and Pill (1998), Corsetti et al. (1998), and Frankel (1998).

put emphasis on the inherently volatile nature of unregulated financial markets and the deficiencies of the international financial architecture.[2] Despite the more recent ascendancy of the second view, the first view still predominates. Therefore, in this section I critically examine five popular varieties of this first view that tries to explain the Korean crisis by virtue of institutional deficiencies of Korean capitalism, and then present the second view that I believe shows the 'real' causes of the crisis.

Industrial Policy[3]

Especially in the early days of the crisis, many commentators argued that industrial policy that went against the market logic was the root cause of the Korean crisis.[4] The argument is that the Korean government put pressure on the banks to lend to favoured industries regardless of their prospects, leading to the accumulation of non-performing loans. It is also argued that those who were running the favoured industries regarded their projects as at least implicitly under-written by the government, which naturally encouraged lax management and excessive risk-taking. This argument is best summed up in the following passage from *The Economist*: 'Most of the financial mess is of Asia's own making, and nowhere is this clearer than in South Korea. For years, the government has treated the banks as tools of state industrial policy, ordering them to make loans to uncreditworthy companies and industries'.[5]

In discussing this view, it should first be pointed out that, contrary to the widespread assumption, state guarantee through industrial policy need not be bad. There are all kinds of 'market failures' that justify socialisation of risk through industrial policy as revealed in the recent debates on industrial policy.[6] Of course, as we are all familiar with, there are many examples of failed industrial policy attempts all over the world, but these failures have occurred because of poor design and implementation, and not because the principle of socialisation of risk itself is inherently wrong.

Moreover, whether or not industrial policy can be theoretically justified, the recent crisis cannot be blamed on industrial policy, as it was more or less dismantled by the early 1990s.[7] Indeed, many of the key bankruptcies

---

2   Interestingly, this camp includes both 'mainstream' economists such as Stiglitz (1998, 2001), Furman and Stiglitz (1999), Radelet and Sachs (1998), and Feldstein (1998) and 'heterodox' economists such as Taylor (1998), Kregel (1998), Singh (1999) and Chang (2000).
3   The following four sections draw heavily on Chang (2000).
4   For example, *The Economist*, 15 November 1997; Brittan (1997).
5   *The Economist*, 15 November 1997.
6   Chang (1994), chapter 3; Stiglitz (1996); Lall (1998); Chang (1999).
7   For details, see Chang (1998) and Chang et al. (1998).

that shook confidence in the Korean economy (for example, Kia, Hanbo) were direct results of the lifting of government control on entry into industries with large fixed capital requirements, which created serious excess capacity problem in the short- to medium-run.

Cronyism

According to the explanations of the Asian crisis that emphasise the 'cronyistic' nature of the crisis countries, those Asian enterprises that had cronyistic connections with the government were seen by their lenders as having no downside risk (as the government would rescue them if they got into trouble). This meant that the financial institutions were willing to lend them as much as they wanted, which in turn inflated the asset bubbles that led to the crisis.[8] In the Korean case, the corruption scandal surrounding the collapse of Hanbo Steel in early 1997, which was a key moment in the making of the Korean crisis, was often cited as a 'proof' that the country's crisis can also be seen as an outcome of cronyism.

One obvious problem with this story is that corruption has been prevalent in Korea (and the other Asian crisis economies) throughout its high growth period, and therefore that it cannot explain why it did not cause similar crises before. If anything, corruption was seen as diminishing in the country in the build-up to the crisis. For whatever its worth, according to the corruption index released by Transparency International (on the scale of 0, very corrupt, to 10, very clean) Korea's corruption problem became slightly worse in the late 1980s and the early 1990s (the index fell slightly from 3.93 during 1980–85 to 3.50 during 1988–92) but showed a marked improvement in the mid-1990s (the index rose significantly to 5.32 by 1996).

However, the 'crony capitalism' story is more relevant than is suggested by the aggregate corruption figures. The aggregate corruption indexes are problematic, as they comprise both generalistic and cronyistic corruptions. In the traditional Korean system, corruption was usually of generalistic kind, as the bribes were rarely directly related to particular projects *in the main manufacturing sectors* (areas like urban planning and defence contracts were different). Under the Kim Young Sam government (1993–97) that created the crisis, 'cronyistic' corruption started affecting the key manufacturing sectors (Hanbo steel case, Samsung automobile case).

However, whatever its true extent was, it is not clear whether cronyism can ever be a major explanation of the Asian crisis. Cronyism by definition has to be selective. It does not make sense to argue that all (or even the bulk of) those Korean financial institutions that borrowed money from abroad had such good political connections that they could expect to be

8   Krugman (1998b); Frankel (1998).

bailed-out in times of trouble. If some foreign creditors thought this was the case, they should have practised themselves those 'advanced' credit risk assessment techniques that they are now so eager to preach to the Asian financial institutions.

Deposit Insurance

Some people find an important source of the recent Asian crisis in explicit and implicit deposit insurance that created moral hazard on the side of the banks, which then lent to misconceived or speculative projects.[9]

The main problem with this view is that deposit insurance does not necessarily create moral hazard on the part of bank managers. By definition, it is the depositors who are protected from this arrangement, and not the bank managers. Therefore whether deposit insurance gives the bank manager the incentive to make imprudent lending decisions will be critically determined by the degree to which his/her job security and remuneration depends on the quality of his/her decisions, and not merely by the existence of deposit insurance. If the bank managers lose their jobs following a government bailout, for example, the fact that their banks are bailed out by the government does create moral hazard on their part. Of course, in practice the bank managers do not necessarily get punished for their poor decisions, but this is the result of a poorly designed incentive system for the bank managers, and *not* the result of deposit insurance per se.

The empirical limitation of the deposit insurance story is that it cannot really explain why, if deposit insurance was what was driving over-lending, it was the non-bank financial institutions (for example, the Korean merchant banks, the Thai finance companies) or the non-financial sector corporations (for example, Indonesian corporations) that did not have same kind of government guarantee, rather than the banks, that led the over-lending process in the crisis countries.

The Logic of 'Too Big to Fail'

Many observers of the Korean crisis argue that the country's large conglomerates, or the *chaebols*, took excessive risk because they believed that they were 'too big to fail' (henceforth TBTF).[10]

The logic of TBTF seems difficult to dismiss, especially given that it is indeed practised by all governments in all capitalist countries, including the ones that claim to be the most market-oriented. The rescue of the US hedge fund, Long Term Capital Management (LTCM), is one prominent recent example, but the late 1970s rescue of the bankrupt Swedish shipbuilding industry through nationalisation by the first right-wing govern-

9   McKinnon and Pill (1998); Krugman (1998a).
10   For example, Yoo (1997); Pyo (1998); Burton (1998).

ment in the country for over 40 years or the early 1980s rescue of the car-maker Chrysler by the avowedly free-market Reagan administration seem to demonstrate the power of the logic of TBTF.

However, there is a confusion in the TBTF story between the rescue of a firm and the rescue of its owners or managers who are responsible for creating the situation whereby the rescue is needed. To the manager or the owner, it is not much of a consolation that his/her firm is saved by the government due to its large size, if the rescue operation involves the termination of his/her contract or, in the case of the owner, the loss of his/her control over the firm. In other words, whether government bailouts of large firms encourage moral hazard by the managers of other large firms depends on whether they are accompanied by punishments for bad management.

The evidence from Korea is not on the side of the TBTF story. Especially in the 1960s and the 1970s, when the country was going through rapid structural changes, it was not infrequent to see even some of the largest *chaebols* going bankrupt. The Donglip *chaebol*, which ranked ninth in the early 1960s, went bankrupt by the end of the decade. The second largest *chaebol* during the 1960s, Samho, and the Gaepoong *chaebol*, which ranked between third and fourth during the 1960s, virtually disappeared by the late-1970s. These are striking statistics. Collapse of these three *chaebols* of the 1960s is equivalent in US terms to the disappearance by the early 1980s of Standard Oil (New Jersey), Ford Motor Co. and IBM, which ranked second, third and ninth respectively in the US enterprise ranking in 1964.

After the mid-1980s, and especially in the 1990s, the ranking of the top ten *chaebols* remained highly, if not completely, stable, but among the lesser *chaebols* there was still a high turnover. Between 1990 and 1996 alone, three of the top 30 *chaebols* (Hanyang, Yoowon and Woosung) went bankrupt, and in 1997, in the build-up to and at the beginning of the crisis, six of the top 30 *chaebols* (Kia, Halla, Jinro, Hanbo, Sammi and Haitai) went bankrupt, again debunking the TBTF story.

Of course, all this is not to deny that the Korean government not infrequently injected money into ailing large enterprises. However, these financial injections were conditional, with very few exceptions, on a change of ownership and top management, and were always accompanied by tough terms of financial restructuring.

The Peculiar Nature of the Corporate Sector[11]

Another popular explanation for the Korean situation is that the Korean economy was bound for a trouble in the long run anyway because of the

---

11 This section draws heavily on Chang and Park (1999), where more detailed arguments and more data can be found.

peculiar nature of its corporate sector that was characterised by, among other things, high leverage and low profitability. This view is well reflected in the corporate governance reform agenda that has been pursued by the IMF and the two Korean governments since the crisis. However, as we shall see below, these characterisations are misleading and it is doubtful whether these characteristics can 'explain' the crisis.

Low Profitability

The first thing to note when discussing profitability as a measure of enterprise performance is that it is not necessarily a good indicator of a firm's social contribution, given various market imperfections.[12] Moreover, it is difficult to decide which measure of profitability should be used. And, needless to say, different measures give very different results. In addition, comparing profitability across countries is notoriously difficult, as different countries have different accounting standards.[13]

It is also doubtful whether we can 'explain' the 1997 financial crisis in Korea (and other Asian countries) with low corporate profitability. For example, according to a study by Calessens et al. (1998), Korea had the 44th lowest returns on assets among a sample of 46 countries,[14] apparently supporting those who point out low profitability as the cause of the Korean crisis. However, Korean profitability has not been so low if profitability is defined differently (see below), and, more interestingly, the other crisis economies had very high returns on assets. Thailand and Indonesia ranked first (by a huge margin) and third in these sample countries (second was the Philippines, a semi-crisis country), and Malaysia ranked a very respectable eighth.

There were insufficient data available to decide whether Korean corporate profitability was exceptionally low by international standards, but Table 6.1 gives us some insights. The table's limitations are clear (very limited sample size, the particular types of profitability measures, etc.), but it shows that, while net profitability (ordinary income to sales) of the Korean firms was the lowest among the four countries in the sample, their gross profitability (operating income to sales) was the highest.

The data from Claessens et al. (1998) also confirm this observation.[15] They show that the 'operational margin' (which is similar to the notion of

---

12 For example, Blaine (1993); Chang and Singh (1993).
13 Some, for example, claim that, the Japanese corporate profitability has been underestimated because of the differences in accounting methods from those used in other, especially Anglo-American, countries (e.g., Blaine, 1993).
14 Claessens et al., p. 5, figure 1.
15 *Ibid.*, p. 7, table 3.

gross profitability)[16] among the Korean firms during 1988–96, at 19.6 per cent, was higher than that in the USA (14.4 per cent) and Germany (14.6 per cent), although it was lower than that in five of the eight other East Asian countries for which figures were available (Japan, Indonesia, Taiwan, the Philippines and Thailand; Hong Kong, Singapore and Malaysia had lower figures).

Table 6.1: Structure of Profit in the Manufacturing Sector in Korea, Japan, the USA and Taiwan (per cent, average during 1988–97)*

	Korea**	USA	Japan	Taiwan
Operating Income to Sales	7.0 (7.1)	6.6	3.3	6.5
Ordinary Income to Sales	2.1 (2.7)	4.2***	3.3	4.5
Financial Expenses to Sales	5.6 (5.3)	n.a.	n.a.	2.1

*   Taiwan's figures are for 1986–95.
**   Figures in parentheses are for 1986–95.
*** Net profits.
Source: BOK website, BOK (2000), Chang and Park (1999).

High Financial Leverage
High financial leverage of the *chaebols* has been widely blamed as the primary cause of Korea's financial crisis of 1997 and efforts have been made to reduce corporate leverage in the country (see below), but it is not clear whether this argument is correct.

First of all, there is a well-known and still-inconclusive debate in financial economics on the relative merits of equity financing and debt financing.[17] Moreover, the debt-equity ratio of Korean corporations (historically between 300 per cent and 350 per cent, depending on the phase of business cycle) is not exceptionally high by international standards. A World Bank study covering the period between 1980 and 1991 shows that, at 366 per cent, the average debt-equity ratio for Korean corporations was simi-

16   The notion of 'operational margin' used by Claessens et al. is defined as the difference between sales and the costs of goods sold as a share of sales. This is slightly different from the notion of 'gross profitability', as it does not subtract selling and administrative expenses from the numerator.
17   Harris and Raviv (1991); Brennan (1995).

lar to that in Japan (369 per cent), France (361 per cent) and Italy (307 per cent).[18] Rather surprisingly, it was much lower than the norm in Scandinavia, that is, around 500 per cent to 538 per cent in Norway, 555 per cent in Sweden and 492 per cent in Finland.[19]

Many people believe that the high financial leverage of the Korea firms, especially the *chaebols*, was the result of a peculiar ownership structure, where the 'owning family' avoids financing through the stock market for fear of diluting their control. This has been a driving theme behind the recent corporate governance reform efforts in the country

However, there is no evidence that the dependence of the Korean *chaebols* on the stock market is exceptionally low by international standards. A number of recent studies have revealed that, together with the large corporations in other developing countries, large Korean firms, most of them *chaebol* subsidiaries, have actually relied *more* on equity financing than their counterparts in the advanced countries, which rely mostly on financing through retained earnings.[20] For example, in Table 6.2, one can see that the contribution of stocks in investment financing in Korea during the 1970s and the 1980s was, at 13.4 per cent (1972–91), much higher than that in Germany (2.3 per cent), Japan (3.9 per cent), the UK (7.0 per cent), or the USA (-4.9 per cent).

Table 6.2: Gross Sources of Finance in Selected Countries (1970-89) (per cent)

	Germany	Japan	UK	US	Korea*
Internal	62.4	40.0	60.4	62.7	29.0
Bank finance	18.0	34.5	23.3	14.7	18.9
Bonds	0.9	3.9	2.3	12.8	5.7
New equity	2.3	3.9	7.0	-4.9	13.4
Trade credit	1.8	15.6	1.9	8.8	n.a.
Capital transfer	6.6	n.a.	2.3	n.a.	n.a.
Other	8.0	2.1	2.9	5.9	n.a.

Sources: All figures other than those for Korea are from Corbett and Jenkinson (1994, p. 9). The Korean figures are calculated from Chang and Park (1999).

18   Demigruc-Kunt and Maksimovic (1996).
19   The average debt-equity ratio in Japan during the 1970s was also around 500%.
20   See Mayer (1988 and 1990); Corbett and Jenkinson (1994); Singh (1994 and 1995); Singh and Hamid (1992). According to one World Bank study, Korea had higher stock market capitalisation as a proportion of GDP than several advanced countries such as Canada, France, Italy and Sweden (Demirguc-Kunt and Levine, 1996).

Thus seen, there is no substance to the claim that Korean corporations, especially the *chaebols*, have avoided financing through the stock market. They have large debts not because they eschewed stock financing, but only because they have found even these large sums raised in the stock market insufficient for the aggressive investment strategy that they have pursued with impressive results.

The Real Causes of the Crisis

Having rejected the more popular views on the causes of the Korean crisis, I now turn to present an alternative explanation. The first element in this alternative explanation is industrial deregulation. Starting from the late 1980s, Korean industrial policy, especially investment coordination among competitors intended to restrain 'excessive competition' was gradually weakened. The decisive change came in 1993 with the coming to power of Kim Young Sam administration, which symbolically allowed Samsung into what industry experts regarded as an already overly crowded automobile industry.[21]

As is well known, uncoordinated capacity expansion in industries that require large fixed investments can result in 'wasteful competition', where excess capacity leads to low capacity utilisation, at the industry level.[22] For a country like Korea, which is a relatively small economy but specialises in industries with large-scale economies (for example, micro-chips, automobile, shipbuilding, steel, etc.), failure in investment coordination can even have macroeconomic consequences. If excess capacity materialises simultaneously in a number of industries whose combined relative importance in the national economy is large, it can have macroeconomic consequences.

And this is exactly what happened in Korea in the run-up to the crisis. Excess capacity was created in key industries like micro-chips, steel and automobiles, in the absence of government coordination, and this in turn led to deteriorating corporate profitability in a major segment of the economy, damage to 'investors' confidence' due to major bankruptcies (Kia in automobiles and Hanbo in steel), and even balance of payments problems (falling micro-chip prices, to which Korean excess capacity contributed).

More important than the demise of industrial policy was the mismanagement of financial liberalisation and opening-up that occurred during the early- to mid-1990s.[23] The inherent instability of a liberalised, open financial market, possibly except for the most advanced economies, is well known and does not need repetition here. Therefore it is not clear whether Korea should have liberalised and opened up its financial market at the point it did.

21   For further details on this, see Chang (1998).
22   For further theoretical discussions, see Chang (1994), chapter 3.
23   Details of this process can be found in Chang et al. (1998), p. 737, table 1.

However, even supposing that financial liberalisation and opening-up was beneficial, the process itself was very poorly managed. First of all, the Korean government allowed too many new entries into the financial industries too quickly, which lowered the average quality of decision-makers. For example, 24 additional merchant banks were licensed between 1994 and 1996, as opposed to the six that had existed until 1994.[24] Second, and even more importantly, financial liberalisation and opening-up was *not* accompanied by a commensurate upgrading in the financial supervision system. There was virtually no monitoring of, for example, foreign debt maturity structure, which was the key to the country's fall.[25]

The Management of the Crisis

I have documented the chronology of the crisis in detail elsewhere,[26] so in this section, I want to point out a few problems that emerged from the strategy of crisis management followed by the IMF and by the Korean government, which more or less accepted the IMF line.

First of all, many people have criticised the IMF for 'crying "fire!" in a crowded theatre'.[27] By rubbishing the Asian economies as being in need of a fundamental structural reform, it encouraged investors' panic and undermined the purpose of its own bailout operations. In this context, one could also point out the highly negative role that the credit rating agencies played in the crisis. These agencies, which magnified investor euphoria in the boom leading to the crisis by awarding improving ratings to the Asian crisis economies before the crisis, completely changed their tune and magnified the panic encouraged by the IMF prognosis on the crisis economies once the crisis began.

Second, others criticised the high interest rate policy maintained during the first half year of the crisis for its contractionary effect. Stiglitz especially emphasised that, contrary to the IMF belief that it would attract more capital inflow by offering the holders of Korean-won-denominated assets higher rewards, high interest policy can easily undermine confidence in crisis economies, as it increases the chance of bankruptcy and therefore loan default.[28]

Third, and a less discussed aspect of the IMF macro-financial policy, is the introduction of the Bank for International Settlements (BIS) capital adequacy ratio as a banking regulatory measure. Despite the fact that the high interest rate policy was relaxed by May 1998, credit crunch continued in the econ-

---

24   Chang (1998), p. 1558.
25   For further elaboration on this point, see Chang (1998).
26   Chang (1998) and Chang and Yoo (2000 and 2002).
27   For example, Radelet and Sachs (1998).
28   See his essays cited above.

omy, as banks tried to keep this ratio high for fear of becoming objects of future take-over and forced merger. How serious the credit crunch was during the 1997 crisis is shown by the fact that loans by deposit money banks *fell* by 0.1 per cent in 1998, whereas they *grew* by about 36 per cent in 1980, when Korea had another economic crisis and an IMF-style programme. Even the fall in exports following the 1997 crisis, which contrasts with the continued rise in exports after the 1980 crisis, owed significantly to the squeeze on export credits, rather than to an over-valued currency or to the depressed world market conditions (the world economy was in a deep recession in the early 1980s, whereas it has remained relatively buoyant since 1997). In other words, the pro-cyclical nature of the BIS standards aggravated the crisis.

Last but not least, issue needs to be raised with the IMF's mandate. The IMF is, in its original charter, mandated to deal with current account balance of payments problems. Since the 1980s there has been 'mission creep', as the IMF got involved in more and more policy areas. Initially, this was done by the introduction of the so-called 'monetary theory of balance of payments' in the IMF operations during the 1970s, which justified its intervention in budgetary and monetary policies on the ground that these are sources of all balance of payments problems. With the Debt Crisis in the 1980s and the 'structural adjustment programmes', there was another expansion in the virtual (if not legal) mandate of the IMF. This 'mission creep' has reached another height during the recent Asian crisis, especially in Korea, when the IMF demanded a fundamental institutional overhaul, including hitherto-untouched areas such as corporate governance system and labour law. One may or may not agree that these institutional changes are necessary, but it seems clear that the IMF is now engaged in policy issues that it has neither the mandate nor the expertise to deal with.

The Recovery

As the contractionary policies led to a disastrous collapse in the economy (with more than 100 firms going bankrupt every day in the early months of 1998), the IMF belatedly took a U-turn and allowed the Korean government lower interest rates and (in the face of the continued aversion of the Korean government to budget deficits) pushed it to increase the budget deficit (the fourth agreement in May 1988). And largely as a result of this U-turn, the speed of contraction of the economy slowed down from the fourth quarter of 1998. By the end of the first quarter of 1999 the economy had started to recover rapidly and achieved an impressive 10.7 per cent growth (GDP) in 1999, although given the 6.7 per cent fall in output in 1998, at the end of 1999 the country's income was only 3.2 per cent higher than it was in 1997. The economy posted a strong growth at least for the first three quarters of 2000, with 9.3 per cent overall growth rate for the whole year.

What can one make of this rapid recovery? Does it prove that the IMF policy was a success, as the IMF and its supporters claim? My contention is that it does not. First of all, I must point out that a large part of the recovery was due to a natural reaction to the easing of the initial macro-economic policy that was excessively tight and shrank the economy unnec-essarily. The fact that the financial markets did not stabilise until May 1998, when the IMF abandoned its earlier policy, suggests that the country could have recovered much more quickly, and much more strongly, had the IMF policy not been so restrictive.[29]

Secondly, the quality of the recovery is not as impressive as it looks. The output recovery may have been quite impressive, but the country's performance in unemployment and equality has been poor, even com-pared to similar situations before. Unemployment rose from 2.5 per cent just before the crisis (and from the trough of two per cent in 1996) to a high of 8.6 per cent in February 1999 (it has fallen since March 1999), in contrast to the rise from 3.8 per cent in 1979 (or from the trough of 3.2 per cent in 1978) to 5.2 per cent in 1980. Income inequality also worsened markedly following the crisis. The ratio of the income of the top quintile to that of the bottom quintile rose from 4.49 before the crisis to 5.38 by 1999[30] and the ratio of the income of the top ten per cent to that of the bottom ten per cent rose from 7.1 in the first quarter of 1995 to 9.8 in the first quarter of 1998 and 10.2 in the first quarter of 1999.[31] In contrast, the worsening of income inequality in the aftermath of the 1980 crisis was not very significant, if at all.[32] Labour market casualisation has progressed fast, with 52 per cent of the workforce not having a permanent contract at the end of 2000, according to a research report from the highly respect-ed Korea Labour Research Institute.[33]

More importantly, the recovery has proved unsustainable in the medi-um term. The recovery was initially led by a consumption boom created by the wealth effect following a stock market bubble, which started deflating in the autumn of 2000. The stock market price index, which fell below 300 (297.9, to be precise) in the second quarter of 1998 went up to 562.5 by the fourth quarter of 1998, and broke the 1,000 barrier in July 1999. Final consumption expenditure started growing from the first quarter of 1999, while investment started growing only in the second quarter of 1999, and

---

29 See Chang and Yoo (2002).
30 *Joongang Daily Newspaper*, 18 June 1999.
31 *Daehan Maeil Newspaper*, 25 June 1999.
32 Of the five estimates of trends in income inequality reviewed in Ahn (1996), two showed a small fall in Gini coefficient between 1980 and 1982 (from 0.389 to 0.357 and from 0.409 to 0.393) and three showed a small rise during the same period (from 0.386 to 0.406, from 0.356 to 0.385, and from 0.337 to 0.376).
33 *Chosun Ilbo*, 4 November 2000.

outpaced investment growth throughout 1999 (consumption grew at 8.5 per cent, while investment grew at 4.1 per cent). During the first half of 2000, investment demand led the recovery, but its growth peaked in the first quarter of the year (22.4 per cent in the first quarter, 12.9 per cent in the second quarter) and stopped being the leading growth factor from the third quarter of 2000. The stock market index started its climb-down from its height of just over 1,000 in the autumn of 1999, fluctuated between 700 and 800 throughout the first several months of 2000, and started another fall below this level at the end of the summer 2000. Reflecting this, consumption demand has started to fall since July 2000.

As I argued elsewhere earlier,[34] the stock market inflation was unsustainable, as it was the result of a number of factors that were either one-off or unsustainable. First of all, the opening-up of the stock market to foreign investors enabled them snap up bargain-price blue-chip stocks following the post-crisis asset price collapse. This is a one-off event that is unlikely to repeat itself. Secondly, the liberalisation of the domestic financial industries, especially licensing of unit trusts, made stock trading accessible to an unprecedented number of people, thus initially creating a huge inflow of new money into the stock market. Apart from the fact that many of the unit trust companies are in tatters now due to poor management and unlawful trading, this was another one-off event. Third, the stock market inflation was fuelled by the excess liquidity created by the easing of monetary policy (from the third quarter of 1998) in the face of a dramatic collapse in real investments.

The Future

What is more worrying than the shakiness of the recovery in the medium-term is the impact of the post-crisis institutional changes, especially the ones regarding the financial system but also regarding the corporate governance system, on the economy's long-term dynamism.

The policy package that was adopted in order to manage the 1997 crisis was not entirely in the mould of the standard IMF package and still showed some traditional Korean streaks. For the most important example, the Korean government pushed the *chaebols* into a 'voluntary' industrial restructuring programme involving mergers and business swaps in eight industries (semiconductor, automobile, power-generating equipment, naval diesel engine, aircraft, petrochemicals, petroleum refining and railway carriage) — the so-called 'Big Deal' programme. More recently, the Ministry of Commerce, Industry and Energy announced that it intends to restructure six industries (synthetic fibre, cotton spinning, pulp and paper, electric

---

34   See Chang and Yoo (2000).

furnace, cement and petrochemicals) that are suffering from 'overcrowd-ing'.[35] Although these programmes are not parts of a coherent long-term industrial policy as in the case of previous industrial restructuring pro-grammes, it is similar to their earlier counterparts in their spirits.[36]

However, in general, the crisis management package implemented since 1997 has resulted in institutional changes that have significantly trans-formed the nature of the Korean economy. Are these changes for the bet-ter or for the worse? Important changes were made in other areas too (for example, employment institutions, bureaucratic recruitment and appoint-ments), but in this chapter the discussion will be confined to institutional changes that concern the financial system and to a lesser extent the cor-porate governance system, and what these mean for the future of the Korean economy.

First of all, one needs to talk about the institutionalisation of the 'pro-finance' policy stance that characterised the macroeconomic policy in the early days of the current crisis.[37] To begin with, the role of the central bank was redefined into a fundamentally monetarist (i.e., pro-finance) one. In the old central bank act, the Bank of Korea (BOK) Act, the BOK was supposed to maintain the 'soundness of the banking and the financial sys-tem' (which can mean a lot of things in practice) as well as price stability. The new act that took effect from April 1999 specifies that price stability should be the sole aim of the BOK. This change, while appearing minor, has profound implications for the Korean financial system, as it de-legit-imises the kind of pro-investment, pro-growth monetary policy that char-acterised the Korean financial system until the crisis. Moreover, the bank-ing law and other financial laws were revised in a way that strengthens the shareholder interest in the running of the banks, thus making it possible and, more importantly legitimate, to defend financial interests at the cost of industrial interests (something that was not allowed before).

The second important institutional change in the Korean financial sys-tem that followed the current crisis was the introduction of the BIS stan-dard on capital adequacy ratio into the financial system. The BIS standard has certain merits (such as simplicity and transparency), but, as was men-tioned earlier, its pro-cyclical nature has made the crisis worse — in reces-sion, increased bankruptcy and fall in asset prices shrink the banks' asset bases, which makes them withdraw their loans in order to meet the stan-dard, thereby making the recession even worse. It should also be noted that the introduction of the BIS standard in Korea was carried out at the worst time — in the middle of the deepest recession in the country's modern

---

35   *Chosun Ilbo*, 13 November 2000.
36   On earlier industrial restructuring practices in Korea, see Chang (1993).
37   In contrast to the 'pro-industry' stance that characterised previous Korean policies, including crisis managements; see Chang and Yoo (2000).

history. Moreover, the very way in which the BIS standard is defined encourages the holding of liquid assets and therefore a strict enforcement of the standard, to which the Korean government claims to be committed, will make the banks reluctant to lend to industrial projects that involve large sunk costs.

The third important institutional change made after the current crisis was a radical capital market liberalisation and capital account opening, including the full-scale liberalisation of corporate borrowing from abroad (which makes government regulation of foreign debts much more difficult) and the complete opening of the stock and bond markets to foreigners. These changes have increased volatility in the financial market, which is not conducive to long-term investments and therefore harmful for the country's investment-growth dynamics.[38]

Also problematic was the demand made to the *chaebols* that they bring down their debt-equity ratio from above 400 per cent to 200 per cent by the end of 1999, which made them cut down on new investments as well as engage in 'distress selling' of their existing assets.[39] The short-run effect of this change was to create a downward investment spiral. But more importantly, in the long run, if they continue to meet this demand, the Korean corporations are unlikely to be able to mobilise the funds necessary for the kind of aggressive investment strategy that they have traditionally pursued. The hope held by the policymakers who introduced this rule was that the deregulation of the stock market would lead to a greater reliance of the *chaebols* on direct financing. However, although this hope seemed to be realised for a while following the stock market inflation, especially for the 'internet' companies, this has proved to be unsustainable. Given the well-known short-term orientation of the stock market, which is markedly worsening in Korea at the moment, it is unlikely that the Korean firms are going to be able to mobilise through the stock market enough 'patient' funds needed for the investments in large-scale industries.

Concluding Remarks

The 1997 financial crisis in Korea has led to some dramatic changes in the institutional structure of the economy. The problem is that these changes were made on the basis of, as I endeavoured to explain, of flawed analyses of

---

38   For more detailed information, see Chang and Yoo (2002).

39   As a result, the average debt-equity ratio of manufacturing firms has fallen from 369.
3% in 1997 and 303% in 1998 (Samsung Economic Research Institute, *Korean Economic Trends*, 25 November 2000) to 215.7% by the end of 1999 and by November 2000 it had fallen to 193.1%, the lowest since 1967 (when it was 173.4%) (*Chosun Ilbo*, 14 November 2000). The same ratio for the *chaebols* was not available, but is probably somewhat higher than this average, if the traditional pattern has held.

the causes of the crisis. In my view, the IMF and the so-called 'reformers' in Korea have failed to recognise that it was the weakening, rather than persistence, of the country's traditional economic system that caused the crisis.

The most worrying change is that the traditionally strong link between industry and the banking sector, which had served the country so well throughout its high growth period, has been significantly weakened. My prediction is that in the medium to long run, this will seriously damage Korea's ability to raise investment finance and therefore will make it difficult for the country to further catch up with the more advanced economies, with whom it has up to now quite successfully caught up.

CHAPTER 7

Globalisation and Industrial Restructuring: The Case of South Korea

Jang-Sup Shin

Introduction

Industrial restructuring in Brazil in the 1990s was driven mainly by macro-economic factors. There were no visible microeconomic policies directing industrial restructuring. But the market opening and tight monetary policy pressed Brazilian companies to restructure for their own survival. And this restructuring was by and large a process of gaining dynamism, which had lacked in the Brazilian industry in the 1980s.[1]

Korea also underwent industrial restructuring in the 1990s as the pace of external liberalisation was accelerated. But major changes in industrial structure took place after the financial crisis in 1997 as the Korean government and the International Monetary Fund (IMF) carried out comprehensive microeconomic polices to reform the country's industrial structure. The guideline was the so-called 'global standard', on the perception that Korea's institutional structure was far behind what globalisation required. And the central target was the *chaebol* structure, on the diagnosis that it had brought about 'over-expansion without accountability'. In contrast to the Brazilian case, industrial restructuring in Korea was a process of taming 'excessive' dynamism and emphasising financial prudence.

Industrial restructuring is still going on in Korea and it may be too early to assess its appropriateness and effectiveness. It will take more time to have a clear picture about its net benefits (or costs) because new costs are still being added to the system and long-term benefits are yet to come. This chapter, however, tries to assess it by looking at the *chaebol* structure in historical perspective and examining real challenges of globalisation to *chaebols*. It also makes a broader discussion on the 'government-banks-*chaebol* nexus' because the *chaebol* structure has evolved as integral part of Korea's overall catching-up system.

The chapter argues that the *chaebol* structure is still useful to latecomer firms in competing with their forerunners, although Korean *chaebols* failed in managing the financial risks involved in global competition. The post-crisis industrial restructuring was overly conscious of financial prudence

---

1   See the chapters by Goldstein and Amann in this volume.

and, in a hurried attempt at removing the supposed problems of *chaebols*, discarded positive elements of *chaebols* as well and incurred an unnecessary burden of system change. The chapter also explores a possible second-stage catching-up system for Korea.

The Challenges of Globalisation

Globalisation is a trend increase in mobility of products, services and factors of production across national borders. The mobility in the world economy was led by exchange of products and 'the basic division of labour within the productive process was primarily organised within national economies' for more than two centuries after the Industrial Revolution, as Hobsbawm points out. It was only a recent phenomenon that factors of production and services became mobile across national borders.[2]

Multinational companies (MNCs) took off in the 1960s. Foreign direct investment (FDI) grew at twice the rate of growth of the world output and 40 per cent faster than world exports in the decade. After a short period of deceleration in the 1970s, FDI flows quadrupled in the 1980s, growing three times faster than trade flows and almost four times faster than GDP.[3] It was also only from the 1970s that financial markets began to integrate globally.

The underlying forces behind this transformation are ever-increasing competition, technological progress and regulatory changes. As Schumpeter (1934, 1943) observes, firms are incessantly competing for 'new combinations', chasing new markets, new factors of production, new organisations and new products and processes. The earlier MNCs like Standard Oil were primarily interested in locating its production facilities near the place of raw material extraction. The globalisation of the semiconductor industry in the 1960s began as a competitive response by Silicon Valley firms in their attempts to lower production costs by relocating assembly lines to developing countries. The proximity to local markets and availability of local engineers were major factors considered by the US car manufacturers when they started investing in Western Europe in the 1970. Currently, ever-increasing costs and risks involved in new technology development drive MNCs towards widespread cross-border mergers and acquisitions (M&As) and alliances. More and more MNCs are also setting up their facilities abroad for local market penetration both in developed and developing countries.

This relocation of production process was greatly facilitated by the development of information and communication technologies (ICT). Since the Industrial Revolution, the expansion of the world economy has been paralleled with the rapid development of 'space-shrinking' technolo-

2   Hobsbawm (1979), p. 313.
3   Dicken (1992); Julius (1990); Ernst (1999).

gies like transportation and communication.[4] The principal role of the ICT Revolution, which earnestly began in the 1980s, was to enable firms to co-ordinate their operations on a global scale more easily thanks to a drastic fall in the costs involved in information creation, processing, transfer and storage. ICT created 'new opportunities for knowledge sharing and interactive learning without co-location' and increased flexibility in firm operation.[5]

The pace of globalisation also gained momentum by regulatory changes in the world economy. Major developed countries like the USA and the UK initiated progressive liberalisation of their domestic economies and pushed for liberalisation of international trade and finance from the 1980s. The wave of liberalisation spread to other developed countries and also to developing countries. The World Trade Organisation (WTO) was formed and the Multilateral Agreement on Investment (MAI) has been discussed as a way to create stable new regulatory frameworks for the free flow of products and investments. Bilateral and regional agreements to liberalise trade and finance also progressed.

The increased mobility in the world market poses new challenges to industrial restructuring by providing companies and national governments with a new set of opportunities and constraints.

First, MNCs have acquired more leeway to organise their activities on the global scale and became a more dominant force in the world economy. Their share of world production and services is on a trend increase. They have also won an ideological battle. In the 1960s and 1970s when East Asian countries and Latin American countries began their industrial development, MNCs were widely regarded as entities to be accepted cautiously and therefore it was a norm that they operated under heavy regulations. But now they are enthusiastically welcomed by both developing and developed world. On the other hand, competition among MNCs has become more intense as more MNCs emerge and the scope of their competition widens and deepens. They are under constant pressure to restructure in order to remain competitive.

In the process of expanding their global operations, MNCs also press for restructuring of local firms. Responses by local firms are broadly in two directions: attempting to rise as fully-fledged MNCs or participating in the MNCs' global network as subcontractors. In the former case, local firms need to make heavy investments to protect their local markets from entrance of competing MNCs and to penetrate in foreign markets. In the latter case, local firms are required to restructure in line with the restructuring and changing needs of their partnering MNCs.[6]

---

4   Dicken (1992); Crafts (2000); Frankel (2000).
5   Ernst (1999).
6   It should be noted that these two responses are not mutually exclusive. There are also rapidly increasing incidences of alliances among MNCs. MNCs are also diverse in their technological capability, specialisations and so on, thereby creating great scope for subcontracting network among MNCs.

Secondly, national governments are under pressure to change earlier practices of economic management as national borders become more 'porous'. Above all, national competitiveness has been redefined as having competent firms within national territory regardless of their origin. Although there are still many routes for the national governments to support their local industries, available tools for such support are being reduced, and, in formulating and implementing economic policies, national governments increasingly face a question of 'who is us'.[7]

One ironic thing about globalisation is that, as more and more factors become mobile, national competitiveness is more critically dependent on more immobile assets, i.e., less globalised ones. If immobile assets do not complement mobile assets sufficiently, mobile assets are free to take the option of leaving the territory. The character and quality of immobile assets determine the 'stickiness' of mobile assets in a given territory. Among any others, the national government is most immobile. In this respect, it can be said that the functioning of the government has become more important in the economic wellbeing of a country.

Thirdly, the financial sector has rapidly emerged as a leading sector of globalisation. In terms of technologies involved and characteristics of businesses, financial services are more mobile than physical products. They are easy to duplicate with low marginal cost and easy to move from place to place at the speed of light. But the globalisation of the financial sector had been lagging behind that of the manufacturing sector mainly because of regulations. In most countries, the financial industry has remained principally a domestic industry under heavy government regulations.

The collapse of the Bretton Woods system and the need to circulate oil dollars worldwide in the 1970s helped the growth of the global financial market. Financial liberalisation started in earnest in the USA and the UK in the early 1980s, spread to other developed countries and reached developing countries in the 1990s. Once regulations were removed, the financial sector became the most decisive force in globalisation leveraging on its high mobility. The possibility that a large amount of money can move across borders at a touch of button is threatening, and, in managing companies and national economies, the view of international investors increasingly prevails in the name of 'investors' confidence' whatever that may be.[8]

7   Reich (1990).
8   For instance, Greider (1997, p. 258) argues that '[t]he power of global finance includes an extraordinary ability to create its own version of reality and persuade others to believe in it'.

Korea's Industrial Structure as a Catching-Up System

The growth of East Asian Newly Industrialising Countries (NICs), like Korea, Taiwan, Hong Kong and Singapore, is characterised by export-oriented or outward-oriented development. In catching up with their forerunners, the governments of these countries, except Hong Kong, employed various forms of industrial policy and were actively engaged in promoting economic growth.[9]

However, there were also significant differences among East Asian NICs. Singapore has developed mainly through attracting MNCs. Local firms were underdeveloped, although government-linked companies (GLCs), Singaporean versions of public enterprises, filled areas in which MNCs were not interested but which the Singaporean government regarded as strategic to the country's development. As a city-state depending for its survival on trading, Singapore barely had room to exercise protections for the domestic market.[10] It took the most international route of development among East Asian NICs. Since its industrialisation was spearheaded by MNCs who already had their own financial and technical resources, Singapore did not face any great difficulty in financing its industrialisation.

Taiwan initially developed through nationalistic route relying on three pillars, public enterprises, local medium-sized business groups, i.e., *guangx-iqiye*, and small and medium-sized companies (SMEs). It underwent a short period of import-substituting industrialisation and imposed heavy regulations on foreign direct investment. But it swiftly moved into reducing protection and attracting MNCs as means to compensate for the lack of big businesses in the domestic market. The Taiwanese industrial structure is based on complex relations between four major players: namely, public enterprises, *guangxiqiye*, MNCs and SMEs.[11] Among East Asian NICs, it can be said that Taiwan developed through the semi-international path of catching-up among East Asian NICs. Partnering with MNCs in high-risk projects and the dominance of SMEs also reduced the need for external funding for its industrialisation.

Compared to Singapore and Taiwan, Korea took the most nationalistic route to industrialisation. Unlike Taiwan, which developed heavy and chemical industries by means of public enterprises owing to a chasm between mainlanders and local Taiwanese, Korea, with a homogenous population, entrusted the heavy and chemical industries to local private entrepreneurs. Through state-controlled banks and various taxation measures, it provided *chaebols*, diversified conglomerates, with subsidies and protections. Unlike Singapore, Korea generally discouraged foreign direct

9   Wade (1990); World Bank (1993); Lall (1994); Rodrik (1998); Chang (1999).
10   Mirza (1986); Low (1998); Toh and Tan (1998); Wong (2000).
11   Wade (1990); Whitley (1992); Hou and Gee (1993); Field (1995).

investment and financed its economic development through domestic resource mobilisation and foreign loans. The government-owned and government controlled banks played important role in domestic resource mobilisation and foreign loans were guaranteed by the government until the mid-1980s. *Chaebols* relied heavily on Japanese producers for the parts and intermediate goods necessary to gain international competitiveness for their export items, resulting in the relative underdevelopment of local SMEs. In the industrial structure of Korea, the nexus between the government, banks and *chaebols* was central, leaving MNCs and SMEs on the periphery.[12]

These differences brought about differences in relative strengths and weaknesses among East Asian NICs although they have achieved almost equally high-powered economic growth for more than three decades until the Asian financial crisis in 1997. Singapore and Taiwan, through actively participating in the international subcontracting network rather than attempting to build 'one set' industries of their own, ventured less into projects with high financial risk, and, when they did, they normally arranged schemes to share risks with MNCs. They have therefore been virtually free from debt crisis. But they have relative weaknesses in the depth of their industrial structure and have lagged behind in accumulating broad research and development (R&D) capability. On the other hand, Korea has succeeded in building up relatively high level technological capacity in some industrial segments and developing a handful of its own high-profiled MNCs.[13] But this process was financed largely by external funds supported by heavier interventions from the government. Korea was thus the only country among East Asian NICs that feared the possibility of debt crisis when Latin American countries fell into debt crises in the 1980s.[14]

Korea's corporate profitability figures can be better understood in this context. One distinctive feature of corporate finance in Korea is a wide discrepancy between operating income to sales and ordinary income to sales. Operating profit of the manufacturing sector in Korea was relatively high, 7.4 per cent on average during 1973–96 and 7.0 per cent during 1988–97. This is slightly higher than those of Taiwan (6.5 per cent on average during 1986-95) and the USA (6.6 per cent on average during 1988–97), and comparable to that of Japan during its high growth period

---

12   Jones and Sakong (1980); Amsden (1989); Chang (1994); Song (1997).
13   Reflecting this, the gross expenditure of R&D to GDP in 1997 was 2.89% in Korea, similar to the levels of developed countries, while corresponding figures were 1.92% for Taiwan and 1.47% for Singapore, although they were similar in number of researchers, science and engineers to their labour force (Pacific Economic Cooperation Council — PECC, 1999; National Science and Technology Board — NSTB, 1999).
14   Korea in fact underwent a debt crisis in the early 1980s though on a smaller scale. For details, refer to Chang and Yoo (2002).

(7.2 per cent on average during 1961–73). But ordinary profit in Korea was very low, historically around 2.8 per cent (average during 1973–96 and 2.1 per cent during 1988–97). The comparable figures were 4.5 per cent for Taiwan (average during 1986–95), 4.2 per cent for the USA (average during 1988–97, net profit) and 4.3 per cent for Japan (average during 1955–73 and 3.3 per cent during 1988–97). (See Figure 7.1 and Tables 7.1 and 7.2.)

Figure 7.1: Trend of Profitability in the Manufacturing Sector in Korea

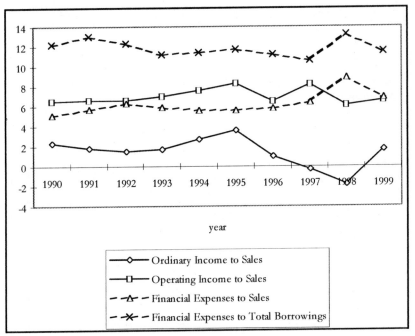

The discrepancy between operating profit and ordinary profit is basically a consequence of difference in financing, rather than that in corporate efficiency. If a company relies on the stock market for investment funds, the payments should be made from ordinary income. On the other hand, if a company gets its investment fund through external financing, the payments should be made from operating income. Financial expense to sales was 5.5 per cent for Korea (average during 1973–96), while it was 2.1 per cent for Taiwan (average during 1986–95). The difference in ordinary profit between Korea and Taiwan is largely explained by difference in financial expenses.

**Table 7.1: Structure of Profit in the Manufacturing Sector
in Korea, Japan, the USA and Taiwan
(per cent, average during 1988-97)***

	Korea**	USA	Japan	Taiwan
Operating income to Sales	7.0 (7.1)	6.6	3.3	6.5
Ordinary income to Sales	2.1 (2.7)	4.2***	3.3	4.5
Financial expenses to Sales	5.6 (5.3)	n.a.	n.a.	2.1

* Taiwan's figures are for 1986–95.
** Figures in parentheses are for 1986–95.
*** Net profits.
Source: BOK website, BOK (2000), Chang and Park (1999).

**Table 7.2: Major Business Indicators for Korea and Japan (manu-
facturing, per cent)**

	Korea (1973–96)	Japan (1955–73)
Current growth rate of sales	24.6	17.3
Operating income to sales	7.4	7.2*
Financial expenses to sales	5.5	3.4
Ordinary income to sales	2.8	4.3
Debt ratio	338.4	320.7

*1961-73
Source: Chang and Park (1999)

In general, a high dependence on external funds and low net profitability is certainly a soft spot of an economy. The economy becomes vulnerable to financial shocks when demand conditions deteriorate or cost factors like interest rates, prices of raw materials and so on are pushed up. However, this weakness was an opportunity cost involved in Korea's push for heavy and chemical industrialisation (HCI) in the face of capital shortage. If Korea had already accumulated enough capital to embark on the HCI, it would not have needed to rely so heavily on external funds. If the country did not precipitate itself in the HCI, it would not have required such extensive funds in a short period.[15] The debt-equity ratio of the Korean manufacturing sector had remained at 119 per cent on average during 1963–69. But it shot up to 342 per cent on average during 1970–79 and reached its peak of 487 per cent in 1980. Later, largely as a result of success in the HCI, the ratio was brought down to less than 300 per cent by the end of 1980s (Figure 7.2). This historical pattern is similar to that of Japan, whose debt-equity ratio reached around 500 per cent at the height of its push for the HCI and dropped subsequently.[16]

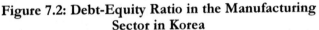

Figure 7.2: Debt-Equity Ratio in the Manufacturing Sector in Korea

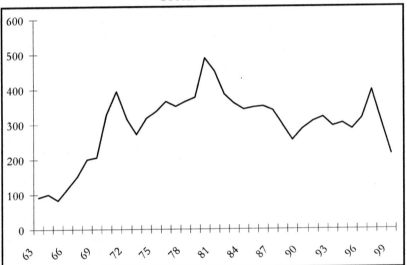

Source: BOK

Moreover, there were institutional mechanisms working on the economy to reduce the financial risks involved in this growth strategy: one was the government's industrial policy and the other was the *chaebol* structure.

15   There was also a taxation consideration in *chaebols'* reliance on debt financing because dividend income was liable to 'double taxation': it was taxed on corporate income before it was distributed to shareholders and was then taxed again on personal income of shareholders, while interest payments were deducted from taxation base of companies.

16   Chang and Park (1999).

As a 'developmental state', the Korean government employed various industrial policy measures both to maximise growth rate and also to make economic growth sustainable. One basic theme of the government intervention was to make those strategic industries internationally competitive. To this end, the government limited the number of firms in targeted strategic industries. It also pressed and helped them to start by attaining minimum economies of scale in the world market. It provided them with protection and subsidies as well. On the finance front, the government tightly controlled capital flows. It also guaranteed foreign borrowings of the private sector and supported commercial banks to keep providing it with 'patient' money.

Loan guarantees and other forms of mutual assistance among affiliates of *chaebols* helped a further creation of credit by reducing risks on the side of commercial banks. Diversification is also an effective mechanism for exploiting economies of scope. Transfer of money within the business group makes up for the insufficiency of investment funds and lessens liquidity pressure. Intra-group transfer of other resources like technologies, personnel and so on also provides advantages in entering and sustaining new long-term projects. Diversification, loan guarantee and intra-group resource transfer are an essential part of *chaebols'* strength in competition. *Chaebols* have thusfar been, when compared with non-diversified firms, not bad at generating profits but better at expansion, although they can criticised for unfair competition and concentration of economic powers within the domestic market. The diversified business portfolio also works to mitigate possible fallout from uncertainties. For businesses are hit unevenly by external shocks, and some businesses less affected by the shocks act as a buffer for the whole group.[17]

Looking back on history, this kind of system was not uncommon in other countries. The Japanese system of the developmental state and the *keiretsu* was a precursor of the Korean catching-up system. Catching-up processes of Germany, France and other continental European countries in the nineteenth century were also based on bank financing and the government's broader involvement in economic activities. And a large part of those institutions developed in their catching-up period have sustained well into the late twentieth century.[18] Business grouping is also more a general feature of industrial structure in developing countries than an exception. Although business groups are different across countries in terms of size and dominance in the economy, this structure is an effective mechanism to compensate for underdevelopment of capital markets and scarcity of managerial and technological capacity.[19]

17   Chang and Hong (2000); Chang and Choi (1988).
18   Gerschenkron (1962); Trebilcock (1981); Chandler (1990).
19   Leff (1978); Strachan (1976); Shin (1996).

Globalisation and the Financial Crisis in Korea

From the early 1980s the Korean economy began a gradual transition from its archetypal catching-up system to a more liberalised one. Liberalisation and stabilisation became a main policy agenda. This shift was more a response to correct imbalances brought by the HCI in the 1970s than a response to globalisation. It was also a transition towards gradual maturity of the economy. The actual pace of liberalisation was slow.

It was only in the late 1980s, when Korea accumulated substantial trade surpluses, that the pace of liberalisation was accelerated and the force of globalisation was felt seriously in the Korean economy. Domestically, increasing abundance of capital eased the need to allocate financial resources in preferential ways and led to a move towards more market-oriented resource allocation. Internationally, Korea began receiving pressures from the USA and European countries to open its product and financial markets further.

Korea's product market opened nearly to the levels of Western European countries by the mid-1990s. Subsidies were also trimmed substantially.[20] At the same time, the investment coordination mechanism was dismantled, the government hardly coordinating investment competition among *chaebols* in the 1990s.[21] Domestic financial liberalisation also progressed. Interest rates and foreign exchange rates were substantially liberalised. Licences for new financial institutions were more liberally given, resulting in tremendous growth of the non-banking financial institutions (NBFIs) in the 1990s.[22] Capital market opening was accelerated especially with Korea's accession to the OECD in 1993. Foreign commercial loans were allowed without the government's approval in so far as they met some guidelines and foreign investment by local financial institutions was also significantly liberalised. President Kim Young Sam's government (1993–97) drove 'globalisation' (*Se Gye Hwa* in Korean) as part of the national agenda and the nation was pre-occupied with the changes required to cope with globalisation.

Economic reforms after the financial crisis instituted under the IMF stewardship were based on the diagnosis that previous market opening

---

20 For instance, Korea's average tariff on manufacturing industries was reduced from 35.7% in 1978 to 18.1% in 1988, and further to 6% in 1996, comparable to that applied in developed countries. Most quantitative import restrictions were lifted except those targeting some Japanese consumer products, which have been practised in the name of the 'import source diversification' policy. By the early 1990s, the amount of subsidy as a percentage of the manufacturing value added reached 2.8%, also comparable to that of developed countries (Lee 1999).

21 Chang (1998).

22 The share of banks deposits among the total financial savings declined from 46% in 1980 to 24% in 1993. In contrast, the share of non-bank deposits increased from 38% to 68% during the same period (Park, 1996, p. 253).

and liberalisation was too slow. The pace of both product and financial market opening was thus accelerated. The remaining import barriers, such as 'import source diversification', were removed. The upper limit to foreigners' domestic shareholdings was eliminated, the bond market was completely open and commercial loaning was further liberalised. As far as the market openness is concerned, Korea became a full First World country after the financial crisis.

At the same time, reforms on 'structure' were carried out. In the financial sector, the most serious structural problem was regarded as the supervision and monitoring system. So the Financial Supervisory Commission was launched as an over-arching agent for financial supervision. Supervision standards were tightened by applying the Basle capital adequacy ratio (the so-called BIS ratio), changing the classification of bad loans and so on. Monitoring and transparency within financial institutions were strengthened by introducing the external board system. The government also closed many commercial banks and NBFIs and forced mergers and acquisitions to prevent bad loans from increasing.

In the corporate sector the *chaebol* structure became a main target of the reforms, as it was accused of causing 'over-expansion without accountability'. The *chaebols* were forced to reduce their debt-equity ratios radically to 200 per cent in a period of less than two years. Some basic pillars of the group structure, such as loan guarantee, mutual subsidisation and so on, were prohibited. The *chaebols* were also requested to concentrate on 'core' businesses by selling, closing and swapping 'peripheral' businesses. Corporate governance was particularly emphasised given the perception that a 'dictatorial' management style by the owner families was a cause of 'reckless' expansion.[23]

In a nutshell, the structural reforms were directed at moulding the Korean economy into the Anglo-American system, in the name of a 'global standard'. External liberalisation was pursued full tilt. The financial sector was assigned as the centre of economic and risk management. The role of the government was confined to supervising financial institutions and maintaining competitive market order. Companies were supposed to compete as individuals, rather than as a group.

Is such a transition desirable to the Korean economy? Does globalisation necessitate this kind of transition in developing countries? Has the financial crisis vindicated the necessity of the transition? Let me try to answer these questions by looking at challenges of globalisation for the *chaebols* first and extending the discussion to the overall system of the Korean economy.

---

23   For instance, the rights of minor shareholders were strengthened and the responsibility of governing shareholders was reinforced. Big companies were also required to appoint more than half of their directors from outside.

The challenges of globalisation to *chaebols* can be understood in two different dimensions: that of the product market and that of the financial market, both of which provided their own opportunities and constraints. With globalisation in the real sector, *chaebols* came to have new market opportunities in other countries, especially in emerging economies, while they faced stiffer competition in the domestic market. Responses by the Korean *chaebols* can be epitomised by 'global management': they attempted to emerge as true MNCs by investing overseas to capture new market opportunities as well as investing locally to maintain their domestic market. [24]

This response tended to stretch *chaebols* and increase their financial risks. After the financial crisis, the *chaebols'* active participation in global investment competition was therefore criticised as 'over-investment', itself often attributed to their structure allowing 'irrational' behaviour. However, the over-investment argument requires several qualifications. It is true that 'investment efficiency' as measured by the ratio of gross value added to property, plant and equipment in the manufacturing sector dropped rapidly from 73.3 per cent in 1995 to 56.3 per cent in 1997.[25] But this should be balanced by strong operating profit figures, which recovered to 8.24 per cent in 1997, the second highest of the 1990s (Figure 7.1). It might be said that, facing an export price shock and pressure on their profitability, Korean firms had already started restructuring though in substantially milder fashion than after the financial crisis. It is not certain whether 'corporate efficiency' dropped significantly before the crisis.

Moreover, their investment, in general, can be understood as a natural response to the challenges of globalisation. Given the situation, Korean companies had to take part in global competition whether the possibilities of over-investment and financial risks were increased or not. Actually, this participation in the global investment competition was not unique to Korea, but common to East Asian countries. For instance, the year 1996 was characterised by a general and rapid slowdown of exports in East Asia (Table 7.3). Over-investment, if any, can be seen rather as a general glut in the region than as a malaise of a country. Arguments about 'irrationality' or 'moral hazard' of the *chaebols* are not convincing in explaining the *chaebols'* strategies and behaviours.[26] The corporate reforms after the crisis assumed that, implicitly or explicitly, Korean firms should have been passive in investment competition in the 1990s. But participation in investment competition looked an inevitable course of action at that time.

---

24   This term became popularised by the Daewoo Group, declared bankrupt in 2000.
25   BOK website.
26   Also refer to Chang (2000) and Chang and Park (1999) for further details on criticisms of moral hazard arguments.

Table 7.3: Export Performance of East Asian Countries
(per cent, year-on-year)

	1991	1992	1993	1994	1995	1996	1997	1998	1999
Malaysia	16.49	18.30	16.05	24.53	25.95	5.66	0.54	-6.94	15.45
Thailand	23.37	14.18	13.85	22.38	24.76	-1.25	3.41	-5.70	7.67
Hong Kong	19.98	21.21	13.19	11.95	14.76	4.03	4.04	-7.47	-0.07
Singapore	11.96	7.67	16.31	30.57	22.51	5.97	0.32	-12.26	4.49
Indonesia	13.50	16.56	8.41	8.78	13.39	9.68	7.29	-8.6	-0.37
China	15.81	18.12	7.10	33.06	22.92	1.61	20.95	0.39	6.30
Korea	10.54	6.63	7.31	16.75	30.25	3.72	4.97	-2.83	9.40
Taiwan	13.54	6.86	4.00	9.73	20.12	3.74	4.62	-8.72	9.93

Source: IMF (2000).

On the other hand, the *chaebol* structure itself still retains strength in global competition, especially in entering emerging markets. With their diverse resources and centralised decision-making, *chaebols* can make 'package deals' with the governments or companies of developing countries. For single product companies, it is difficult to invest in emerging markets because backward and forward linkage industries are not developed. But business groups can enter these markets with their diverse business portfolios. For example, when they establish automobile factories, they can also bring along their own mechanical engineering and steel businesses. Their construction units may oversee and execute the overall process of building the factories. In some cases they even set up commercial banks to provide consumer financing for their products. In this respect, the *chaebol* structure is better at 'market creation' in developing countries. Reflecting this strength, Korean companies' investments in emerging markets resulted in fast growth in sales with reasonable profits though their investments in developed countries did not show profits even with rapidly increasing sales (Table 7.4). And one reason why some *chaebols* became vulnerable to the financial crisis would be that, after the South East Asian financial crisis broke out, their new ventures in emerging markets suddenly looked precarious.

Table 7.4: Business Indicators of Foreign Direct Investment by Korean Companies (per cent, 1995)

	South East Asia	China	Europe	North America	Latin America
Growth rate of sales	62.77	105.94	111.14	48.62	33.11
Growth rate of assets	18.80	33.06	75.41	30.98	14.57
Operating income to sales	6.78	-3.92	-0.14	2.85	4.16
Net income to sales	3.95	-4.86	-2.44	-0.10	2.18
Debt-equity ratio	324.86	270.04	682.62	318.25	609.80

Source: Wang (1997).

The financial globalisation also provided *chaebols* with both opportunities and constraints by allowing better access to financial resources, but at the same time increasing financial risks. Since the cost arising from financial expenses was so decisive for profitability and there was a big gap in interest rates between domestic and international markets, the *chaebols* clamoured for liberalisation of the financial market. Easier access to foreign money was what they needed, especially when they had invested heavily to cope with increased competition. This domestic pressure matched perfectly well with external pressure by developed countries to open Korea's financial market.

However, in retrospect, *chaebols* were blind to of the dark side of the financial globalisation at their own peril. Broader exposure to international financial markets meant dealing with less committed bankers and investors, willing to withdraw their money any time things looked to be going wrong. Exchange rate risk was also hardly taken into account since the main concern in the mid-1990s was to slow the pace of appreciation of the Korean won due to the rapid inflow of foreign capital. But, as it turned out, they faced the calling-in of their loans after the bankruptcy of the Hanbo Group in February 1997.

Evidently, the *chaebols* failed in managing the financial risks involved in global competition. But corporate profitability figures in 1997 suggest the need to investigate the causes of this failure beyond the corporate sector. The deterioration of ordinary profit in the manufacturing sector in 1997, recording minus 0.33 per cent, was mainly due to foreign exchange losses, which amounted to 3.1 per cent of sales income. It could have recovered to the historically normal level if the sharp depreciation of the Korean won had been resisted (Table 7.5 and Figure 7.1). Numerically, the single largest factor in the profitability decline in 1997 was the exchange rate shock. We need to explore the wider causes of this failure to draw balanced implications for corporate restructuring in Korea.

Table 7.5. Anatomy of Profits (Losses) in the Manufacturing Sector (per cent)

	1996	1997	1998
Operating income to sales	6.5	8.3	6.1
Financial expenses to sales	4.7	8.0	6.7
- FX loss to sales	0.4	3.1	-0.1
- interest payments to sales	4.3	4.9	6.7
Other expenses to sale	0.8	0.6	1.2
Ordinary income to sales	1.0	-0.3	-1.8

Source: BOK (1999).

Prior to the financial crisis, the overall system of Korea was in disarray. This was mainly because Korea underwent a 'transition without building a system', as Lee (1999) points out. The pace of liberalisation was a major issue with fewer considerations as to how the overall system should be re-moulded in view of its historical development and current challenges. Despite some concerns and warnings regarding the ways to deal with liberalisation, appropriate actions were not taken.[27]

One potentially problematic area of Korea's catch-up system was the underdevelopment of the financial sector. Decisions on lending and investment, decisive in determining the competitiveness of financial institutions, were not ultimately in the hands of banks, especially in big projects. So the incentive to improve the risk management capacity of the financial sector was generally weak. Moreover, unlike the industrial sector, which had been exposed to international competition from the beginning, the financial sector had remained cosily under government protection and regulations. It can be said that the gap with forerunners was much bigger in the financial sector than in the industrial sector. And to survive the challenges of globalisation, it was more urgent for Korea to strengthen its financial sector.

But the Korean government responded to the challenge by liberally licensing financial institutions while maintaining strict divisions among dif-

27   For instance, see Park (1998).

ferent financial services. This was quite opposite to the worldwide trend then when financial institutions in developed countries were growing bigger and moving towards universal banking through merger and acquisitions (M&As) and alliances. The result was dismal. Too many weak financial institutions mushroomed.[28] A significant proportion of the bad loans accumulated in the financial sector in the 1990s can be attributed to taking higher risks for survival and the imprudent management of assets by the financial institutions.[29]

With financial liberalisation, financial supervision should also have been strengthened. But, here again, Korea failed in this transition. Earnest efforts to improve supervision function were not made. It actually deteriorated because of the increasing rivalry between the Bank of Korea and the Ministry of Finance and Economy, which shared the responsibility. Information on the status of financial institutions did not flow well between the two agents, providing companies with loopholes to exploit by under-reporting their total liabilities and making it difficult to monitor changes in financial risk in the whole system.[30]

There is currently consensus among economists and policymakers regardless of their ideological differences that the capital market liberalisation was poorly managed in East Asian crisis-hit countries. The rapid build-up of short-term debt was an immediate cause of the crisis, and this was a result of failure in 'sequencing' of liberalisation in which short-term borrowing was liberalised ahead of long-term borrowing.[31] Korea's overall size of foreign debt was manageable, but heavier reliance on short-term debts left the economy vulnerable to external shocks.[32]

The abandonment of industrial policy also looks premature. In Korea's catching-up system, the role of promoting growth and managing financial risk was shared between the government, banks and *chaebols*, with industri-

---

28   By the early 1990s, five new commercial banks were chartered, 17 short-term finance companies, 57 mutual savings and finance companies and 12 new life insurance companies came to existence. The number of merchant banks, which contributed significantly to the loss of foreign 'investors' confidence' due to their involvement in short-term foreign financing, increased from six in 1993 to 30 in 1996. (Park 1996).

29   According to an unpublished internal report by the Korea Economic Research Institute in 1998, more than one third of financial sector's losses in the 1990s until the outbreak of the financial crisis were due to their investment failure in stocks and fixed-income assets.

30   So the government and the financial sector did not know the actual size of outstanding loans of the Hanbo Group and Kia Group even well after they went under. The government had to wait until all the claims from creditors were gathered.

31   Radelet and Sachs (1998a); Chang (1998); Lane et al. (1999); MOFE (1999).

32   After the financial crisis, this weakness was corrected by a rescheduling of the debt structure by paying higher interest rates to foreign banks with the government's guarantee.

al policy providing an over-arching framework of coordination. The departure from industrial policy practice meant entrusting the role to the financial sector. But, as I mentioned above, Korea's financial sector was far from being developed to undertake the role. Coupled with the financial liberalisation that placed financial institutions under increasing pressure, the result of abandoning industrial policy was a vacuum in the risk management system.[33] After the financial crisis, the Korean government, contrary to its stated commitment to the 'free market economy', had to undertake a comprehensive ex post investment coordination through arranging the swapping of businesses, namely 'Big Deals', and forcibly closing down other businesses. Of course, all of the government's involvements were not conducive to the economy. But it looked inevitable when the financial sector does not function.[34]

More than anything else, it seems that the degradation of government leadership is important for an understanding of the crisis. I have emphasised that, with the increased pace of globalisation, the role of the government, i.e., a major immobile asset in a territory, becomes more important. It needs constant upgrading to meet the challenges of globalisation. This is because the government is the ultimate system manager in a territory and the market cannot substitute this role. But the Korean government failed as regards reforming and providing a vision for transition. It was increasingly overwhelmed by corruption scandals and lost coherence in implementing economic policies in the 1990s. As I mentioned above, the financial supervision function deteriorated and it had neither the will nor the capacity to clear bad loans to strengthen the financial sector. After the Hanbo collapse, it also failed to act swiftly to remove the system risk in its financial sector.

A Tentative Appraisal of Industrial Restructuring in Korea

In comparison with other East Asian NICs like Taiwan and Singapore, the challenges of globalisation to industrial transition were more formidable in Korea. Taiwan had its own MNCs like Acer, Tatung and so on, but its overall industrial structure complemented rather than competed with the major MNCs in developed countries. The MNC-led industrial structure of Singapore could never be in conflict with the MNCs' global activities. But Korean *chaebols* were on a course for head-on collision with major MNCs, and therefore faced the more daunting task of competition. And the financial crisis showed that they failed in surmounting this challenge.

---

33   Refer to Chang (1998; 1999) and his chapter in this volume for details on the lack of industrial policy and its consequences in Korea.
34   Shin (2000).

As mentioned above, the Korean government carried out structural reforms aimed at swiftly shifting the Korean economy over to the Anglo-American model. The direction of the reform was set by the IMF programme. The Korean government also enthusiastically agreed to the need for those 'fundamental' reforms.[35] The relative success of the Anglo-American economies over the Japanese and Continental European economies in the 1990s helped form public opinion in Korea in favour of a transition to the Anglo-American model of economic management.

It may be true that the Anglo-American model was triumphant in the era of accelerated globalisation and that, among East Asian NICs, the more international models of economic development of Singapore and Taiwan were more adaptive to challenges of globalisation. But this does not necessarily mean that it is desirable for other countries to change over to those models, as there are also costs involved in transition. Khan's (1995) concept of 'transition cost' seems relevant here.[36] The 'transaction cost' of a new system may be lower than that of the old system. But the net gain from transition to the new system is not simply determined by the difference in transaction cost. If transition cost is too high, it could be more beneficial to maintain the previous system and try to improve on it. The desirability of an institutional transition is determined by considering both transaction and transition costs, and the calculation of net benefit (cost) can be undertaken only in context of the system concerned.

What, then, are the benefits of Korea's system of transition after the financial crisis? A popular perception is that the economic recovery from 1999 on was mainly due to the structural reforms. But reform measures were basically geared to preventing future crisis, even sacrificing short-term economic performance. It is difficult to establish robust relations between the reforms and the short-term recovery. The most frequently cited route would be the inflow of foreign investments due to change in 'investors' confidence'. In fact, foreign direct investment into Korea sharply increased from US$6.9 billion in 1997 to US$8.8 billion in 1998 and further to US$15.5 billion in 1999, a 114 per cent increase in two years (see Figure 7.3).

---

35   The Korean government, led by the newly elected President Kim Dae Jung, reluctantly agreed to the IMF's tight macroeconomic policies but it came into power with an economic policy platform of 'democratic market economy', the central tenet being to reform the previous economic system dominated by *chaebols* and government intervention (Kim 1997; Shin 1999). In his speech on National Liberation Day, 15 August 1999, President Kim Dae Jung said that he wanted to go down in Korean history as 'a president who reformed *chaebols*' (*The Maeil Business Newspaper*, 16 August 1999).

36   He developed this concept mainly by focusing on political costs in industrial transition. It seems to me that his concept can be extended to understanding different paths of industrial transition even when the political costs may be the same.

Figure 7.3. Trend of FDI Inflow in Korea
(US$ million)

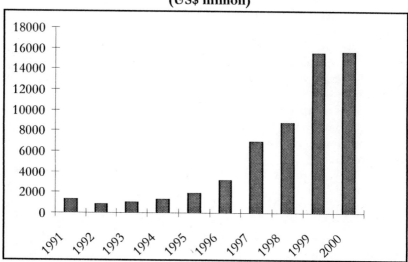

Source: MOCIE website. Figure for 2000 is an estimate.

However, on closer inspection, it seems that foreign money returned to Korea because the economy began picking up, not the other way around. Foreign investment seriously began returning to Korea from November of 1998, only after uncertainties surrounding the Korean economy were reduced substantially.[37] Among many reform measures, the swift recapitalisation of commercial banks by injecting 64 trillion won (about US$50 billion) of public funds in September 1998 is regarded as crucial in the turnaround. But this is not really a structural reform since the injection of public money is necessary to revive the financial sector after the crisis, whether or not a government is committed to reform.

The factors behind the turnaround were mainly macroeconomic. In other words, the Korean economy recovered through typical Keynesian policy. First, an unprecedented reduction of interest rates was a major boost to the corporate recovery. For instance, the three year corporate bond rate dropped to 8.7 per cent in 1999 from 15.1 per cent in 1998. The rate stood at 12–13 per cent before the crisis (Figure 7.4). It was the first

---

37   For example, foreign direct investment flows into Korea remained at US$545 million per month on average until October 1998 and then increased to $1,370 million in November, and US$1,943 million in December. The monthly FDI inflow reached US$1,295 million in 1999 (MOCIE website).

time since the beginning of industrialisation in the 1960s that the market interest rates remained at one digit level for a year.[38]

Figure 7.4: Changes in Interest Rates in Korea

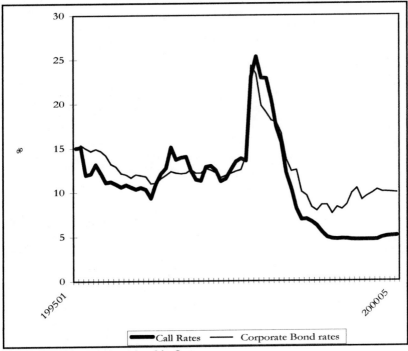

Source: BOK website. Monthly figures.

Secondly, the depreciation of the Korean won contributed to the recovery of the corporate sector. The won-dollar exchange rate in 1999 was 1,189 won per dollar on average. Although it appreciated by 14.9 per cent from its level in 1998, it still depreciated by 25 per cent from the 1997 level. Thirdly, the budget deficit was substantially increased to recapitalise financial institutions, to provide a 'safety net' and to carry out public works. By

38 The financial expenses to sales in the manufacturing sector therefore dropped by 2.1 percentage points from 9.0% in 1998 to 6.9% in 1999. The interest rate cuts also boosted demand. The Korea Stock Price Index (KOSPI) shot from below 300 up to 1,000 in a year and the recovery in consumption contributed to domestic demand growth.

August 2000 the Korean government had injected 110 trillion won of public money into the economy.[39]

It should be noted that this aggressive Keynesian policy was by no means part of the IMF structural adjustment package. The initial macroeconomic policy direction was retrenchment and, by sharply raising interest rates during the crucial period of crisis, corporate failures soared, making corporate adjustment more difficult.[40] Korea's monetary policy remained cautious well into the summer of 1998. Korea could lower interest rates markedly only after the G7 countries took concerted action to lower interest rates and expand monetary supply in order to avoid financial turmoil after crises in Russia and Brazil and the near-bankruptcy of Long Term Capital Management (LTCM), a hedge fund based in New York.[41]

It is also doubtful whether the corporate reform actually contributed to lowering the financial risk of the corporate sector. It would appear that the greatest achievement in this regard was the enforcement of a swift reduction of corporate debt-equity ratio. The *chaebols* were mandated to lower their debt ratios to below 200 per cent by the end of 1999, and, as a result, the debt ratio of the manufacturing sector in Korea dropped form 396 per cent in 1997 to 214 per cent in 1999, the lowest since 1968. But the reduction of interest payments was not quite realised. Although financial expenses to sales in the manufacturing sector dropped to 6.9 per cent in 1999 from 9.0 per cent in 1998, this was still higher than in 1997 (6.4 per cent) and than the average during 1990–97 (5.8 per cent) (Figure 7.1). This was because Korean companies carried out the debt ratio reduction mainly by issuing new stock, asset sales and asset revaluation, with less repayment of debt. In this respect, the corporate reforms have not succeeded as yet in correcting the structural weakness of high debt and low profitability.

39 The ratio of budget deficit to gross domestic product (GDP) therefore dropped to -3.2 % in 1998 and -3.0% in 1999, from slight budget surpluses during the 1990s before the crisis. Despite this substantial increase in budget deficits, the ratio of budget deficit to GDP was only 23.4% at the end of 1999, still one of the lowest among the OECD countries (MOFE, 1999).

40 Even Mr Lee Hun-Jay, the former chairman of the Financial Supervisory Commission, whose nickname was 'Mr Restructuring', observed, in a diplomatically mild tone: '[C]omponents of the IMF programme, such as tight monetary policy, complicated our recovery efforts by deepening the recession … In managing the crisis, the IMF programme could have been more properly calibrated in line with the structural characteristics of the affected countries' (speech at the Asia Development Bank Workshop, 16 March 1990).

41 The call market rate, over which the central bank exerts almost deciding power with its distribution of central bank funds among commercial banks, was in a steady decline from the second quarter of 1998 and reached 13% in July, the level before the crisis. The BOK subsequently lowered the rate rapidly to 6% in December 1998 and to 4.7% in April 1999. The rate was maintained during the rest of the year (Figure 7.4).

On the other hand, this pressure to reduce radically the corporate debt ratio incurred several costs, both tangible and intangible. Above all, companies with high debts were categorically regarded as potentially non-viable regardless of their corporate efficiency or long-term prospects. Financial institutions, facing stiffer supervision standards and being preoccupied with their own survival, called on or stopped offering their loans to those companies, driving them to bankruptcy or near-bankruptcy. A large part of the build-up of non-performing loans after the crisis was due to an abrupt change in the financial environment as it became overly negative to high debt.[42]

From the beginning, a basic policy dilemma in Korea after the financial crisis lay in the fact that the structure of high debt and thin profit margin was not a matter that could be corrected in a short time though it had made the Korean economy financially vulnerable. If the structure was forced to change radically, an inevitable consequence was credit crunch, bringing about more corporate failures and more bad loans in the system. The corporate reforms took this aspect lightly and costs arising from attempting this radical transition were supported by public money. So the debt reduction in the corporate sector was paralleled with the debt increase in the public sector.

The debt ratio reduction drive also forced *chaebols* to sell their assets at bargain prices although what price represents a bargain is arguable. But they were only able to sell those assets that were profitable and had good market potential, while foreign investors did not have any incentive to buy risky assets when all the regional companies were on 'fire-sale'. According to the BOK (2000), extraordinary income in the manufacturing sector, mainly from asset sales, amounted to 1.0 per cent of total sales, i.e., 4.6 trillion won (US$4 billion). The debt ratio was also reduced substantially by asset revaluation.[43] The 30 largest *chaebols* were able to reduce their debt ratios by 56 percentage points on average in 1999 simply by revaluing their assets.[44] But this compromised

42 It is arguable whether companies that went bankrupt after the financial crisis were already non-viable or became non-viable due to exchange rate shock and ensuing credit crunch. Both cases must have prevailed, but views are diametrically opposed as to the relevant proportions. Given the difficulties in verifying those proportions, it is likely that diverging views will remain.

43 The Korean government did not allow revaluation of corporate assets from 1981 for fear that the *chaebols* might make use of it for speculation in real estate. Once the debt level became a critical issue, the *chaebols* persuaded the government to allow revaluation of their assets to get a fair valuation of their financial status following the denumerator, the value of their debt varied with price movements while the numerator, the value of their equity, was fixed for accounting purposes.

44 *The Maeil Business Newspaper* 13 November 1999. For instance, the Hyundai Group reduced its debt-equity ratio by 120% points solely by revaluation. Business groups with sound financial balances did not revalue their assets because of huge taxes and other transaction costs involved in revaluation.

the profitability of the corporate sector as it incurred transaction costs such as valuation fees and transaction taxes, and depreciation costs in accounting had to be raised as assets were revalued. Depreciation costs to sales increased from 4.7 per cent in 1997, to 5.4 per cent in 1998 and 5.5 per cent in 1999. The BOK (2000) attributes this increase mostly to asset revaluation. The end result was that Korea's manufacturing sector improved its profitability by one percentage point through asset sales, but lost as much by revaluing its assets, neither of which might have been necessary if the debt ratio itself had not been targeted as a major objective of the corporate reforms.

Corrections of 'excessive diversification' and the dismantling of the internal resource transfer mechanism of *chaebols* also have a dark side. Surprisingly, to date there has been no empirical study to prove that diversification increased the financial risk of *chaebols*, although such contentions were rife.[45] I find, on the contrary, that the degree of diversification was negatively correlated with the *chaebol* bankruptcy during and after the financial crisis (Table 7.6). There have been some corporate failures due to ill-managed diversifications, such as the cases of the Kia Group, the Hanbo Group and others. But it is also the case that the diversified business structure provided *chaebols* with a sufficient buffer to survive external shocks through channelling internal resources to weaker business units.

Table 7.6: Factors Affecting Bankruptcy of *Chaebols*

	Before Crisis	After Crisis
Debt ratio	+	+
Total asset	–	–
Rate of fixed asset increase	+	+
Diversification	–	–
Transfer of management to the second generation	n.s.	n.s.

Source: Lee and Eo (2000).

As emphasised previously, the diversification and the internal transfer of resources constitute a basic strength of the *chaebol* structure and can be understood as an institutional mechanism for latecomer firms to compete

---

45   Lee and Eo (2000).

with their forerunners in the international market. A critical question here is whether the Korean companies have now grown sufficiently to compete with their forerunners on the basis of individual firms without utilising the group structure. More fundamentally, it is questionable whether it is desirable that the government and international organisations set an ideal type of business structure, and force companies to move to the new structure. With the increased pace of globalisation, the *chaebols* were already facing pressure for change. They were destined to reduce 'excessive' diversification, if this existed, because the increased competition both in the domestic market and in the international market should make it more difficult for the *chaebols* to subsidise non-viable affiliates. Facing tougher financial institutions, they had to improve the transparency of internal transactions in any case.

The corporate reform after the crisis, in a hasty move to eliminate the supposed weaknesses of the *chaebol* structure, removed its strength as well. The previous mechanism for mobilising resources and reducing financial risks in large-scale projects was dismantled.[46] Instead, a rigid debt-equity ratio was put in place and the standard of financial supervision was significantly strengthened. In this environment, it is difficult to expect that the banking sector will provide the corporate sector with enough financial resources for future growth.

The Korean government is currently trying to find alternative engines of growth from foreign direct investment and venture businesses. This is in line with its attempt at adapting the Korean economy to a more international model of development. It is certainly desirable for the Korean economy, which has been dominated by the state-bank-*chaebol* nexus, to be complemented by foreign companies and small and medium-sized enterprises (SMEs). However, this transition was attempted by weakening *chaebols*. And the result of promoting inward FDI and SMEs is not that impressive on closer inspection.

The FDI, though rapidly increasing, still comprises a small portion of economic activities in Korea, with the FDI stock to the domestic gross product (GDP) being 7.7 per cent in 1999.[47] And a large portion of the increase in 1998 and 1999 was related to asset sales of Korean companies. Therefore, the growth rate of the inward FDI in 2000 was nearly stagnant, estimated at one per cent from 1999 (Figure 7.3). Moreover, it should also be noted that the FDI was already on a trend increase even before the financial crisis and subsequent corporate reforms. It increased 65 per cent

---

46   A leading Korean businessman said in an interview with me in August 2000: 'It has been possible for major *chaebols* to mobilise a large amount of investment funds through their internal mechanisms without letting foreign competitors or foreign financial institutions know about their plans. But now they have to go to the international financial market if they need an investment over 1 trillion won (US$870 million).'

47   MOCIE website.

to US$3.2 billion in 1996 from US$1.9 billion in 1995 and further 117 per cent to US$6.9 billion in 1997. This implies that, even without corporate reforms and national efforts at attracting FDI, the market opening and relaxations of regulations on FDI, combined with the strong growth of the domestic economy, were enough to bring about a trend increase in FDI. There is no clear evidence that Korea needed those fundamental corporate reforms to increase the volume of FDI.

From 1999 Korea experienced a venture business boom in line with the worldwide Internet boom and influenced by the government's active promotion of venture business and venture capital. However, KOSDAQ, the Korean version of NASDAQ, crashed spectacularly in the latter half of 2000 just as it had previously risen spectacularly. Its market capitalisation, which stood at seven trillion won (US$6 billion) in 1997 and 7.9 trillion won in 1998, jumped to 106.2 trillion won at the end of 1999 and further to 126.4 trillion won in March 2000. But, after the crash, market capitalisation was decreased to 29 trillion won at the end of 2000, nearly one fifth of the figure at the peak in 2000.[48] It would have been greatly beneficial to the Korean economy if the investment funds for SMEs had increased directly from 7.9 trillion won in 1998 to 29 trillion won in 2000. But the policy-propelled boom and subsequent crash of the market has several downside effects like a sudden change in flows of resources and resulting credit crunch in the economy.

Considering that the structure of the Korean economy is still dominated by big businesses, FDI and SMEs are at best supplementary engines of growth and the success of industrial restructuring after the financial crisis hinges on reviving big companies.[49] But the record here is far from satisfactory as yet. Since the increase in bad loans was greater than expected, the Korean government added 40 trillion won of public funds on top of 110 trillion won it had already spent to clear non-performing loans in the financial sector.[50] It remains to be seen how much of this public fund will eventually be recouped after the Korean government cashes bad loans and stocks of financial institutions that it purchased in the process of recapitalising or closing them.

The final assessment of industrial restructuring in Korea can be made only after taking into account all the benefits and costs raised above. And, evidently, this cannot be completed in the near future. It is also highly likely that, given difficulties in calculating and comparing those benefits and costs, divergent views will remain. But it seems to me that the actual costs of the radical industrial transition may be larger than is popularly perceived and that its supposed benefits should be re-examined.

48   You (2000), KOSDAQ website.
49   For example, the 30 largest *chaebols* constituted 45.8% of total sales and 46.2% of total assets in the Korean economy in 1998 (Choi, 1999).
50   MOFE (2000).

Conclusions

Even if the current momentum of globalisation can be maintained in the future, the fact remains that Korea is still a middle-income country. Its per capita income was US$8,581 in 1999, nearly one fourth of that of the USA.[51] According to Lee's (1999) estimate of 'relative backwardness', Korea in 1995, when the country's per capita income reached US$10,000, was approximately at the level of Japan in the mid-1960s when the Japanese catching-up system was at its height.

A basic question regarding Korea's transition is, therefore, whether it is possible for a middle-income country to catch up with its forerunners without a catching-up system. I have argued above that we need to calculate both transaction and transition costs involved in the transition and that, when considering transition costs, it seems premature to discard the catching-up system altogether, though the previous system might have some problems. Gerschenkron (1962) suggests that latecomers devise different economic systems in order to compensate for the lack of capital, technologies and so on in competing with their forerunners. From a historical perspective, transiting directly to the forerunner's system amounts to an attempt at becoming a forerunner by wearing forerunner's clothes before one grows big enough for them.

What is needed for Korea is a second stage catching-up strategy and institutional changes to support it, rather than a transplantation of its frontrunner's system. The catching-up system is, by definition, destined to undergo constant change as the gap with the forerunner is narrowed as a result of successful catching-up. However, also by definition, the system's objective is not fulfilled until that gap disappears. The financial crisis seems to have made it all the more important to build a new catching-up system for Korea. To respond to the challenges of globalisation, Korean companies needed to take part in global investment competition to deepen and widen their industrial base, but the financial risks involved in international competition were greatly increased. It appears that a sharp trade-off between financial prudence and industrial catch-up has emerged.

The corporate reforms after the crisis focused primarily on the side of financial prudence. But even the achievement here is questionable because the structure of high debt and low profitability has yet to be corrected, while large costs, both in the corporate sector and the public sector, have been incurred. Considering the fact that alternative growth engines have yet to emerge, and the possibility of financing new long-term investment is constrained, it is still difficult to justify the costs involved in the restructuring.

---

51   BOK website, current prices. The plunge in the per capita income in 1998 was due to the combination of the sharp depreciation of Korean won and the contraction of the economy in the year.

For developing countries, it is not a matter of choice whether they should give priority to financial prudence or industrial catch-up. They have to achieve both. It is certainly true that it has become more difficult for them to do that with the accelerated pace of globalisation. But the increasing difficulty does not negate the necessity of such a strategy. It simply provides stiffer challenges and requires more creative responses. The new system should also give due consideration to the current stage of economic development; that is, the fact that Korea has so far succeeded in the first-stage of catch-up but it has a long way to go to reach an advanced country status.

In general, a new system should be a step forward from the previous system, not a complete abandonment of it. First, the strength of the *chaebol* structure should be maintained, although some readjustments are certainly needed. As I have emphasised, the *chaebol*'s diversified structure is an effective mechanism in international competition. Mutual subsidies and other intra-group resource mobilisation, which make it possible for several affiliated companies to work as a team when they embark on strategic projects, are major sources of the strength of the *chaebol*. The negative consequences of the *chaebol*'s dominance, like unfair competition with small and medium enterprises (SMEs) in the domestic market, should be addressed by finding an alternative way. Japan has achieved the development of strong SMEs during the period when the *keiretsu* system was at its height. In the same vein, the inflow of FDI could be increased without intentionally weakening *chaebols*.

Secondly, the role of the state should be revitalised. If the financial sector is only required to stick to tight supervision standards, it becomes risk averse in credit creation. And, if the same supervision standard and same risk management systems are applied between advanced countries and developing countries, it is likely to reduce credit creation in developing countries given that the credit risks are higher. One way to reduce credit risks in investment projects while sustaining the level of credit creation would be government involvement. In fact, industrial policy was practised in Korea on this basis. By providing government support to some strategic industries, credit risks on the part of commercial banks were also reduced. It would be neither possible nor desirable for Korea to return to the old style practice of industrial policy. However, by establishing a new national system of consultation involving government, the financial sector and the corporate sector, industrial expansion can be maintained while shielding the economy from unnecessary financial risks (Figure A7.1).

Figure A7.1: Changes in the Government–Finance–Industry Relations in Korea

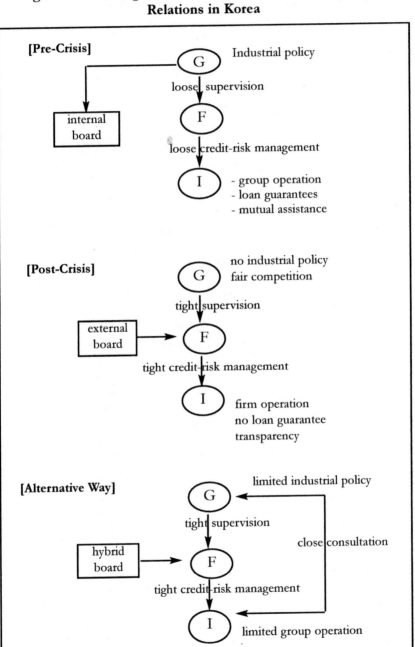

CHAPTER 8

The Labour Market and Korea's 1997 Financial Crisis

Louise Haagh[*]

Introduction

Since Korea's financial crisis of late 1997 there has been much speculation about the solidity of the state-led model of development practised in East Asia and, with particular vigour, in Korea. From being a
model performer and a champion of 'market enhancement' policy, the
wisdom or otherwise of the state's role in the economy has come under
intense review. Throughout the 1990s international development agencies
like the World Bank had engaged in constructive criticism of the successful East Asian NICs, even co-opting economic policy in South Korea as a
model of 'market enhancement'.[1] Many scholars felt that this was an
attempt to nullify the important role that state intervention did play in
directing development in Korea by institutions that were at the time advo-
cating market neutral policies to developing countries around the world.[2]
Their suspicions were confirmed when the economic crisis led to the general conclusion that the state-led model had been seriously flawed from the
outset (inevitably bringing the crisis on). The general mood was one of
vindication of neoclassical development economics.[3] The 'lessons' now
drawn from Korea turned to emphasise the 'don'ts' instead of the 'do's'.
This lessons debate is of course misplaced. As has been shown, Korea's
model was never as market-driven in its general economic management as
claimed, nor was it as state-driven, or as selective or corrupt, in its industrial policy as is now commonly being presented.[4] The labour market is an
interesting arena in which to explore the lessons debate.

[*] I would like to thank Yonsei University's Graduate School for International Studies
     for hosting me as a visiting fellow during the conduct of this research and the British
     Academy and the Nuffield Foundations for their support during different stages of
     my research.
[1] The World Bank, *World Development Reports*, 1992, 1995, 1997, Oxford.
[2] A position of market neutrality is one that sees markets and institutions as separable
     (for instance Hayek 1984), and which advocates the minimisation of intervention in
     markets. Lall (1995) and Hirschmann (1993) provide good discussions of related
     arguments.
[3] Neo-classical development economics is the term used by Lall (1995) to refer to the
     application of neo-classical economic principles to development policy in the Third
     World.
[4] See, for instance, Chang (2000).

According to the vindication hypothesis, the shock produced by the crisis should have virtually crowded out non-market rational behaviour in internal and external labour markets, thereby making the labour market work more efficiently and removing the bases for state guidance in labour affairs. This view implies three hypotheses that this chapter will dispute. As regards the first, the crisis did produce great changes in labour institutions, but not the kind of wholesale transformation that the neoclassical school would predict. The Korean is a good case for showing that labour markets do work as a set of social institutions. Secondly, the changes that the crisis did produce in a more market-rational direction did not appear unequivocally to lead to greater efficiency outcomes, where efficiency is understood as the development and flexible use of human resources. Finally, the longer-run changes in labour institutions which the crisis helped to accelerate did not point towards a lesser, but towards a changed and, if anything, greater, role for the state. This argument can be made in two ways. First, the changes in labour markets produced a need for an enhanced role for the state. Secondly, looking at a selected area of social policy, the employment insurance system, we can see that, despite the efforts to deregulate in many areas, Korea's state bureaucracy did find the means to reinvent itself. Hence, in both labour relations and in public policy, institutional memory survived the crisis. Below we first discuss changes in labour relations and labour markets produced by the crisis. We then look at some of the consequences of these changes, before turning, in the last section, to look at the system of employment insurance.

Labour Markets and Employment Systems

The idea that Korea moved from a closed to an open labour market as a result of the 1997 crisis does not do justice to the complexity of labour markets and institutions. It ignores some important analytical issues and historical facts. First of all, it presupposes that the Korean labour market before the crisis was not free.[5] It also presupposes that there is such a thing as a free labour market that can easily be defined. For instance, is freedom in labour markets to do with minimising wage regulation, or is it to do with absence of restrictions on the management of human resources, or with open hire and fire laws, or are all these required before a labour market is truly 'free'?[6]

---

5   It is indicative of the extent to which the ground has shifted since the crisis that scholars critical of the World Bank interpretation only a few years ago had to prove the point that the labour market in Korea was *not* free. See You and Chang (1993).

6   For analyses that suggest that absolute freedom in labour markets is possible, and that counterpose regulation with rigidity (unfreedom), see Hirsh (1992), Addison and Chilton (1993). Blank and Freeman (1993) have a good discussion of different notions of flexibility.

Apart from the issue of areas of freedom, there is the question of who the agents are whose freedom should concern us. Is it firms' freedom or is it freedom of the moving agents of labour, wage earners, or indeed is it the freedom of both?

The reality of labour markets and institutions in most countries is more complex than the notion of absolute freedom allows. This reality inevitably involves choices and accommodations between areas and agents of freedom. In fact, on some counts, labour markets that we know as the most regulated in the world are at the same time the most free. Take for instance the case of Denmark, where national regulation of wage rises (though not necessarily levels or bonuses) predominates, where the development and exchange of qualified wage labour is certified strictly and incentives to look for work are mitigated by fairly generous social assistance, all of which go against classical notions of labour market freedom. In fact, social provision in Denmark is one of the most extensive in Europe.[7] Yet the country also has, according to the OECD, one of the highest rates of labour mobility (low tenure)[8] as well as virtually no restrictions on firing.[9] How could the level of social protection be so generous and Denmark *at the same time* have one of the highest rates of labour mobility (turnover rates) and one of the most liberal sets of firing laws in the EEC, if it were true that all areas of freedom listed before are required for labour markets to be truly free, or if it were the case that freedom in one area of the labour market is ultimately dependent on freedom in all of the others? The Danish example shows that freedom of movement can sometimes presuppose regulation.

We may take another example, Chile, where, on the face of it, the labour market is free on virtually all the counts mentioned above. Chile has no national wage regulation, no certification of skills in a market of hundreds of unconnected training providers and virtually unrestricted freedom by employers in the area of hiring and firing and in the organisation

7   Denmark in 1998 spent 5.63% of GDP on labour market programmes, the highest
     in a recent OECD comparison of selected countries, followed by Sweden at 3.93%,
     Germany at 3.56%, France at 3.22%. By comparison, the USA spends 0.43% and
     Japan 0.52%. Korea spent 0.2% only in 1998, up from less than 0.1% in the early
     1990s. Betcherman et al. (2001), pp. 344 and 357.

8   On average 25% of the workforce is affected by unemployment each year, but aver-
     age unemployment spells are quite short (just over one third of the year, and some-
     times less. Between the third quarter of 1997 and the second quarter of 1998, the
     average period was around 15 weeks. ILO (1999), p. 2. Average tenure is eight years,
     lower than that of most countries in the OECD group studied, as cited in Smith
     (1998), p. 109.

9   The degree of freedom enjoyed by Danish firms in this domain was only overtaken
     by the USA in a sample of 16 member countries assembled by the OECD (*Ibid.*)
     Close to 40% of all existing jobs are opened each year. ILO (1999), p. 17

of work. In this case, freedom in particular areas where short-term gains can be made (for instance in hire and fire and random modifications of work contracts), has been shown to have costs in terms of freedom in other fields. For instance, relatively high levels of labour turnover in a system with little skill certification entailed disincentives for individual employers to invest in training and hence a collective problem of scarcity of skilled labour when firms wish to hire.[10] Firms' unwillingness to share job information (which protects their freedom to organise work and pay) also entailed restrictions on informed labour movement and especially relocation of workers in the wake of downturns such as that experienced in Chile as a result of the 1997 East Asian financial crises.[11] In addition, the Chilean case shows that, even where voluntary organisations are kept to a minimum, social institutions and legal rules that restrict absolute freedom in some way inevitably form. For instance, it has been found that where local unions were stronger, investment in training was greater.[12] Moreover, since labour inevitably needs some form of social protection, employers may end up paying a high cost for not engaging in collective forms of market governance (for instance in setting up systems of unemployment insurance and job relocation), in the form of high indemnity payments, as has been the case even in Chile. This indirect restriction on firing older workers in turn led to far higher turnover rates of younger people (cheaper to fire) and hence further inefficiencies in developing human resources of the young labour force.[13] Chile, then, is a good case for showing how an excess of freedom, or freedom in labour markets understood in absolute terms, can lead to unexpected forms of rigidity.

The point to note is that in both the Danish and Chilean cases the distribution of freedom between areas and agents in labour markets varied but in neither case, not even in the 'best of cases' following a neoclassical model, in this case Chile, was freedom absolute. In both the cases of Denmark and Chile, freedom depended on forms of regulation, whether directly or indirectly, through labour institutions and the public policy framework. Accordingly, we could call the institutional settings within and between firms and in labour policy, both legal and social, that direct the patterns of movement that individuals and firms are faced with in labour markets the 'employment system'.[14] The two examples show that labour markets are embedded in employment systems.

10   These problems are extensively discussed in Haagh (1999, 2000a).
11   As a result of the impact of the Asian crisis, unemployment nearly doubled, to over 11% and stayed around the 10% mark for several years after, a performance that is worse than Korea's own.
12   Haagh (1999).
13   Younger workers was the group most likely to face dismissal (at 25.8%) compared with older workers (at 15.2%), followed by unskilled workers (*Ibid.*) p. 470.
14   Kongshøj Madsen (ILO, 1999, p. 14) uses the term 'the employment system' to describe the 'interplay between the labour market and the public sector'. My definition is somewhat broader.

The notion of an employment system as exemplified by the two cases helps to solidify the critique from areas of institutional economics and sociology of neoclassical models of labour markets that have been growing in recent years. Both cases show that it is indeed difficult to separate internal from external labour markets,[15] that legal regulation affects decisions in firms, even in the freest labour market (the Chilean) and certainly in a free labour market (in hire and fire) that works over time (the Danish). The relationship works counterfactually. In Chile, absence of regulation, for instance the weakness of unions in firms, on some counts even contributed to the rigid nature of labour markets.[16] Labour markets do work as social institutions, and labour relations affect how markets work. This was an insight developed earlier, but ignored to long, in Hirschman's delineation of the relationship between exit and voice,[17] in Solow's admission that the labour market is a social institution,[18] and finally in the distinction made by institutional economists and organisation theorists between forms of contracting (for example relational versus contingency contracting).[19] Relational contracting built on reciprocity over time is more efficient in that it enables compromises between labour and capital that allow scope for immediate flexibility without hurting long-run goals such as the development of human resources. In this context, the labour market agreements in Denmark on wage restraint coupled with systems of labour rotation involving apprenticeship constitute an example of a sophisticated network of relational contracts.[20] The notion of the employment system as the nuts and bolts that connect labour markets brings together such insights.

In summary, the employment system in Denmark was characterised by high levels of movement between firms both for employers and workers, a fact made possible without great restrictions on the development and

---

15   For a good recent discussion of the relationship between internal and external labour markets, see Grimshaw and Rubery (1998), pp. 200-2.

16   A survey of local labour labour leaders in manufacturing sector firms, carried out in 1992, supports these findings. For instance, among firms where training was high (training of more than 9.99% of the workforce in the last two years), 53% had a functioning health and safety committee, compared with only 20% of firms where less than 9.99% of workers were trained in the same period (Haagh, 2002a). Moreover, the odds were more than 3:1 that firms in which unions were established before 1973 (with no new unions in the sample of older firms being formed between 1974 and 1980, during the most repressive period of the Pinochet dictatorship) would belong to the high training group, compared with firms with younger unions (Haagh, 1999, p. 471).

17   Hirschman (1970), especially chapters 7–9.

18   Solow (1990).

19   See, for instance, Williamson (1985, pp. 70-3) and Eggertson (1990, chapter 2) for a good review of this side of institutional economics.

20   On these schemes, see ILO (1999), and Haagh (2001).

reproduction of human resources due to the certification and public development of skills and support for individual movement. The social institutions underlying this system included union-employer cooperation on wage regulation and skill certification, and a public system of social assistance and job rotation supported by unions and firms at local level and upwards.[21] Meanwhile, the employment system in Chile was characterised by ample freedom of hire and fire for firms, with high degrees of freedom of firms to determine working conditions and training with weak unions and weak public policy measures to support training and movement for workers. The system provided ample short-run flexibility for firms, but low flexibility for workers in finding new jobs and for employers to re-hire and develop skilled labour.[22]

The Korean Case

The debate about Korean labour markets in the context of the 1997 crisis is relevant to this broader discussion. As we saw, some of the same dichotomies that characterise the general debate about the Korean economy pre- and post-crisis also motivate the discussion about labour markets. The financial crisis which Korea experienced at the end of 1997 led to an immediate crisis of employment. From a level of 3.1 per cent in December 1997, open unemployment rose to 6.8 per cent in 1998 and to 8.7 per cent in early 1999 (See Table 8.1). Since then Korea's unemployment rate has fallen significantly. It fell to 3.4 per cent in October 2000, and continued to hover just under the four per cent mark well into 2001. The general data suggests that Korea's employment crisis has been overcome. In the interpretation of many observers, including international agencies like the World Bank, and in line with the general conclusions about the Korean economy's downward drift and then upturn, Korea's labour markets recovered in large measure due to long overdue liberal reforms, which the crisis made possible. Both interpretations, however, represent too superficial a picture. The crisis did have a significant impact on labour markets, but this was more long lasting and institutional in nature than the down- and then upswing hypothesis allows analytical room for. Korea, too, pre-crisis was governed by an employment system that combined freedoms and constraints in areas and for agents in labour markets in peculiar ways. In this context to suggest that the country moved swiftly from an unfree to a free labour market makes little sense.

---

21   See Haagh (2001) and ILO (1999).
22   See Haagh (1999, 2001).

Table 8.1: Unionisation, Strikes and Conflict, Korea 1963–99

No. of unions	No. of union membs.*	Ave. size union	Unionisation	No. of Strikes	Ave. Size of Strike	Coll. bar	Cov. rate of lab-man councils+	Real wage rises**	Unemployment
2,150	224	104	9.4						
2,634	302	115	11.6						
3,500	473	135	12.6	4	250		-	-	4.4
4,091	750	183	15.8	52	192		-	-	4.1
2,635	948	360	14.7	407	120		-	-	5.2
2,551	1,004	396.2	12.4	265	109		38.7	-4.7	4.0
2,675	1,036	387.3	12.3	276	170		38.6	7.4	3.8
4,103	1,267	310.1	13.8	3,749	337		38.4	6.2	3.1
6,164	1,707	277	17.8	1,873	157		67.2	8.3	2.5
7,883	1,932	345.1	18.6	1,616	253		74.7	11.6	2.6
7,698	1,887	245	17.2	322	416		77.1	18.3	2.4
7,656	1,803	235.5	15.9	234	748		75.6	10.7	2.3
7,527	1,735	230.4	15.0	235	447		69.7	6.9	2.4
7,147	1,667	233.2	14.2	144	757		69.5	8.8	2.8
7,025	1,659	236.2	13.5	121	860		69.5	5.8	2.4
6,606	1,615	244.5	12.7	88	568		67.8	8.7	2.0
6,424	1,599	248.9	12.2	85	929		67.4	5.2	2.0
5,733	1,484	258.9	11.2	78	564		69.5	7.0	2.6
5,560	1,402	252.2	12.6	129	1,132		59.6++	0.7	6.8
5,637	1,481	262.7	11.9	198	465			-9.1	6.3

* thousands

** In manufacturing

+ firms with more than 50 workers

++ firms with more than 30 workers.

Source: KLI - Profile of Korean Human Assets, Labor Statistics (2000).

This characterisation is also historically flawed. The most important legal changes to facilitate changes in labour relations occurred prior to the crisis. They were brought on initially by the reaction of employers and the state to the unsustainable wage gains of the late 1980s and the attempt to weaken the strike capacity of *chaebol* unions and introduce wage regulation (Table 8.1). Later membership of the International Labour Organization (ILO) and then the Organisation for Economic Co-operation and Development (OECD) spurred on a series of studies and recommendations for industrial relations reforms, which resulted in the legal changes of 1996, under Kim Young Sam. Meanwhile, a series of changes in labour management practices were beginning to take place, which the crisis merely helped to accelerate. By all these accounts the legal attempt to codify a more Anglo-Saxon form of labour market had taken place prior to the crisis itself.[23]

What the crisis did instead was to accelerate and slightly shift the direction of the trend. By accentuating underlying contradictions between its different elements, it put the existing employment system in a state of disequilibrium. As existing patterns of movement in labour markets were abruptly changed, finding new links between the different institutions that make up the employment system came to represent an immediate challenge.

The employment system in Korea prior to 1997 was underpinned by fairly high levels of job security, particularly in larger firms, quite good economic individual rights, matched by quite poor collective rights, and by relatively high rates, especially in the SME market, of voluntary mobility.[24] Let us take each of these elements in turn and look at how they are joined. It has been common to distinguish broadly between two types of labour market in Korea pre-crisis, each of which has slightly different employment systems. There is the labour market of larger firms, where job security has been greater, with fairly large in-house investment in human resources, good occupational welfare coverage and commonly (though not always) with strong unions, though unions which typically have little actual say in decisions and are either involved in paternalistic semi-close relations with management (as typical in

23   The legal changes that were finally put through parliament in March 1997 included greater flexibility in the system of working hours; facilitation of 'part-time' work; introduction of lay-offs in cases of urgent business reasons (amendments to the Labor Standards Act); prohibition on payment (by employers) of full-time union officials; legalisation of multiple trade unions (with immediate effect for sectoral or national unions, with enterprise unions starting from 2002); elimination of the ban on unions' political activities; elimination of a ban on third party intervention; removal of the ceiling on union membership dues; establishment of a system of mediation (Trade Union and Labour Relations Adjustment Act); among others (see Tables 1 and 2 in the Appendix). The legal changes were first put to parliament in late 1996, but due to strong opposition from unions were legislated only in March 1997 with minor revisions, and the coming into effect of the dismissal laws (lay-off for managerial reasons) being postponed for two years.

24   SME stands for small and medium-sized enterprise.

Lucky Goldstar — or LG), or in highly combative relations with employers focused on primary areas of labour rights, such as wage gains (as in Hyundai Motors). The SME employment system, by comparison, is much less formalised, with less stable forms of work contract and far weaker extension of unionisation.[25] Korea's rate of standard employment is markedly low by international standards, at 32 per cent in 1998, compared with 51 per cent in Mexico, 52 per cent in Spain and 73 per cent in Japan (Table 8.2). Moreover non-standard employment is heavily concentrated in smaller firms (Table 8.3).

However, despite the duality, employment systems in both labour markets were relatively stable and guided in both cases by fairly high rates of voluntary mobility. The issue of mobility often raises controversy, with the commonly held impression that Korea's labour markets were static, particularly those of larger firms. Available data on labour mobility suggests that this impression is flawed. You gathered data on monthly separation rates in 1990 for employees of firms of different sizes. For blue-collar workers the separation rates were higher for smaller firms, although the separation rate was high for all sizes (Appendix 3).[26] For white-collar workers, the rate was more even across sizes but also high. This conforms with Korea's low tenure rates by international standards. Average tenure rates were 5.4 in 1996, compared with an average of 9.8 for European Union countries, 11.3 for Japan and 7.4 for the USA (all in 1995) according to recent OECD figures.[27] What made the employment systems in Korea relatively stable, however, was the largely voluntary form of labour mobility. You, for example, makes the assumption that the separation rate was equal to the quit rate, i.e. that movement was largely voluntary. Although the data generally is quite sparse on this, the survey material that is available in Korea from this period appears to support You's assumption. One survey of 1,354 unemployed of 1990 showed that only four per cent had left their previous employment involuntarily (1.7 per cent due to redundancy dismissal and 2.2 per cent due to early retirement).[28] Since the

---

25 In 1986 there were just over 2,500 company unions (this type of union accounting for over 90% of total unions). By 1987 the number had climbed to around 4,000, and by 1989 to nearly 8,000 (Table 8.1). However, the larger the company the more likely it was to have a union. In 1989 around 80% of firms with more than 1,000 employees had a union (Korea Labor Institute). Many of these had union shop clauses (29% of firms in a 1998 Korean Employers Federation [KEF] survey), a feature not common to SME firms. Firms with between 50 and 99 workers had a unionisation rate of 9.5% (compared with 60% for firms with 300 workers or more and 26.4% for firms with between 100 and 299 workers). For firms with 10–49 workers, the unionisation rate was 1.7%, descending to less than 1% for firms with less than nine workers (Korea Labor Institute).

26 You (1997), p. 360.

27 Martin and Torres (2001) p. 367.

28 Too little income, future prospects, personal dissatisfaction, setting up of a private business or marriage, old age or health accounted for 80% of quits, other reasons for 7% and shut-down for 9.1% (Keum, 1997, p. 38).

Table 8.2: Composition of Workforce by Type of Work

	Korea (thousands) Employed			Korea Unemployed		Other countries						
	June 1997* (%)	June1998 (%)	June 1999 (%)	June1998 (%)	June 1999 (%)	1	2	3	4	5	6	7
Total	21,927 (100)	20,253 (100)	20,604 (100)	1,292 (100)	1,019 (100)	100	100	100	100	100	100	100
Regular	6,102 (27.8)	6,471 (31.9)	6,036 (30.3)	293 (22.68)	173 (16.98)	81	73	51	52	35	81	n.a
Temporary	2,487 (11.4)	3,982 (19.7)	4,161 (20.2)	427 (33.05)	354 (34.74)							
Daily	7,238 (33.0)	1,718 (8.5)	12,427 (11.8)	361 (27.94)	312 (30.62)							
Temporary + daily.	44.4	28.2	32.0			9	10	10	25	8	6	n.a***
Self-employed	4,139 (18.9)	5,864 (29.0)	5,923 (28.7)	190 (14.70)	159 (15.60)	8	12	29	20	31	12	8
Unpaid family Worker	1,961 (8.9)	2,218 (10.9)	2,057 (10.0)	21 (1.63)	21 (2.06)	1	6	10	3	25	1	0
Employment rate**	64											

Thousands. **Source:** *Trends in Employment Data* (National Statistics Office, Korea, 1999), no. 7.

* Based on year-on-change figures from the June 1998 report.

1. Denmark. 2. Japan. 3. Mexico 4. Spain. 5. Turkey. 6. United Kingdom 7. United States

** Based on Martin and Torres (2001), pp. 364-65. Martin and Torres' statistics differ slightly. I have used the employment/population ratios for Korea (year-on rates), and their 'total employment' figures for other countries (year-on 1999 rates). For Korea the two statistics do not differ markedly.

*** The figures for temporary and daily workers are amalgamated in this column.

survey was conducted at random, the number of SME workers would be high, making for a reasonably broad-based figure. This being said, some caution probably needs to be exercised in terms of what we should interpret as voluntary in SME firms in particular. For instance, the 9.1 per cent for shutdown indicates business failure and hence hardly reflects a voluntary quit. Still, the point to note is that movement was to a large degree voluntary in nature.

This relative stability in the employment system was made possible by a careful balance between intervention and markets. As in other employment systems, freedom in some areas was sustained by regulation or intervention in others. SME firms, for instance, operated with de facto semiformal contractual forms that were not to the same degree as in the sector of larger firms either defended by unions or enforced in the courts. At the same time, they were able to rely on workers with good educational backgrounds only due to the state's investment in good quality, broad coverage secondary education and post-schooling training.[29] Their freedom presupposed continuation of socialisation of this investment by the state, as well as state protection for individual movement in other ways. For example, freedom of movement for agents in SME markets was protected by the state's indirect support for job creation in this particular sector. A similar balance of sorts between regulation and freedoms pertained in the labour market of larger firms. Employers, to a large extent, could rely on the retainment of highly skilled labour, thereby maintaining fairly good incentives for the development and protection of human resources, in exchange for high degrees of freedom in the organisation of work. Unions were mainly concerned with the negotiation of economic aspects of labour rights and were never able to attain significant influence on labour management. Hence, the system was stable and protected the development and reproduction of human resources in so far as relatively high rates of job stability for core workers generated incentives to invest in company-specific skills. At the same time, Korea's employment systems rested on a careful exchange between economic and political rights.[30] Labour's lack of

29   Korea's ratio of completed secondary and/or tertiary education in the labour force, at 73% in 1995, ranked with Canada's, at 79%, Japan's, at 80%, hovered over that of the UK, at 67%, and far exceeded those of neighbouring countries, with Thailand at 16% and Malaysia at 50%. Tertiary education, at 21%, was similar to that of the UK, at 23%, though still lower than Japan, at 31%. On the subject of education and the labour market, see also earlier work by You and Chang (1993), Park (1994) and Jeong (1995).

30   For a detailed discussion of this exchange and how it compares with Chile, see Haagh (forthcoming). Figure 1 in the Appendix presents a summary of this argument. In this article, the term 'political rights' refers to a particular aspect of collective rights. The latter may be necessary for the former, but does not provide any guarantee for the former. This point is particularly valid in the Korean case, where the capacity for strike and wage gains by larger unions did not necessarily provide these with legitimate formal or informal sources of influence over the design of labour management

Table 8.3. Composition of Workforce by Type of Work, June 1999

	*Korea June 1999 (%)		**Period (months) of				By firms size per cent (no. of employees)				
			Tenure 1.	Employment 2.	Unemployment 3.	Nonemployment 4.	1-9	10-49	50-299	300-	Total
Total	20,604										
Regular	6,471	31.95	10.5	11.6	0.1	0.3					
Temporary	3,982	19.66	7.5	9.7	0.6	1.9	57.4	29.5	10.1	3.0	100.0
Daily	1,718	8.48	4.3	7.4	1.2	3.7	65.5	25.5	6.3	2.7	100.0

* Thousands. **Source:** *Trends in Employment data* (National Statistics Office, Korea, 1999), no. 7.

** Figures are from the Economically Active Population Survey, in Hur (2001), p. 31.

1. Period in regular employment as wage or salary worker in a firm.

2. Period in employment as wage or salaried worker, not necessarily tied to one firm or establishment.

3. Period of active job search during unemployment.

4. Period of active job search as well as period where the person is out of the labour force.

political power was offset by arrangements that restricted employers and led employees to have relatively high degrees of economic power compared, for instance, with many counties in Europe. The state intervened quite heavily to protect occupational welfare and training, and the courts enforced long-term contracts.[31] The clearest manifestation of the exchange between political and economic rights was the ability of unions to sustain high wage rises throughout the late 1980s at the same time as the emergent democratic union movement was struggling to establish the legality of its existence. At the firm level, good occupational welfare and employment stability were virtually inseparable from a tradition of bargaining that emphasised combinations of company loyalty and economic justice (including wage bargaining) but which rarely admitted a fair and reasoned exchange of views based on organisational independence of unions and management.[32] Nevertheless, the state's policies of job creation in the SME sector and relatively high job stability and state and judicial regulation of employment practices in larger firms meant that Korea's employment systems remained fairly stable.

There were sources of instability emerging from the mid-1980s in these employment systems. For instance, in the labour markets of larger firms poaching of skilled workers became more common, and a collective action problem in investing in skills was emerging partly as a result of this practice and the state's decision to move towards a more market-based training system.[33] The scheme of compulsory levies was replaced by one of in-house training for firms of a certain size, and a market of private training providers was encouraged as the state was seeking slowly to replace the system of state-provided initial training (intended primarily for employment in the SME sector).[34] The weakness of workers' political rights was also unsustainable over the longer term. The fact of labour's weak politi-

---

31   For example, compulsion in respect to the operation of labour-management councils, introduced in 1963 and governed by an independent act since 1980 (most lately extended in 1997) was quite effective by comparative standards. Meanwhile, the courts consistently protected the pattern of long-term employment. The civil courts might allow a dismissal, but the individual firm had to make a special case. See further Haagh (forthcoming).

32   The phenomenon of full-time paid union leaders is probably the best expression of this curious relationship. Although union leaders are at pains to insist that the relationship does not affect their independence vis-à-vis management, it is difficult to dismiss the observation that had leaders been paid from outside funds, it may have been easier for them to withstand appeals to company loyalty and establish a reasoned dialogue on workers' rights. The payment by firms of full-time union officials was banned with the legal revisions of 1997 and 1998, to commence from 2002. Strong union opposition during the winter of 2000–01 led to a further postponement till 2006.

33   Park (1994), Kang (2000).

34   See Ryan (2000) and Kang (2000).

cal rights in the firm was only officially recognised by the Korean state with membership of the ILO in 1991 and with the initiation of a slow process of democratisation in labour affairs. In a broader sense, the tenuousness of labour's ties to the political system, its lack of party-political links and lack of say in tripartite fora was oddly out of step with the process of democratisation of the political system which had been underway for over ten years. However, it took the crisis to bring these incipient sources of instability in the employment system to a real institutional shift. When the vital links in Korea's employment systems, the largely voluntary nature of labour mobility and labour's assurance of economic security were unhinged, the whole chain of inter-locking checks and balances, of freedoms and regulations, was broken.

Table 8.4 shows the number of firms in a survey of 285 firm-based unions that had engaged in some form of employment restructuring by the end of 1999. 70 per cent had already done so and 40 per cent were either extending or initiating a plan. The *chaebols* in particular cut large numbers of staff. Samsung cut roughly 30 per cent of its personnel during 1998 and 1999, LG cut just over 20 per cent of its employees. The massive increase in involuntary mobility upset the existing equilibrium in both Korea's labour markets. The state's usual employment-generating policies were no longer able to absorb the level of involuntary unemployment in the SME sector, or for that matter of the labour market of larger firms. The basis for firm-specific investments in training was also upset and the sources of legitimacy and loyalty that had previously bound employees were put into question.

A political imbalance within Korea's institutions of labour therefore also emerged. One of the political factors of incipient instability in the employment system by the mid-1990s was the question of how large labour unions would influence changes in labour management which were beginning to dilute previous features of in-house labour protection, including seniority wages, and which unions were becoming incapable of defending with the established combative methods of collective action.[35] Between 1997 and 1999 the use of merit-based pay systems increased from 3.6 to 18.2 per cent of firms in surveys carried out by the Labour Ministry. An additional 30 per cent in 1999 had plans to introduce one in future. Moreover, the large wage rises of the late 1980s could no longer be attained, thereby removing union leaders' established sources of legitimacy vis-à-vis their constituency, and leaving a void to be filled. The degree to which this was the case is exemplified by the novel concern with organ-

---

35   Table 8.4 shows some of the changes in work patterns affected in the wake of the crisis. Even before the crisis, however, performance wage systems were being introduced in larger firms. See below.

ising the unemployed, as expressed most immediately in the frustration union leaders felt at losing members as a result of the slowly changing patterns of hire and fire. The crisis turned these pending issues into an instantaneous challenge.

The impending task was one of how to re-establish a functional link between the different economic and political institutions of labour and between these and other relevant institutions that support employment systems, such as the social policy framework. However, it was certainly not one of moving from an unfree to a free labour market. Indeed, the process of market reforms in Korea, including the crisis, put some of the assumptions behind the legal reforms undertaken in the mid-1990s in Korea in question. The legal changes of 1996–98 emphasised the promotion of more market-rational behaviour in the areas where, as described, legislation in both the Danish and the Chilean labour markets allowed for greater immediate flexibility, particularly in hiring and firing, and conversely placed less emphasis on adjusting other areas of the employment system which, as we saw for the Danish case, may be crucial to the functioning of labour markets overall.

Prior to 1998 dismissals were basically regulated by precedence established at the Supreme Court. Larger firms would occasionally get consent to dismiss, but on the whole the assumption was that the legal one-year contracts commonly used in Korea would be renewed unless grave reasons existed for this not to be the case. The 1997 legislation itself was essentially based on a court ruling of 1989, where the justifications for dismissal under *strict circumstances* were set out. The four conditions included: (i) urgent managerial reasons; (ii) the exploration of all other avenues first; and (iii) adherence to certain procedures for selection of the employees to be dismissed in cases where lay-offs could not be avoided. Finally, (iv) employers were required to consult with employees or the labour union (where it existed) on the forms of the dismissals and the selection of the workers to be dismissed.[36] The 1997 legislation repeated basically the same conditions, but by taking the issue out of the hands of court precedence and into a legal code, the spirit, interpretation and actual usage of the provisions changed. The requirements could be interpreted in a more liberal way, as the expectation of a lengthy and potentially costly court process was removed. This liberal usage was enhanced with the impact of the financial crisis. When it hit in late 1997, IMF conditionality required the lay-off laws to come into effect earlier than planned, and the Tripartite Commission established by Kim Dae Jung was made, in February 1998, to recommend the coming into force of the new legislation a year early, as well as give its blessing to the legalisation of temping agencies for the first time in Korea. A special session of the National Assembly then ratified the changes later that month.

36   See also Park et al. (2001), p. 127.

The new more liberal spirit in the understanding of lay-off conditions was in accordance with the leaning within the policy-making community in Korea at the time towards a more neoclassical model of labour markets that subsumed issues of organisation of labour under problems of the exchange of labour. The developmentalist leaning spearheaded in the past by institutions within the state bureaucracy such as the Korea Development Institute was being replaced by a more laissez-faire approach implying fair regulation, but reduced intervention. Core state planning institutions from the mid-1980s onwards increasingly became populated by scholars educated in the USA and influenced by monetarist and Anglo-Saxon common law visions of market neutrality, and more expansionist ministries, such as the Ministry of Labour, were reined in.

It is a curious reflection of the degree of de facto employment stability previously enjoyed by employees of larger firms in Korea that neoliberal reformers and international institutions like the World Bank and the IMF favour a *more detailed* legal code in the context of Korea, where in Latin America the emphasis since the 1980s has been on simplifying and reducing the scope of state regulation of labour relations. This goes to confirm again the point that 'free' labour markets do not necessarily presuppose less regulation, but simply regulation of a different form, a form which, because of our acceptance of the organisation of firms, appears in the Anglo-Saxon tradition as 'natural' and free rather than institutional or as combining freedom and regulations in a particular way.[37] In other words, in Korea multilateral institutions and neoliberal reformers wanted the country to shift not away from *an* employment system, but towards an Anglo-Saxon type, and fairly extensive new codification was felt to be necessary in order to achieve this objective.

Whichever way, this marked emphasis on one area of freedom, hiring and firing, and freedom for one set of agents — employers — addressed itself primarily towards one element of the employment system and therefore failed to resolve important contradictions enhanced by the crisis. The crisis itself, as noted, led to a more marked emphasis on the areas of the new law that allowed for greater freedom in hiring and firing, at a time when political aspects of labour reform had not had the time to seep

---

37   For good recent discussions of the historical specificity of the organisation of firms in Western capitalism see Chomsky on the 'legal personification of firms', in Burchill's interview with Chomsky (Burchill, 1998), Pagano (1985), and Arestis et al. (1997).

38   Many of the 'political' changes were deliberately phased to come into effect several years later, as in the case of the right to form multiple trade unions (2002), and, as mentioned, the prohibition on the firm's payment of full-time union officials. Although labour leaders resented some of these reforms (as in the case of the latter) these reforms nevertheless clearly formed part of a shift towards a new and more transparent logic of negotiation at firm level that may be envisaged would match the more

through.[38] Leaders of Korea's two labour centrals who agreed to the 1998 pact had hopes of extracting significant concessions, thus explaining the labour movement's surprising cooperation on a matter that conflicted not only with the unions' tradition of defiance, but also their defence above all of traditional labour rights of wage gains and employment stability. Union leaders of the KCTU (the more radical of the two national centrals) who entered the pact also felt that the state of crisis warranted cooperation from labour, thus prompting what in historical terms was an unprecedented act of goodwill and faith in the political system on labour's part.[39] However, when the gap between what the government was willing to concede to labour and the expectations held by base-level labour level leaders became apparent, it turned out to be extremely difficult to establish a new consensus to facilitate political changes in labour relations that might act as a counter-balance to the economic aspects of the labour reforms.

The interplay between the new legislation and the crisis is an interesting one. One would have thought that the crisis would have accelerated the transition to a more exchange-based labour market, where labour mobility both voluntary and involuntary is the norm. In fact, the sequence of legislation and then crisis provides the best possible scenario for showing the difficulty of moving very rapidly from one employment system to another, *especially* if the latter is an imagined rational free labour market. Indeed, in many ways it is not so much the degree to which the labour market changed in response to the crisis that is surprising, but the ways in which labour relations *did not*. In both positive and negative ways legacies of the past manifested themselves in the reactions of social actors and the

---

directly contractual or contingent nature of economic bargaining. Other reforms that were important in giving political and organisational support to unions from intermediary-level and national-level organisations were proving extremely difficult at this time, as in the delay on legalising the Korean Confederation of Trade Unions (KCTU), and not least in the difficulty sectoral level organisations faced in establishing a legal existence, as well as any kind of dialogue with employers at this level. In the case of the metal sector, for instance, the Korean Metal Workers' Federation (KMWF), probably the strongest private sector union federation, had no relationship of dialogue with employers above the individual firm level *at all*. An important source of explanation for this is of course the *chaebol* system, which provides employers not connected within an economic group with little incentive to form a joint strategy on almost any matter. See further Haagh (forthcoming).

39   Interviews with Yoon Youngmo, international secretary of the KCTU and with Kim Yoo-Sun (August and September 1999), vice-director of the Korea Labour and Society Institute. Kim was one of the elected high-profile KCTU leaders who in 1998 entered the tripartite pact, and in the KCTU's subsequent annual congress was forced to resign along with the entire KCTU executive as a result of local leaders' anger at what they saw as a sell-out by the national leadership. Kim left the KCTU for a period to head the Korea Labour and Society Institute, a think tank closely linked to the KCTU.

state to the crisis. The legislators of 1996–98 overlooked the degree to which the labour market is a social institution. Legal changes, even changes designed to expand markets at micro-level, are not likely to be as effective when introduced from above. In Korea they exposed the political difficulties involved in labour market reform. One indication of this was the unexpectedly small impact that the attempt to introduce a more transaction-based and notionally free labour market with the 1996–98 legislation actually had.

Challenges to the employment system brought on by the crisis can be summarised by dividing them into areas that have to do with industrial relations (and thereby into problems of generating human resources, and political problems of negotiating the social contract) and areas that have to do with welfare reform and the state. Below I look first at industrial relations and then at labour policy.

Economic Crisis and Labour Reforms

Human Resources

The large majority of Korean firms carried through employment restructuring during the crisis, and an unprecedented number of lay-offs occurred. Nevertheless, it appears that Korean firms did make notable efforts to avoid dismissals. This clearly emanates from Table 5 of the same survey cited before. It shows that out of the 285 firms surveyed only 7.7 per cent had turned to direct lay-offs in the first round of employment restructuring. If one discounts from the total the number of firms that either faced partial closure, were privatised or sold off, the figure is still only 10.3 per cent. This is a remarkably low figure given the context of crisis that Korean firms faced and the level of lay-offs they eventually had to concede. The most significant sources of employment restructuring by a very large margin were wage and benefit reduction (22.2 per cent) and merging departments (21.4 per cent). If discounting merger and acquisition, privatisation and closure of firms, the figures rise to 29.8 per cent and 28.7 per cent, respectively. In short, over 89 per cent of firms emphasised internal forms of employment restructuring in the first round.[40] This shows that historical patterns established in labour relations do matter to economic behaviour, which from neoclassical theory we should expect to be characterised by reflex reaction to external forces. Such patterns matter *even* in a crisis of great magnitude such as that which Korea faced.

---

40 Even in the second round attempts to use wage and benefit reduction took precedence. 23.5% of firms (or 25% if discounting privatisation, closures, etc.) emphasised wages and benefits reduction and only 29.4% (or 31.5% when discounting the factors mentioned) relied mainly on lay-offs.

Table 8.4: Implementation of Employment Restructuring Plan

	Already implemented	Plan to implement or to extend	Number of establishments surveyed.
	198 (70)	117 (41)	Total: 285
Chemicals	40 (66.7)	17 (28.3)	60
Textiles	15 (57.7)	7 (26.9)	26
Metal	45 (64.3)	34 (48.6)	70
Construction	15 (78.9)	11 (57.9)	19
Finance	29 (78.4)	12 (31.6)	38
Other service	54 (76.1)	36 (50.7)	71
Public	40 (83.3)	30 (61.2)	49
30 major chaebols	40 (71.4)	30 (53.6)	56
foreign	11 (47.8)	6 (26.1)	23
non-chaebols	106 (70.2)	47 (31.1)	151
SME	82 (68.3)	37 (30.8)	120
Large	110 (66.7)	76 (46.1)	165
Implemented	141 (91.6)	49 (31.8)	154
Planning to implement	51 (58)	68 (77.3)	88
No plan	7 (16.7)	1 (2.4)	42

Source: KLSI Survey (1998).

This particular lag in labour relations obviously contained some positive features. For example, it showed a continued willingness to emphasise internal flexibility and to protect investments in human resources. When compared with efforts in Chile during periods of modest downturn, this response by Korean firms is remarkable.[41] The evidence of path dependency is certainly clear. At the same time the behaviour of employers bears witness to the tensions in the employment system that I referred to above. The lag in political relative to economic rights made it difficult to accommodate labour management to the change in markets. Many human resource managers of top conglomerates stated the wish to change the employment stability expectation of employees of the past, but these conflicted with other objectives. Managers

41   Rates of dismissal (involuntary quits) in Chile were always high. For instance in the early 1990s, annual dismissal rates were found to be as high as 17% in manufacturing and 26% in services, not counting job terminations imputing fault to workers (Haagh, 1998, p. 160). A survey of local unions indicated that the total size of the workforce in a set of manufacturing firms varied on average by over 30% over two years (taking the maximum and minimum number of employees into account, Haagh, 2002a, chapter 8) This tendency to use workforce numbers as the first point of call in economic restructuring also helps to explain the extent of the impact of the Asian economic crisis on the Chilean economy, as unemployment stayed at double the levels of the early 1990s for several years after the crisis, an impact that was not only as great as that on Korea itself, but more sustained.

valued the loyalty that job stability inspired in employees as well as the retention of human capital that it entailed. Two-thirds of respondents to a pilot study stated these as the most important reasons for keeping the system. If second priorities are included as well a far greater number said so. Yet they also wanted to rely more on merit-based pay systems (which as noted earlier had increased) and to concentrate on hiring employees during their lifetime peak productivity spells.[42]

The picture that emerges is one of poor adjustment to the changes that labour markets had traversed. Employers wished to retain employee loyalty, have greater freedom of hiring and firing *and* retain an available stock of skilled labour. This combination would not be possible without changes to the representation of workers in firms or without the development of an efficient system of labour recycling outside them. Below I look in turn at the issues of representation and welfare policy.

Rights of Movement and Political Freedoms

The 1996–98 legal reforms in Korea established greater freedom in hiring and firing for firms, but did not strengthen workers' political capacity to negotiate the terms of labour mobility. Rights of movement in this context refer to the effective access that workers have to exercise control over their labour market movement.[43] On the face of it, the legal reforms of 1996–98 did make for a reasoned dialogue with labour unions about dismissals. By letter of the law this legislation was far less liberal than either the Danish[44] or the Chilean (even prior to 1973)[45] discussed earlier on. While it established, for the first time, an independent legal code governing dismissals (the freedom of employers), a development much welcomed by international economic actors,[46] it also sought to satisfy unions' demand for inclusion by stipulating apparently strict rules for consultation with labour. Following the 1989 precedent, lay-offs were justified in two cases: (i) employers had to show urgent managerial reasons, and provide a detailed justification. This justifi-

---

42 These answers emanate from a pilot of in-depth interviews with top managers (at executive board level) of 16 of Korea's largest firms during 1999 and 2000. These include affiliates of Samsung and LG (Lucky Goldstar), in the latter case the group's eight largest member firms.

43 For a longer discussion of membership of labour markets understood in this sense, see Haagh (2002a), chapters 1 and 2.

44 In this case firing laws have traditionally been extremely lax. Occupational citizenship has been supported instead by inter-linked systems of unemployment insurance, training and income support (Haagh, 2001).

45 See Haagh (2002c).

46 As key figures in the Labour Ministry and the Korea Labor Institute pointed out, the World Bank and IMF were at pains that the Korean state should use the opportunity presented by the crisis to further consolidate a more contingency contract-based labour market (interviews with leading figures in the KLI and one of the director generals of the Labor Ministry, who wished not to be named, July–August 1999).

cation could not, as in Chile's highly liberal legislation (Article 3), refer to any 'necessities of the firm, establishment or service; such as those deriving from rationalisation, modernisation, falls in productivity, changes in market conditions or in the economy, which make it necessary to dismiss one or more workers'.[47] Moreover, (ii) management had to (a) make serious efforts to seek alternatives to the dismissal and (b) conduct sincere consultation with labour leaders about such alternatives and discuss the form that the dismissals would take. In addition, the dismissals would have to be projected and planned over a period of time.[48]

In this way the new code appeared to be a rational attempt to unite an expansion of exchange relationships with greater involvement of unions, market expansion with democratisation, a marriage that became politically popular in Korea in the 1990s.[49] The legislation was politically weak, how-

47   See Haagh (2002c).
48   Ministry of Labor, Republic of Korea (1997), p. 5.
49   Kim Dae Jung clearly saw the project of deepening political democracy in Korea as closely intertwined with developing freedom in the economic sphere, a fairly nebulous vision. Although his rationale for doing so was undoubtedly based on the attempt to fight the inter-familial form of rule of the *chaebols*, widely seen as politically corrupt in Korea (and conversely to strengthen the power of small share-holders), a 'democratic' vision, there was in practice a close overlap with the thinking and reform programme of neoclassical market reformers in Korea and with the policies and outlook of multilateral development institutions seeking to convert the Korean economy and economic policy away from a developmentalist orientation involving integrated forms of support for technological and human development, to one based on discrete competition between individual agents reliant on 'finding' sources of support for short-term survival. Put simply, the romantic aspect of this vision lies in the failure to distinguish between the desire for corporate reform (in particular shareholder and corporate governance reforms), on the one hand, and wholesale reform of the state and private-public sector networks, on the other. The 'democracy equals market reform' vision applied to Korea threw the baby out with the bathwater: it is not necessary to withdraw the state from providing forms of long-term support for business or human development in order to make private-private and state-private sector relations more transparent. The Kim Dae Jung government was forced to take the easy way out: attempting all-out reform rather than a careful transition, moving towards an interpretation of free enterprise that was more doctrinaire and imposing than even the contemporary Anglo-Saxon model (in practice), to the extent that the state, heavily influenced by encouragement by the IMF and World Bank (see note 39) was prepared to force conglomerates towards wholesale *de*-diversification, and placing strict limits on the sectors in which they can operate, on a strangely outdated and romantic model of the small firm concentrating in a single industry. One can to some extent understand the frustration of Korean managers at the time who saw their US conglomerate counterparts and competitors happily diversifying into ever more diverse strands of economic activity, at home and worldwide, with the staunch support of their government. How far the practical content and direction of the economic reform programme was an unknown in Korea is expressed by a top economist and advisor to Kim Dee Jung based at the Korea Development Institute (KDI) School in Seoul, 'We know what we are destroying (the *chaebol* system), but we have no clue where we are going or with what we wish to replace it' (interview September 1999).

ever, because it failed to take into account the ways in which labour representation remained immature in Korea. Legislators cannot be blamed for this, of course, but it shows the difficulty of introducing legislation that is not profoundly intertwined with social agreements and without taking the wider dimensions of the employment system into account. A tradition of actual compromise between independent agents (unions and employers) on the shop floor, such as that which the legislation seemed to presuppose, had never taken root in Korea. It was barely existent at the national level and virtually non-existent at the federal (sectoral) level, as noted. At the national level, labour was involved in some discussions within the Labour Ministry prior to the legislation of 1997, but a formal public body, the Tripartite Commission, since May 1999 with a legislated permanent status (put through by the Kim Dae Jung administration as a gesture to union leaders) only became established in 1998, and for the most part the KCTU remained outside. The two labour centrals did not have any permanent independent relations with either the Korean Employers Federation (KEF) or FDI, the two main employers' organisations.

Unions also remained financially and, to a large degree, socially dependent on management in Korea, as noted. Even as of the mid-1990s, union leaders of the democratic trend that began to gain force a decade before were struggling to establish authority vis-à-vis the leaders of the older generation who typically were able to extract concessions from, and enter unilateral deals with, the management ranks.[50] Unionists particularly of the democratic trend in Korea were very combative, and willing to risk long terms in jail for minor offences, in order to demonstrate their independence and their readiness to do all that is necessary to defend the economic justice of members. For instance, the imprisonment of Dan Byung-ho, president of the Korean Metal Workers' Federation (KMWF) during 1998–99, on the common charge of involvement in illegal strike activity, greatly contributed to his legitimacy and standing with the base, and to his election as KCTU president in the autumn of 1999, upon his release from jail on special presidential pardon.[51] Yet it is fair to say that a country in which close to 100 union leaders at any one time either await trial or spend long terms in jail for what are fairly regular trade union activities has barely begun to experience what democratisation in labour relations might mean. Union leaders, particularly in larger firms and specific *chaebol* groups, have been able to

50 Interview with 12 local leaders in the auto and metal industries, and especially with former president of Kia Auto Workers Union, Na Yong Gon (interview, August 1999).

51 A total of 703 KCTU members were subject to legal action during 1998 and 1999, and not a few were charged on counts of involvement in illegal political activities under the National Security Law. Further details can be found in Haagh (forthcoming).

achieve spectacular wage gains and even protect employment security against incredible odds, such as those of the 1997 crisis.[52] The fact, however, remains that the firms in which unions had achieved a true political voice remained few and far between. Gains such as those in Hyundai were achieved at very high cost and are imaginable in only a minority of firms. The lack of union involvement in social welfare institutions more broadly also tended to reinforce a firm-centred relationship with employers, based narrowly on economic rights, as did a culture of company loyalty that rarely permitted open discussion of organisational alternatives between firm members belonging to different ranks. To this should be added the fact that most local unions in SME firms have been de-linked from a broader political network and remain largely defenceless.

The preferential ranking of unions by the late 1990s understandably was not strongly formed, as control gains have been virtually impossible to develop in Korea. An internal survey conducted by the KMWF found that only 6.7 per cent of firms had employment stability committees in 1998. The figure increased markedly for firms with over 1,000 employees (to 11.5 per cent) and in the final assembly plants (33.3 per cent), but these represent the best possible case in Korea. The average of 6.7 per cent is low considering that the metal sector probably represents the most cohesive segment of organised labour.[53] The economic crisis enhanced union leaders' consciousness of this situation. As a consequence sectoral and national-level leaders were by the late 1990s becoming more acutely aware of their weakness in reflecting a broad spectrum of labour interests, a sensation that was most clearly expressed in the new concern with organising the unemployed.[54] Even this concern, however, had a ring of desperation

52   Hyundai motors originally planned to cut 11,672 employees, but managed to bring the workforce down by only 1,538 workers, and of these 1,261 were sent on unpaid leave (which effectively means that they had first right of refusal when the firm was ready to hire again).

53   Korean Metal Workers Federation (1999), p. 135. Moreover, out of a group of ten local union leaders in the metal sector interviewed by the author in August 1999, only one leader had had any experience of bargaining on matters of organising work. Yet all the leaders regularly bargained on economic issues like wages, welfare benefits, working conditions and training.

54   This became a core concern in particularly the more radical national union federation, the KCTU. However, the concern emanated from the sectoral level, where the immediate loss of union members as a result of the crisis was most directly felt. Union leaders were thinking along a model of the occupational union in Germany, but were not too clear about the implications of such a model for union financing and union organisation, and relations with employers and the state more broadly (interview with Kim Seung-Ho, director of Research and Statistics Unit, Korean Metal Workers' Federation, August 1999). The KCTU's proposals for allowing unionisation of the unemployed were looked at in the Tripartite Commission, but were not taken seriously by the Kim Dae Jung government.

rather than thoughtful planning about it. Union leaders wished to ensure that dismissed workers retain membership of their union primarily so that their chances of re-employment with the same firm would be enhanced. This reflected the firm-centred, paternalistic dynamic of labour relations characteristic probably of the great majority of firms in Korea, and represented a logical, immediate response to the situation brought about by the dynamics unleashed from the combined effect of the 1997 legal changes and the crisis. However, it also reveals just how far this incipient broader concern with unionising was from the broader involvement with rights of movement that is characteristic of union movements that have successfully mixed organising with broad-based political and welfare advances and that have come close to erasing the distinction between workers' and citizens' rights.[55]

Table 8.5: Type of Restructuring Plan Pursued

	1st round	2nd round
Selling off	9.7	2.1
Privatisation	3.2	0.4
M & A	9.7	3.8
Closure	2.8	0.4
Changing of business	1.2	0.4
Separation of departments	4.4	2.5
Contract out	3.6	2.5
Merger of departments	21.4*	6.3
Introduction of team system	5.6	6.3
Management and ownership restructuring	3.2	5.5
	1.6	2.5
Computerisation	22.2*	23.5*
Wages and benefits reduction	7.7	29.4*
Lay-offs	2.8	10.9
Restructuring of wage system	0.8	3.3
Personnel management system		

Source: KLSI Survey (1998).

---

55   For a discussion of occupational citizenship, see Haagh (forthcoming, chapters 1 and 2), and as applied to recent labour market reforms in Europe, Asia and Latin America Haagh (2002a).

Table 8.6: Most Important Forms of Employment Restructuring

	Measures adopted		Measures by priority		
	No. of firms	Frequency (%)	1st priority	2nd priority	%
Adjustment of work	152	53.3	32	24	12.8
patterns	33	11.6	6	9	3.1
• Reduction of regular	99	34.7	13	6	4.6
work hours	75	26.3	6	6	2.6
• Reduction of	52	18.2	5	2	1.7
overtime work	24	8.4	0	0	0.0
• Increase of vacation	36	12.6	2	1	0.7
• Temporary closure					
• Temporary leave	226	79.3	172	86	62.4
• Change in shifts	157	55.1	45	12	14.7
	132	56.3	102	22	32.5
Adjustment of number of	10	3.5	0	5	0.8
workers	61	21.4	7	12	3.8
• Natural reduction	31	10.9	11	7	4.2
• Honourary	22	7.7	2	3	1.0
retirement	84	29.5	2	15	2.9
• Reduction of	51	17.9	3	10	2.4
retirement age					
• Projected lay-offs	133	46.7	7	13	4.0
• Unfair/punitive lay-	30	10.5	3	3	1.3
offs	60	21.1	3	0	0.9
• Reduction of	14	4.9	0	0	0.0
irregular labour force	106	37.2	1	10	1.8
• Increase of irregular labour force					
• Strongly-advised retirement					
Functional adjustment					
• Sent out to affiliated/related company					
• Training in or outside of company					
• Temporary dispatch outside the company					
• Change of occupation within company					
Total	-	-	**233**	**218**	**100.0**

Source: Korean Labour and Security Institute Survey (1998).

In this context it is perhaps hardly surprising that the new laws on consultation failed to work as intended. Indeed, the second, and perhaps less positive, element in employment restructuring worth noting is the way in which involuntary job terminations have been pursued. Of particular interest is the little use of the new laws on dismissals that we mentioned before. Looking at Tables 8.5 and 8.6, we can see that they were used by just 21.4 per cent of firms. Only 3.8 per cent used them as their first or second priority. In other words, firms continued to use the methods of laying off workers of the past, but just on a more massive scale. We might say that this represents a more negative side of the lag in labour relations.

As we saw, the new laws on dismissals of 1998 did actually by letter of the law provide for quite extensive consultation with unions despite the controversy to which they gave rise. However, this mechanism failed to work. Unionists disliked the new laws because they believed consultation was used by management as a way to legitimise and legalise layoffs. The dismissal laws presupposed an atmosphere of trust and reasoned bargaining that did not exist. Employers' leaders in turn saw the new law as a way to socially sanction their right to cut employees. 'Now it is possible to say that the dismissal is fair,' as a top leader of KEF remarked.[56] However, as we saw, employers hardly used the dismissal option that entailed an open negotiation of the dismissals. Their own faith in the legitimacy of dismissals was clearly in question. The leader from KEF suggested that employers perceived that the new law created an expectation of dismissals amongst employees, which prolonged potential conflicts over lay-offs and made this conflict pronounced in a way that undercut relations with existing staff. Local union leaders confirmed this impression of the new laws, describing their sensation that employers proposed lay-offs to the union which they had no intention of actually discussing, a 'strategy' that was followed initially by other measures of restructuring (which, as the law stipulated, had to be attempted first), and then by dismissals, when employers felt confident enough to show that other efforts had been made. In other words, consultation, as union leaders saw it, was merely a token gesture.[57] From the description of both parties it seems quite apparent that the practical implications of the new laws were that employers planned the alternatives to dismissals in a unilateral way, in contravention to what the legislation foresaw.

56 Interview with Lee Dong-eung, director of the Labor Relations Department, KEF, August. 2000.
57 Interviews with Kim, Seung-Ho, director of Research and Statistics Unit, Korean Metal Workers' Federation and the union presidents of 12 member unions of the KMWF, August 1999, September 2000.

Table 8.7: Forms of Dismissal by Size of Firm

Year	No of employees	Form of dismissal			
		'Strongly advised'	'Honourable retirement'	Lay-off (1997/8 legislation)	Other forms
		Firms (%)	Firms (%)	Firms (%)	Firms (%)
1998	➢ 10	57 (15)	18 (10)	22 (29)	17 (26)
	10-19	61 (16)	22 (13)	11 (15)	8 (13)
	20-29	47 (12)	15 (9)	10 (13)	2 (3)
	30-39	40 (11)	0	2 (3)	5 (8)
	40-49	33 (9)	15 (9)	13 (17)	7 (11)
	50 <	142 (37)	101 (59)	17 (23)	25 (39)
	A: All in category	380 (100)	171 (100)	75 (100)	64
	B: Total	483	483	483	483
	A/B: Percentage (form of dismissal by firm size)	79	35	15	13
1999	➢ 10	89 (27)	20 (24)	25 (57)	13 (24)
	10-19	78 (23)	15 (18)	8 (18)	8 (15)
	20-29	36 (11)	8 (10)	2 (4)	9 (16)
	30-39	24 (7)	7 (8)	0 (1)	3 (5)
	40-49	24 (7)	12 (14)	6 (13)	7 (13)
	50 <	84 (25)	22 (26)	3 (7)	15 (27)
	A: All in category	335 (100)	84	44	55
	B: Total	483	483	483	483
	A/B: Percentage	69	17	9	11

Source: Based on survey of firms conducted in November and December 1999 by Park et al. See Park et al. (2001).

This can be clearly seen in Tables 8.6 and 8.7. Table 8.6 is drawn from a survey of member unions of the Korean Metal Workers Federation (KMWF) of all sizes, whereas Table 8.7 is based on a survey using random selection across a range of sectors, but excluding firms with less than 150 employees. Since unions tend to be stronger in the metal sector and since firms with over 150 employees are more likely to have unions, both surveys approximate a 'best possible scenario' in terms of union strength.[58]

58   This is useful for showing the overall weakness of organised labour. However, there remains a need for surveys which use random selection across sectors as well as firm sizes and independently of whether firms have unions or not.

The results are also broadly similar. Both surveys show that the new lay-off laws are used in only a minority of cases, in 21.4 per cent of cases in the metal survey and in 15 per cent on average in the other survey (both in 1998). By comparison, 56.3 per cent of firms in the metal survey had used 'honorary retirement', 55.1 per cent had used 'natural reduction' and 17.9 per cent has used 'strongly advised' retirement (Table 8.6). The relationships between formal and informal forms of dismissal is similar in Table 8.7, where formal dismissal refers to lay-offs and other forms can be classified as 'informal'. Table 8.7 also shows that the informal forms of dismissal were far more prevalent in cases where larger groups of employees were being dismissed. This is indeed ironic, since the introduction of formal dismissal (lay-offs) was intended precisely to allow for formal forms of dismissal in firms with the greatest economic difficulties, at the same time as dismissals of this kind affecting large numbers of workers should be negotiated with unions.

Table 8.8: Degrees of Union Intervention

Method of reduction	Points (degree of union intervention)
Natural reduction	2.3261
Honourary retirement	3.0773
Reduction of retirement age	3.6291
Voluntary/strongly-advised retirement	2.6810
Lay-offs	3.3522
Illegal/punitive lay-offs	2.8255
Reduction of irregular workers	1.9831
Increase of irregular workers	2.1667

4 points = agreement on reduction of labour force b/t union and company
3 points = consultation b/t union and company
2 points = report before reduction
1 point = report after reduction
0 points = company reduced labour force one-sidedly.

Unfortunately, the surveys available to us at present do not allow us to gauge precisely what the differences are by firm size, but the figures in Table 8.7 at least suggest that it is highly likely that the formal forms of dismissals were used relatively more frequently in smaller firms (in cases with few dismissals), whereas the informal forms predominated in larger firms. It seems, then, that formal dismissals were more likely in situations or firms where unions were weak, whereas informal dismissals tended to predominate where unions were strong. This supposition finds support in the metal survey, where it was shown that the kinds of involuntary dismissal that were least negotiated with unions were the ones most used, i.e. so-called honorary retirement and 'strongly advised' lay-offs (Table 8.8).

What this indicates is that unions in most cases were not strong enough to oppose dismissals outright, nor was management strong enough to push straightforward lay-offs through or to get the unions' consent to them. Labour's weak political rights made unions prone to distrust the intention of managers and the tradition of defiance made it impossible for union leaders seeking re-election to enter a formal bargaining situation on lay-offs. In short there was a self-reinforcing tendency for unions' political rights to remain curtailed, and this in turn undermined workers' rights of movement. Unions were unwilling to give their legitimacy to lay-offs (which a formal negotiation would entail), and preferred instead to be seen to negotiate the 'best deal' for members by reducing legal lay-offs and demanding good pay packages where dismissals could not be avoided.[59] This way unions were not seen to be party to the dismissals.

This probably explains why honourable retirement was more prevalent than 'strongly advised' in firms where unions were likely to be strong (such as the metal sector, as in Table 8.6), and in what we may suppose are larger firms (in Table 8.7). 'Strongly advised' quits are by their nature less likely to lead to generous compensation packages. However, the odd preference for informal lay-offs (as a second worst scenario) by union leaders was a slippery slope. In particular situations it may have served union leaders and union members well, but the risk was a general conversion amongst employers towards the least protective forms of informal lay-offs, such as the strongly advised quits. In fact, Table 8.7 shows that the use of this form of informal dismissal had increased relative to the use of honorary retirement by 1999. There are many negative aspects to this kind of lay-off. They often involve a gradual and degrading loss of status within the firm for the individuals affected. Moreover, problems have been experienced in connecting these types of dismissal with the system of employment insurance.

59   The sensitivity of union leaders on this point clearly emerged in an interview (August 1999) with Kim You Soon, director of the Labour and Society Institute and formerly the KCTU's representative on the Tripartite Commission. As this author used the terms dismissals and lay-offs interchangeably, Kim was at pains to point out that whereas 'dismissal' was a neutral term, 'lay-offs' was a prejorative term. I pointed out that surely in both cases the quit was involuntary, but Kim You Soon seemed to be mainly concerned about the legitimacy of the involuntary quit in the case of (legal) lay-offs. Strongly advised and honorary retirement were also not 'good', but somehow more acceptable because the terms connoted a situation that could not be avoided, where 'lay-offs' implied the legitimacy of 'jumping' to dismissals before all other avenues had been exhausted.

In summary, the political and collective rights of unions in Korea were still so fragile that the kind of transparent negotiation on flexibility that the law envisaged was not in reality feasible. The political and collective rights of unions however need to be seen in the wider context of social sector reform. Clearly, one way of building the representation of workers' interests is to strengthen their political rights in the firm, as I have argued. But closely connected with workers' weak political rights in the firm are their poor rights of exit. Hirschman succinctly captured the relationship between the ability of members of organisations (or countries) to leave, and their power of voice. The ability to leave at a low cost, even if it is not exercised, gives members an implicit power of veto.[60] Hirschman however did not explore in detail what circumstances outside the firm affect members' power of exit (and hence voice). These in any case would be different today than when Hirschman wrote his famous piece. Policies that provide workers with the means to continuous education and skill systems that provide certification of skills that make career continuity between jobs a realistic option are examples of circumstances that strengthen workers' rights of movement today. I have referred to such arrangements as promoting an individual-centred form of labour market flexibility. These may be contrasted with the kind of arrangements facilitated with the 1997 labour reforms in Korea, which concentrated mainly, if not exclusively, on promoting corporations' ability to shed workers at a low cost (a corporation-centred style of flexibility). The kinds of tensions generated by these reforms would clearly be mitigated if workers *also* were given greater effective freedoms to exit. It is possible however to strike some kind of balance between individual- and corporation-centred forms of flexibility, and it could be argued that employment systems that achieve such a balance are more likely to be adaptable and function well.[61] In the case of Korea, as I argued, flexibility for different agents in labour markets existed in pockets prior to the mid-1990s. Small firms had some flexibility because the norm of long-term employment was not strictly reinforced there, whereas larger firms were able to absorb costs in terms of greater employment protection by practising a variety of internal flexibility forms. Meanwhile, workers in smaller firms benefited from the state's active support for employment creation, whereas higher-skilled workers in the larger-firm labour markets were able to and did move around to some extent on the basis of the

---

60   Hirschman (1970).
61   In the case of Denmark, as noted, this balance was achieved through the reproduction through social and union policies of a certain mainstream in skill certification and income support, which allowed individuals a bridge between situations of employment, both in monetary and in occupational terms. On the Danish case, see further Haagh (2001).

implicit mutual recognition of skills value (through poaching) that existed between larger firms. Then, we can see how the almost exclusive orientation of the 1997 law reform towards the corporation-centred side of labour market flexibility would upset the existing set of checks and balances in labour relations which provided both sides with a measure of protection. The rise of involuntary mobility was particularly negative for employees of smaller firms. As we saw there were some indications that lay-offs were more likely to be used here, but employees in this case could not benefit from the potential advantages of this form of dismissal, since they were both less likely to have a strong union (or any union) and less likely to be effectively insured through the employment insurance system (EIS). Workers in this sector were also less able to defend themselves against the use of 'strongly advised' quits or attrition (which increased in 1999) and were not likely to receive significant bonus packages from early retirement. Hence, subsequent to the sudden rise of involuntary mobility no new equilibrium was found *either* within or between firms. Labour's weak rights of exit not only left workers vulnerable and increased the social costs of the 1997 crisis, but also impaired the transparent functioning of the new (corporation-centred) laws, leading employers, as noted, to utilise informal means of laying off workers. Clearly an additional element in labour reform, besides the corporation-centred flexibility laws and the measures to enhance the collective voice of workers, was lacking. This third element referred to measures designed to strengthen workers' economic rights *outside* the firm and may be identified in broad terms with welfare reform. Welfare reform is crucial if you are to develop an approach to flexibility that protects mobile agents, i.e. individuals as well as firms. It is simultaneously reliant upon and in turn extends both political rights and skill rights, and gives unions that are seeking to attain a political voice a stake in shaping members' future welfare and in retaining their membership. In short, welfare reform has the potential simultaneously to strengthen the organisation of unions (depending on its direction and if the opportunity is seized) and to connect the unions with a wider set of public institutions, making them 'responsible' or allowing them to attain influence, depending on where you want to place the weight.

The Employment Insurance System and Social Policy

To summarise I would say that the changes experienced at the micro level in Korea in the late 1990s produced three policy challenges. The first was how to protect individuals faced with involuntary mobility. High rates of involuntary mobility were likely to remain a feature of the labour market long after the crisis. Indeed, the rate of those who lost their employment insurance benefits within two years of acquiring them rose from 48 to 61 per cent of the labour force covered between 1998 and 1999 alone. The second challenge consisted in how to help firms adjust internally, and the third comprised how to provide alternative ways to invest in skills and recycle human resources. Again the established practice of mainly firm-based investment combined with poaching obviously would not suit a labour market characterised by much higher levels of involuntary mobility. Korea's welfare system of the late 1990s was still in its infancy. For instance, nationwide pension coverage (compulsory for all formal sector employed workers) was only achieved in 1988, although public sector workers, soldiers and teachers were covered as early as 1960, 1963 and 1975, respectively. Medical insurance achieved a regionally based nationwide coverage only in 1989.[62] Reforms that would allow individuals of working ability over the age of 18 to receive any form of income assistance were still in a stage of definition in 2000.[63] Less than 50 per cent of those judged as being below the poverty line (around eight per cent of the population in Korea) benefited from the livelihood protection programme, and benefits were very low. Whereas the estimated income required to cover the basic needs of a single (male) in 2000 was Won 1,078,530 using standard international basic needs rates, a Won 324,011 ceiling was used for the livelihood protection programme that year.

However, there is no inherent reason to expect that Korea would need to traverse several decades of institutional development before she would be able to compare her welfare institutions to those of countries that had an earlier start. The logic of learning in late development also pertains to the welfare system. It is too early yet to form a considered judgement about the direction which welfare reform will ultimately take in Korea, or how substantive such reforms will become. However, it is possible to say, based on an evaluation of the early development of the system of employment insurance and the way this institution was used to respond to the crisis, that Korea has started the building of new welfare institutions on a sound footing. In this case it was not the size of the initial institution that mattered as much as the prospects for further development for which its design allowed. The case of the EIS shows that for all the talk

---

62 Special groups like private school teachers were integrated during the 1970s. Problems of integrating informal sector workers remained huge, and even among the formal segment of the labour market Korean Labor Ministry estimates suggest that less than 40% were effectively covered in 1998.

63 Even so, those with employed workers in their extended family considered capable of providing support could not receive public assistance. In 1999 only 2.5% of the population received a form of public income protection (Park, 2001, p. 61). Park (*ibid.*) discusses the prospects of the National Basic Livelihood Guarantee Act put forward in October 2000, and designed to provide a more comprehensive cover.

of reversing the tide of state involvement in the economy, the best in Korea's tradition of developmental public bureaucracy had managed to re-invent itself and adapt to new uses. The EIS had three components, employment stabilisation, support for vocational training and unemployment insurance. The latter was financed by equal contributions of 0.3 per cent of the monthly wage from employers and workers, whereas employers alone contributed towards employment stabilisation and vocational training on a scale depending on firm size (Table 8.9). The state assumed all administration responsibilities and costs.

The Korean EIS provides a contrasting model of social policy reform to that offered in Latin America based on the Chilean experience of separate privately run institutions. Because of their disparate nature, at least in the case of Chile, such services have failed to come together as a network to support individual mobility. The historical strength of the Korean public bureaucracy in development, and vis-à-vis employers, are both important to the more integrated service system that the EIS is likely to be able to offer. A review of central features of the EIS brings out this more integrated approach.

First, as we saw, the scheme covered not just unemployment but also employment stabilisation. This can clearly be seen from Table 8.9, which lists the whole range of subsidies available to firms. In that way the EIS was designed to complement, and hence recognised, the efforts towards internal restructuring that Korean firms typically sought. During 1998 alone the Labour Ministry experimented with over ten different ways to compose the employment subsidies in order to adapt to the situation as it evolved, but also as a way of testing out and developing the subsidy structure. This explains the slightly different composition of the subsidies listed in Tables 8.9 and 8.10. Table 8.10 shows that usage of the EIS by firms increased dramatically during the crisis and shifted from employment promotion towards employment restructuring. Subsidies designed to avoid immediate lay-offs were most in demand. However, as subsidies were redesigned the use of subsidies for training and for leave increased.

Table 8.9: Design and Finance of the EIS

Components and eligibility	Contributions (as per cent of wage)	Schemes	Specific subsidies***
Employment Stabilisation	Employers only 0.2 per cent	• Employment adjustment	- temporary shut-down - manpower assignment - training for job conversion - training to open new business - adaptation training
		• Employment promotion	- active recruiting - regional employment development -child care leave -promotion for elders -re-employment -workplace childcare centre (or loan to build one)
		• Subsidies for construction workers	- retirement
Vocational Ability Development	Employers only Firm size* -49　SM　Large 0.1 %　0.3 %　0.5 %	• Training for the unemployed • In-plant training	- Reemployment training and assistance with transport and fees - In-plant training - Support for educators - Paid vocational training
		• Support for vocational training facilities	- Support for development of facilities.
		• Construction workers	- Re-training
Unemployment Insurance	50/50 employers and employees (0.3/0.3) 0.6 per cent		

* Until January 1998, firms with less than 30 employees did not qualify for the EIS. See Table 8.12.
** SM firms in Korea are usually considered those with fewer than 300 employees.
*** The structure of subsidies changed a number of times during 1998-1999, as policy-makers tried to optimise incentives for employment stabilisation.
Source: Various documents, Ministry of Labor, Korea.

Table 8.10: Utilisation of the Employment Stabilisation Scheme, 1997–98

Name of scheme	No. of cases			No. of people		
	1997 1st ½	1997 2nd ½	1998	1997 1st ½	1997 2nd ½	1998
Total	3,792	4,243	10,513	68,136	174,361	606,218
	100	100	100	100	100	100
Sub-total	7	651	3,694	177	120,329	539,529
Restructuring of Employment	0.2	15.3	35.1	0.3	69.0	89.0
-Subsidy for maintaining employment	4	611	2,636	-	118,865	483,943
(shutdown)	0.1	14.4	25.1	-	68.2	79.8
-Shortening of working hours.	-	8	21	1	-	3,774
-Training	-	0.2	0.2	0.0	-	0.6
-Dispatchment	-	10	300	101	942	35,171
	-	0.2	2.9	0.1	0.5	5.8
-Reallocation of manpower	-	12	78			
	-	0.3	0.7	-	120	702
-Leave	0	2	6		0.1	0.1
	0	0.0	0.1	-	148	345
					0.1	0.1
-Subsidy for promoting hiring	-	-	536			
	-	-	5.1	-	-	10,365
				-	-	1.7
	0	3	100			
-Subsidy for training for changing jobs	-	0.1	1.0	-	169	5,024
				-	0.1	0.8
	1	0	1			
-Subsidy for training for education to open new company	0.0	-	0.0	1	0	10
				-	-	-
	-	5	16	101	85	195
	-	0.1	0.2			
				0.1	-	-
Sub-total	3,723	3,592	6,819	68,034	54,032	66,689
Promoting employment	99.8	84.7	64.9	99.7	31.0	11.2
-Elderly	3,349	3,146	6,437	64,583	49,929	63,466
	89.8	74.1	61.2	94.7	28.6	10.7
- Re-hiring	3	55	49	4	112	178
	0.1	1.3	1.9	-	0.1	-
-Women	247	269	202	2,201	2,662	1,589
	6.6	6.3	1.2	3.2	1.5	0.3
-Childcare within company	125	122	131	1,246	1,329	1,456
	3.4	2.9	0.5	1.8	0.8	0.2

A researcher from the Korean Labor Institute (KLI) explained how the relative insulation of the research (and policy-generating) staff of the KLI allowed for a 'trail-and error' approach during this year of rapid expansion of the EIS. He mentioned the frequent adjustment of the subsidies as representing something of an embarrassment compared with Western more 'stable' approaches to social policy. However, it is also possible to see the capacity for adjustment within the EIS as a source of strength and flexibility of the Korean public bureaucracy that would ultimately benefit firms. Changes were not seen as the result of policy 'mistakes' for which someone had put his or her career on line, but as attempts at improvement. Face-saving manoeuvres did not become necessary when an aspect of policy was found not to work well, and this allowed for a more flexible approach towards developing policy. The capacity to act swiftly combined with efforts towards ongoing research and monitoring seemed to be a positive feature of this aspect of labour policy and institutional change. Obviously, a tendency to change policy frequently may be taken too far, but the case of the EIS employment stabilisation subsidies did not represent modifications of so great a magnitude that those adjustments in themselves deterred employers or entailed a credibility problem. The EIS employment subsidies suffered from under use in the view of some policymakers, but considering how new the system was, and how sudden the crisis, usage was not insignificant. The ratio of benefits to contributions in 1996 was higher for employment stabilisation measures than for either training or unemployment benefits. The usage of unemployment benefits shot up during the crisis (hardly surprising), but usage of both training and employment stabilisation subsidies rose markedly too.[64] Between 1998 and 1999 the use of paid leave schemes (by employers) within the overall population benefiting from EIS-funded training, rose from around one to six per cent.

The second feature of the EIS that needs to be highlighted is the system's public administration. This was a sine qua non for the kind of experimentation discussed, but it also made the effort to link unemployment benefits with employment services, including training, far easier compared with for example the Chilean experience. It also contributed to the adaptability of the system in terms of coverage, both numerically and in the inclusion of new groups, such as employees of small-sized firms. Coverage overall was increased from seven to 15 per cent of unemployed people between 1998 and 1999, as the requirements for receiving benefits were lowered, and as employees of firms of all sizes were gradually entered (Table 8.11). The structure of this expansion is very revealing. In 1998 the growth rate of new member firms exceeded 55 per cent for firms with less than five employees, compared with an average below 20 per cent. The rise in coverage was also fairly equally spread across sectors of economic activity. Manufacturing was in the lead

64   See Table 4 in the Appendix.

with a 24 per cent growth rate, but was closely followed by services at 23 per cent. It is well known that service activities are difficult to cover in terms of social insurance and different forms of employment protection. Hence this high rate of expansion in services speaks well for the system's capacity to adapt. Construction is another area that is notoriously difficult to protect. In this case, the rate of expansion was just over 12 per cent, higher than the hotel and tourism sector, and the financial or educational sectors. The EIS expansion was also well proportioned in terms of gender, and appeared to reflect the increase in female participation in the labour force which characterised the years prior to and especially after the crisis. Female office workers comprised the occupational group with the highest rate of growth, at 39 per cent *in one year.* Females in unskilled jobs also experienced notable growth, at 14 per cent, during 1998. Taking gender and age alone, women between the ages of 19 and 24 represented the highest growth category, at 30 per cent. In terms of education the middle tier increased the most, with high school graduates seeing by far the largest expansion in membership, at over 50 per cent, compared with ten per cent for middle school and university graduates.[65] In general, these figures provide an indication of the degree of penetration within the Korean labour market, at least within its formal segments, that the EIS was able to achieve.

Table 8.11: Expansion of the Eligibility of the Employment Insurance

	1 July 1995	1 January 1998	1 March 1998	1 July 1998	1 October 1998
Unemployment benefit scheme	30 and more workers	10 and more workers	5 and more workers	5 and more workers	1 and more workers
Employment stability and vocational training schemes	70 and more workers	50 and more workers	50 and more workers	5 and more workers	1 and more workers
No. of firms (thousands)	47	129	202	202	1,055
No. of workers (thousands)	4,280	5,785	6,257	6,257	8,586
Rate of eligibility among regular paid workers	35.3	47.9	51.8	51.8	71.0

Source: Ministry of Labor of Korea, internal material, and Ko Yong Bo Hôm Dong Hyang, Trends in Employment Insurance, *KLI*, vol. 4, no. 1 (1999), p. 13.

65   All figures are from the Minsitry of Labor (1999), pp. 16–20.

How can this be explained? In answering this question it is impossible to ignore the leading role played by the state. Indeed, it is difficult to see how the Korean state would have been able to attain the level of compliance achieved with the rapid extension of the compulsion to ensure employees, were Korean firms not already accustomed to state guidance in economic affairs. Despite the overall efforts to deregulate witnessed in Korea during the late 1990s, the Korean state in this instance had not only sustained but extended its proactive role in economic and social development. It is still far too early to say whether this fact would lead to an actual deepening of welfare services or a kind of new deal between the state and employers which would energise the development of human resources and extend occupational rights. Seen in a purely Korean context there was still a thin line between institutional innovation poised to develop a new more inclusive paradigm of welfare protection and merely relying on existing institutional capital to produce an effective but minimal safety net. As of 2001, there was a clear contention between the forces that wished to develop a comprehensive system of public social support within labour markets, led by segments of organised labour, voices in the ministries of labour and health and social welfare and in some ways Kim Dae Jung himself, and those who were concerned to contain the institutional ripple effects of the crisis, led by international institutions like the IMF and the core economic ministries concerned with public spending. Still, seen in an international context, the rapid expansion of the EIS, its comprehensive design and the state's exclusive role in its administration, set Korea apart from the worldwide trend towards private administration and de-linking of welfare domains. The composite nature of the EIS offered a solid set of building blocks towards the development of an employment system that combined aspects of flexibility of both the corporation and individual-based kind.

The institutional capital held by the state contained more than just a well-educated bureaucracy and a legacy of state intervention though the use of varied subsidies and investment support. The accepting attitude of employers towards the state also comprised an element of this institutional capital. Asked about the most favourable and unfavourable elements of labour policy, the top managers interviewed for this research, although critical of what they perceived as giving too much political airtime to trade unions, overwhelmingly regarded the EIS as the most positive feature of employment policy. Employers generally had no problem with the combination of private finance/public operation, in stark contrast with, for instance, the Chilean case, where entrepreneurs had come to demand and expect the opposite mix.[66] The attitude of the Korean side in this regard can be seen in a wider context in which employers valued the long-term

66   See Haagh (2002a), chapter 4 on Chilean entrepreneurs,

credit support for business characteristic of the 1970s higher than the process of financial deregulation experienced in stages since the late 1980s.[67] Coming back to the EIS, it is characteristic that neither of Korea's two national employer associations put up any notable opposition when the Kim Dae Jung government proposed in 1998 to raise employers' contributions to the EIS (the contributions of wage earners remaining frozen).

The direction in which the Korean EIS would develop, as noted, was not certain. One of the key tasks in the development of a more comprehensive welfare service consisted in establishing an effective nationwide system of employment relocation tied closely with labour associations and firms. Korea's public employment service in the late 1990s, although in a period of growth, was still weakly developed. Korea at this stage had 5,816 workers per job counsellor compared with 3,401 in Japan, 364 and 325 in Germany and Sweden, and 745 in the UK.[68] Vocational training and job placement services made up a very large share of spending on unemployment measures in Korea (Table 8.12). This particular structure is noteworthy in an international context where passive assistance has tended to dominate and governments struggle to shift the welfare paradigm towards a composition favouring job placement and training. However, it required a training and job placement infrastructure of much greater maturity and depth than that which Korea possessed. Quantitative changes were obviously required. Increasing the number of job centres was probably advisable in the longer term, particularly if this were to be done parallel with a process of deepening links with employer and labour organisations as well as training providers at local and regional levels.[69] However, a quantitative increase in employment offices, particularly if these were not well integrated with a similar expansion in the infrastructure of the ministries of health and social welfare and education, could not make up for failure to strengthen the links between different ministries, and between these and firms. Given the small size of Korea's welfare budget, and the small likelihood that it would be increased in future, a focus on qualitative changes — building better links with other programmes of social assistance, training providers and social actors, would make the most sense. At the local level

---

67 Of the employers interviewed, 75% made this choice.

68 Korean Labor Ministry, Memo, August 1998.

69 Labor Ministry officials were clearly hoping to expand their administrative power within the state apparatus through what was hoped would be a rapid increase in employment offices administered by this ministry as a result of the crisis. There was an ongoing struggle between the labour and social welfare ministries in the administration of unemployment measures, with the latter ministry in charge of the public works programme. This inter-ministerial conflict of interest would clearly have to be resolved if meaningful and efficient links between different employment related measures were to be found.

the administration of social policy was still divided, with labour policies run through the EIS and the Labour Ministry, and income assistance, public works and educational programmes conducted through the ministries of health and social welfare and education.

Table 8.12. Active and Passive Components in Spending on Unemployment in Korea, 1998*

Unemployment measures*	Budget	No. of persons covered (thousands)
Active measures	20,679	1,582
Vocational training and job placement services	9,011	363
Public works project	10,444	438
Subsidies to employment in the private sector	1,224	781
Passive measures	20,082	1,850+
Unemployment benefits	8,500	530
Loan schemes for the unemployed	7,500	70
Temporary livelihood protection and etc.	4,082	1,250+

* Public expenditures on indirect unemployment measures, such as job creation through social overhead capital (infrastructure) projects, were not included in the table. Nor were expenditures on regular livelihood protection programmes, whose main beneficiaries were frequently those without full working ability. Expenditures on both direct and indirect unemployment and social safety net measures totalled 10 trillion won in 1998.

Source: Funkoo Park and Lee Joohee, 'The Social Impact of the Financial Crisis: Labor Market Outcomes and Policy Responses in Korea,' unpublished paper (Korea Labor Institute, August 1999).

The success of the integration project as a source of enhancement of free individual movement would also depend on the separation of income assistance for people of working ability from the potential for family and extended family support. Meanwhile, the development of meaningful opportunities for movement would depend on the maturing of the training system and of the links of social actors with it. The future willingness of employers to engage more in joint financing and certification of skills would be of the essence. This would make the trade in skills more transparent and therefore empowering to its users. It would also make it easier to identify human resources needs, provide workers with adequate training or employment experiences and find them permanent jobs, or at least jobs that would offer prospects of a long-lasting association with labour markets. Several of the weaknesses in the EIS could not be narrowed down to faults in the public administration per se or even to the design of the system. It is a general mistake to see the success or failure of policy programmes or institutions like the EIS as resting simply on features internal to the state bureaucracy, in isolation from the social economy that such programmes are designed to support. Take the extension of the EIS subsidies towards usage by a more varied set of firms. The distribution of information to firms, especially smaller firms, required improvement,[70] but weaknesses in awareness of the subsidies could be attributed in large measure to the immaturity of social associations previously mentioned. Employer and labour associations alike had little organisational capacity in the area of social policy and, at least up to the end of the 1990s, were not assertive within this domain. Possibly this represented an area where the state would have been well advised to consider taking a proactive role in shaping the training system. In the late 1990s the attitude of policymakers (at least in the Labour Ministry) to the training system had taken on a nonchalant quality. Much was said about the usefulness of a 'demand-led' approach, meaning, for the most part, that leaving more decisions to be made by firms was 'good', a rather vague definition. In practice this would mean firms choosing from the largely unregulated market of private providers that grew from the late 1980s on, an approach which was unlikely to lead to more readily transferable skills, and whose unfortunate consequences have been felt elsewhere.[71]

Taking on a more proactive approach by the state could entail structuring some public subsidies for training deliberately towards jointly made plans between groups of firms and/or unions towards projects designed to build transferable skills. The Labour Ministry had taken some measures to involve various civic groups, including representatives of unions and employer associations, in the administration of the EIS. For instance, in early 1999 committees designed to oversee the quality of training provided were established in some employment stability centres.[72] At the same

---

70   The practical difficulty of incorporating small firms is reflected in the difference between the share of wage earners covered (46% in mid-1999, Park, 2001, p. 56) and the ratio of these to total working population, at just under 30%.

71   As discussed for Chile in Haagh (1999).

72   The author visited one of the more successful of the centres, the centre at Kangnam, in Seoul, where this committee had already met a couple of times.

time, little importance seemed to be attached to the role played by unions and employer associations (although these were represented) relative to the opinions of experts on these committees.[73] One of the standard criticisms of the training provided through the EIS was that re-employment rates were rather weak, at under 15 per cent.[74] One of the possible reasons is that employment expansion in these years occurred mainly within smaller firms, which did not require new skills, but the factors of poor training courses and lack of matching also cannot be ignored. The employment stability centres were forced to rely on new private training institutions. These did not belong to a wider network, and prospective participants found themselves having to choose within a narrow range of what was available locally. This writer found that in some large areas of Seoul no more than six or seven (often similar) course types were on hand. More than that, no prior process existed through which employers had an input into defining training needs. Typically, the courses on offer through the EIS had no tie whatsoever with local employers. In contrast, courses (these were few) offered through the EIS at KOMA (the old state-owned training institution) had re-employment rates of over 80 per cent. The currency of the skills formed there had a historical grounding in labour markets.

In summary, an important downside of labour policy in the late 1990s was the lack of awareness of the importance of social associations in the policy process. At the same time, weaknesses in the social economy of firms and labour institutions hardly detract from the superior core design of the EIS seen in an international context where countries with longer experiences of welfare provision were at the time of the system's founding still struggling to establish an administrative unit through which to link measures of employment stabilisation, social assistance and training.

Conclusion

The behaviour of Korea's labour market in the context of the economic crisis holds surprises both in relation to the debate about the Korean economy and as regards the general analysis of labour markets. Since the late 1980s, at least, Korean employers had called for a greater flexibilisation of labour markets, based essentially on increased prerogatives for firms in terms of hiring and firing and a lowering of union monopoly power. With

73   Interview with the director of Kangnam Employment Stability Centre, Lee Myung Rae, September 1999.

74   For those with high-school diplomas, or university degrees, those under 30 and previously in standard employment, the rates compared with non-participants were best (Kang and Lee, 2001, pp. 251, 258). Kang and Lee's survey was not based on random sampling but discrete selection from cases, and hence is not an ideal representation. A good survey of training and human resource management after the crisis is still lacking.

the combined effect of the legal changes of spring 1997 (fully implemented in 1998) and the economic shock later that year it was thought that a more market-rational mode of operation in labour relations would finally transpire. Indeed, it is difficult to imagine a more forceful inducement to raising corporations' free hand over labour than the coincidence of path-breaking labour code reform and a virtual national economic collapse in the span of less than a year. In theory, this shock and the sustained period of corporate adjustment that followed should break down existing modes of social interaction, establish a more economic–rational modus operandi and help equalise the competition between job seekers as more people would have the incentive to take up available work.

There is no question that significant reverberations were felt within Korea's labour market as a result of the crisis, but the review above raises questions about how far the logic in labour relations in Korea had changed and even to what extent labour market flexibility grew. When Korean employers wished to dismiss employees in the wake of the crisis, they did not use the new dismissal laws, but the more personalised mode of reducing the labour force known from the past. Or, at least, we know that this is the case for larger firms. In an environment where corporate adjustment could not rest solely on internal flexibility measures, these other forms of dismissal offered perhaps the best possible economic protection for employees. However, this timid and semi-protective way of workforce adjustment does not support the expectation of what would happen in the Korean labour market, or indeed any labour market, following neoclassical theory, in response to extensive opportunities for legal and economic liberalisation. Instead, the trade-offs between social and political liberties and economic protection that had characterised labour relations in the preceding period reproduced themselves in a modified form. The socio-personal costs of discrete dismissal were traded for the relatively generous bonus or retirement packages that such dismissals implied. The Korean case offers solid verification of the thesis that labour markets are embedded in social relations.

However, does the greater level of involuntary unemployment, and hence the increased competition for available jobs, not imply that the Korean labour market became more flexible during the crisis? The answer to this question would have to be mixed. Yes, it is true that new forms of employment that implied less long-term responsibilities for firms for their employees were developed. For instance, larger firms in the first years of the crisis relied more heavily on new forms of recruitment, like the method of 'internship', where young college graduates have roughly a 50 per cent chance of continued employment, compared with the virtual certainty of a long-term career of the past. The use of part-timers in other forms — say through the newly legalised employment agencies — also increased. However, the expectation of a greater equalisation of job seekers' conditions was overstated. It is highly unclear how far the great divide between Korea's two job markets was overcome as a result of the crisis. As we saw Korea had before the crisis one of the highest rates of irregular to regular work in the OECD, similar to Turkey's and much lower than Mexico's. Changes in the composition of regular versus irregular work were not as great as one would expect as a result of the crisis (a change of four percentage points).[75] However, the removal of the sources of social and economic support that had sustained a high rate of voluntary mobility and low unemployment in the period before the crisis made the high level of irregular work a greater source of inflexibility in the employment system for both employers and workers.

In addition, we saw that employees dismissed from larger firms typically received high severance payments of one form or another. Workers in smaller firms did not receive such benefits and were less likely to be insured in the EIS. Even those that paid up were less likely to receive benefits compared to employees of larger firms, as Appendix Table 4 shows. Moreover, at the time of the crisis the percentage of workers receiving in-firm training in large companies towered over that of smaller firms by a factor of more than ten.[76] As skill endowments became more significant in the competition for jobs, this skill division between job seekers in Korea's two labour markets almost certainly rose. It is also likely that the firm-specific nature of training helped to consolidate an informal market in skills amongst larger firms. This supposition is supported by data which shows that the gap between average wages of employees in larger firms relative to average wages of employees in small firms began to rise again between 1997 and 1999, following a period of stability since the late 1980s.[77] The crisis only served to increase the exclusion from this informal setting of employees of smaller firms.

But the crisis did not serve the flexibility needs of corporations either. The skills endowments of certain employees placed these in a strong bargaining position, whereas the lack of a more transparent and larger market in tradable skills left employers with a smaller pool of skilled labour to choose from. The intern system also was found not to serve corporations well. The best college graduates avoided the system, realising it did not offer the prospects they expected, and so again the dualised skill structure in labour markets left employers with limited choice.[78] At the same time fewer workers were able to compete in an environment that was likely to

75   Here I differ somewhat from the interpretation by Martin and Torres (2001).

76   Martin and Torres (2001), p. 368.

77   The wage gap increased from a factor of 1.38 to a factor of 1.47 between 1997 and 1999, up from 1.35 in 1989, and 1.12 in 1985 (*ibid.*, p. 369).

78   Interviews with interns in the LG group, with executive director of the Human Resources Division at LG, and with Lee Dong Eung, director for Labour Relations Affairs in the Korean Employers' Federation (KEF).

lead to improved working conditions. Korean labour markets prior to the crisis were already rather flexible on the counts usually employed to measure the movement of labour, such as job tenure. But job tenure alone is a poor flexibility measure.[79] What matters for agents in labour markets is that optimal choices are made when quits and job matching occur. The factors that optimise choices include predictable lines of behaviour and good information. The crisis diminished the first and did not improve on the second in the case of Korea.

The circumstances that helped to equalise conditions between job seekers during the crisis were not markets in this instance, but the activities of a proactive state seeking to increase the inclusion of more workers within a system of employment insurance, work information and skills endowment post-schooling. These measures represented perhaps the greatest inducement to increasing the flexibility of labour markets, by establishing a more level playing field for individuals dependent on income from work. The idea of the 'smart card' put forward by young and enthusiastic Korean policymakers shows the inventiveness and zest for improvement of the public infrastructure in Korea at the time.[80] The proposed smart card would hold employment information for each individual, and employers of all kinds (including employers of daily workers) would be compelled to register wage and employment information on it. Employees could also use the card to access training and social services, by making the cards and the information on them linked to a national computerised employment information system.

At the same time it is fairly clear that the EIS and prospective measures like the smart card by the state would remain incomplete without a more comprehensive institutional shift in Korea's employment system. If Korean employers were to increase their prerogatives in dismissals (increasing the involuntary component in quits), and if this was to happen without great costs to the development of human resources, more rational negotiation procedures and more sophisticated and varied certification of skills and work experiences would have to be found. This is not a job the state alone can take on. Even the 'smart card' idea only provides the

---

79   Average tenure in Denmark, for instance, is similar to that of the United States and Korea, but the nature of flexibility differs greatly between these economies. In Denmark, labour mobility is more secure and led by the individual, and compatible with a more equal skill structure, leaving both firms and workers with better options. See Haagh (2001) for a more detailed argument.

80   The usual definition of a policymaker as an elected parliamentarian does not fit well here. Researchers within the Labour Ministry, including the KLI (as in the case of the employment stabilisation and promotion subsidies), and the different ministerial bureaus, play a key role in the formation of policy. For the smart card idea, see Hur (2001). Hur was at the time a researcher at the KLI.

essential infrastructure, a blank spreadsheet, as it were. Of course the importance of such a spreadsheet cannot be underestimated in an economy where the great majority of workers work in non-standard jobs and where, even after the extension of compulsory coverage of the EIS to firms with *one* employee, only 46 per cent of wage workers are deemed to be covered. Providing an employment information record of each individual worker certainly would be a revolutionary task. It would form the basis for a form of accounting of not only the ad hoc employment situation of both regular, irregular, unpaid and self-employed workers, but also of the *work histories* of these individuals. Still, without extensive and systematic involvement of employers and labour institutions even this revolutionary idea would remain just that, an idea, not a functional feature of the employment system at large. Only the users of human resources would be able to identify meaningful criteria for certification of skills and only the carriers of skills would be able to identify meaningful links between job situations. Ironically, the greatest moment of economic liberalisation witnessed in modern Korean history also represented the greatest challenge hitherto to a democratisation of labour relations and reaffirmed the continued relevance of a proactive state.

Appendix

Table A8.1: Changes in Labour Law in Korea

Date	Legal act	Amendments
November 1987	Labour Standards Act	• Reduction of working hours/abolition of the system of flexible work hours.
		• Priority given to wage payments in cases of bankruptcy (last three months' wages).
	Trade Union Act	• Lessening of restrictions on the formation of unions (depending on number of employees wishing to form one).
		• Ban on multiple unions
		• Reduction of the 'cooling-off' period.
		• Creation of a system of arbitration.
March 1989	Labour Standards Act	• Priority given to wage payments in cases of bankruptcy (industrial accident compensation and retirement pay).
March 1997	Labour Standards Act	• Greater flexibility in the system of working hours.
		• Facilitation of 'part-time' work.
		• Introduction of lay-offs in cases of urgent business reasons.
	Trade Union and Labour Relations Adjustment Act	• Prohibition on payment (by employers) of full-time union officials.
		• Legalisation of multiple trade unions (with immediate effect for sectoral or national unions, with enterprise unions starting from 2002).
		• Elimination of ban on unions' political activities.
		• Elimination of ban on third party intervention.
		• Removal of ceiling on union membership dues.
		• Establishment of a system of mediation.
	Act for the Promotion of Worker Participation and Cooperation	• Changes of rules to elect the Councils.
		• Expansion of matters under consideration by Labor Management Councils.
	Labour Relations Commission Act	• Strengthening the status of the Labour Relations Commission.

Table A8.2: Agreements Reached in the Social Contract to Overcome the Economic Crisis of 9 February 1998*

Area of agreement		Nature of agreement
Basic labour rights		• The unemployed can retain membership of the multi-firm union.
		• Political activities of trade unions will be legalised from 1998.
		• Public sector workers will be allowed to form unions at workplace level from January 1999, and teachers will be allowed to form trade unions from July 1998 (legalising the existing teachers' union).
		• The period of notice to terminate the collective Agreement is raised from three to six months.
Expansion of corporation-centred flexibility.**	Facilitation of temporary work	• Inclusive system for high-skill occupations.
		• Selective system for low-skill occupations
	Easing of rules on lay-offs	• Dismissals for managerial reasons agreed in cases of urgent business problems (take-overs, mergers and acquisitions included).
		• Management must give workers 60 days' notice and consult with them in good faith about alternatives to dismissals (internal restructuring) as well as about the selection of those to be dismissed.
		• Management should make attempts to recall the workers who have been dismissed when hiring again.
		• Management must make an advance report to the Ministry of Labour. [Question: are these more detailed specifications of the March 1997 law or
Expansion of individual-centred flexibility.		A commitment was made to devote more resources to unemployment measures.

* The Tripartite Commission in which the social pact was made was set up on 15 January 1998. The agreement of 9 February was based on the 'Grand Compromise' reached in the Commission on 6 February.

** Corporation-centred flexibility covers the facilities given to management to make changes to labour use. Individual-centred flexibility encompasses measures that ease individual's ability to move and choose in labour and occupational markets. It is therefore an important component of occupational citizenship. See Haagh (2000a) for a discussion of corporation- versus individual-centred labour flexibility.

Figure A8.1: Monthly Separation Rates across Occupation and Firm Size

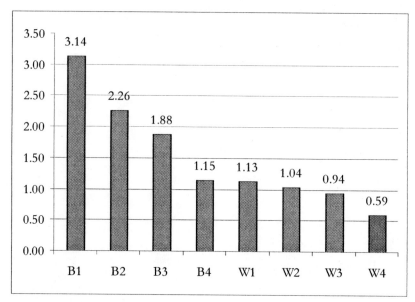

Notes: B = blue collar; W = white collar
Size: 1 = 0–99; 2= 100–299; 3= 300–499; 5 = 500+
Source: You (1997)

Table A8.3: Contributions to and Benefits from the EIS, by Firm Size (1998)

Firm size – No. of employees.	Distribution of benefits	Distribution of contributions	Benefits over contributions
5 or less	0.02	1.1	1.9
5-9	0.6	2.2	4.1
10-29	2.7	6.1	11.2
30-49	2.5	4.0	7.3
50-69	3.3	4.3	76.5
70-99	5.1	5.7	89.5
100-299	19.7	18.4	107.2
300-499	10.1	8.2	122.7
500-999	9.7	10.4	93.3
1,000 and over	46.3	35.7	129.8
Kônsôlkongsa	0.02	4.0	0.5

Source: Ko Yong Bo Hôm Dong Hyang (Trends in Employment Insurance), Korean Labor Ministry (Spring 1999), p. 45

CHAPTER 9

Patterns of Government–Business Relations in South Korea and the Impact of the Recent Crisis

Tat Yan Kong

Evolution of Government-Business Relations 1980–97

Traditional accounts of the cohesive government–business[1] relationship (or Korea Inc.) underpinning Korean economic development have emphasised the following characteristics of interaction:

1. Government economic support for those businesses which advanced national priorities such as exports and strategic industries.

2. Prioritisation by government of its tight relationship with business over other types of societal claim (notably redistribution and the extension of democracy).

3. Convergence of views of top governmental and business leaders on the key issues such as economic policy and the framework of political contestation.

4. Business financial support exclusively for the ruling party and its candidates.

By the time of the 1997 crisis the traditional picture of government–business cohesion had been subject to modification for over a decade. First, the 'targeted subsidy' that had been the cornerstone of government support for business was scaled down after 1985 in the light of policy setbacks (notably the mixed results of the heavy industrial targeting) and liberal international trade rules. Second, under democratisation, government favouritism had to be balanced against the claims of other previously excluded social constituencies. This was manifested in concessions to labour, a shift towards redistributional policies and the official repudiation of the illicit exchange of favours. Third, the traditional convergence of views between government and business was loosened by differences over the pace of economic liberalisation, especially of the financial sector. Recovered from the crisis of the early 1980s and increasingly capable of

---

1   By business, I refer to the top 64 business groups or *chaebol.*

standing by itself, business campaigned vigorously for liberalisation, ironically on the basis of free market arguments. Similar free market and associated 'rule of law' type arguments were deployed by business in opposition to the extension of labour rights and distributional measures. Fourth, democratisation and the concentration of private economic power weakened the dependence of business on the ruling party. Business support for the ruling party, though maintained after democratisation, became more conditional and was no longer exclusive. The weakening of the alliance between the governing party and business was manifested in a number of ways, notably, in open criticism of the government, direct participation in electoral politics, financial support to other parties and the cultivation of personal connections with influential government officials to compensate for the dilution of the state's pro-business orientation.

The government–business relationship changed from being a facilitator to obstacle of economic development during the democratic decade. There were two main aspects to the problem, both related to the weakening of the state's disciplinary powers over business. First, economic restructuring required the constitution of a new developmentalist alliance between state, business and labour. Accustomed to having a fierce anti-labour state on its side, business opposed the inclusion of labour (such as the extension of labour's legal status) and behaved in socially irresponsible ways (such as bribery and land speculation) that magnified labour distrust. The state's limited overtures to the labour movement could not overcome the legacy of confrontation. As a result, policies needed to restore competitiveness to Korea's 'high cost, low efficiency' economy of the 1990s were not implemented. Quite simply it was impossible to get labour and business to apportion responsibility for the 'high costs' of land, borrowing, wages and distribution that dragged down competitiveness. Each insisted the other reform first.

Second, organised labour's complaint about the role of business in the decline of competitiveness was not unfounded. Under two democratic governments between 1988 and 1998 the old pattern of government–business relations had deteriorated to an unsatisfactory halfway house. The state was incapable of enforcing strict performance criteria on the business sector as in the past. At the same time, however, its residual economic powers made it an attractive target for business lobbying. The lessening of the state's pro-business orientation made the securing of friendly consideration by individual officials wielding discretionary power all the more valuable to business. Instead of investing in productivity growth, conglomerates concentrated on speculative activities (notably land and financial activities) and on lobbying for government projects (such as construction) that promised easy profits.

The Asian financial crisis that engulfed Korea in November 1997 put government–business collusion under the international spotlight and intensified the pressure for reform. Previously hailed as the backbone of economic success,[2] government–business cohesion was now blamed for encouraging reckless foreign lending to Korea by lulling investors into a false sense of security. Once said to be 'reciprocal' for the strict performance conditions on which business received governmental favour,[3] Korea's government–business relationship was now said to be 'cronyistic' in a pattern similar to say that of the Philippines or Indonesia. Distancing itself from its previous approval for the conduct of economic policy in Asia, the IMF blamed the incompleteness of liberalisation within an inadequate legal framework.[4] Others attributed the rise of cronyism from 1993 to the practice of intensive business lobbying in an environment where the government had abandoned responsibility for industrial coordination.[5] Both explanations, in fact, highlighted differing aspects of the same problem, namely, that with its capacity to discipline business diminished, the state, by not removing the economic safety net, had also insulated business from the discipline of the market.

The difficulties of reforming the pattern of tight government-business relations stretched back almost two decades. The excesses of the heavy industrialisation programme of the 1970s demonstrated the drawbacks (such as serious over-capacity, monopolisation, underdeveloped small and medium industry) of the old pattern of government–business collusion. Reforms (such as reduced subsidies, partial trade and financial liberalisation, anti-monopoly measures and anti-corruption measures) aimed at weaning the top business groups off government dependence had been implemented by all regimes, authoritarian and democratic, since 1981. Between 1980 and 1997, reforms would follow a typical sequence: some economic blip (slowdowns in 1980 and 1989, external indebtedness in 1985) would trigger government initiatives for reform backed by strong public endorsement; the restoration of growth takes priority and the government finds itself relying on those very big business entities it had hoped to reform; subsequent recovery would then dissipate the enthusiasm for reform. The realisation of the interdependence between growth, political survival and maintaining friendly relations with business similarly dissipated politically driven initiatives for the reform of government–business relations. For example, presidents Chun, Roh and Kim Young-Sam all tried to establish reputations for 'clean government' at the start of their terms

2   The World Bank (1993), pp. 81–7.
3   Amsden (1989).
4   International Monetary Fund (IMF— 2000), pp. 5–6.
5   Chang (1998), pp. 226–9.

of office but eventually all found they had too much to lose from disconnecting collusive links with business.

The summary above indicates that while there were compelling arguments for the overhaul of the system of government–business relations, previous reform efforts have stalled owing to the structural interdependence between business, growth and political survival. The 1997 crisis appeared to have introduced some new factors that were favourable to reform. It was the deepest economic crisis since 1958 and the state of the business sector suggested that it would not be capable of growing its way out of crisis in the old pattern without some major reforms. Economic freefall and the low credibility of the business and governmental elites discredited the old way of doing things and encouraged the public to consider difficult reforms. The political conditions for reform were altered by the victory of Kim Dae-Jung in the presidential election of December 1997, the first ever peaceful power transition. Long identified with the causes of fairer distribution and democracy, Kim (or DJ as he is commonly known) was also noted for his belief in stronger market coordination of the economy in place of government–business collusion. That outlook appeared consistent with the conditionalities mapped out for Korea under the IMF's rescue package of 3 December 1997.

This chapter will analyse the changing pattern of government–business relations during the past three years of crisis and uncertain recovery from the following perspectives: How have government and business perceptions of their relationship changed in recent times? What are the distinguishing features of the current government's policies towards business reform? What obstacles have been encountered in the course of reform? And what is the political environment in which government–business relations exist?

Government and Business Perceptions of their Relationship

The history of the interdependence between governmental and business elites dates back to the 1940s, when the two were drawn together by the illegitimacy which they shared owing to their past colonial associations. In the period of US-financed reconstruction and basic shortages of the 1950s, the connection with the political establishment provided easy pickings for officially connected businessmen. In return for access to officially rationed US aid dollars, these 'political capitalists' gave donations to President Syngman Rhee's Liberal Party.[6] From 1961 the military-dominated regime based its legitimacy on economic modernisation as defined by GNP and export growth. In return for export achievement and for

6   Kim (1976).

undertaking ambitious projects, business was handsomely rewarded, and many of the old malpractices (including domestic monopolisation, land speculation and corruption) were allowed to persist. Under the military's 'guided capitalism', the top business groups enjoyed greater expansion opportunities than they did under Rhee or some alternative free market arrangement (as was originally favoured by US advisers). This more than compensated for the loss of economic autonomy[7] and the payment of political levies to President Park and his Democratic Republican Party.

The outlooks of business and government became even more closely entwined from 1972 when the Park regime entered its hard authoritarian Yushin phase. This period brought the most rapid business expansion and consolidated the pre-eminence of the top *chaebol* groups. The ambitious projects born of economic nationalism enabled business to gain niches in the heavy industrial sectors it could not have entered on the basis of its own resources. The regime's economic nationalism did not impede business' access to international finance and technology. Quite the reverse, the state's gatekeeping enabled business access to the foreign sector on highly favourable terms (that is, without having to concede local ownership or market share to TNCs). Business simply had to follow the government's lead in order to prosper. The articulation of separate business viewpoints on economic and political matters was neither necessary nor advisable. Business ambitions were comfortably accommodated within the regime's ideology of national development.

While it can be safely assumed that business supported the anti-labour crackdown following the 1980 military coup, the early 1980s also marked the beginnings of the divergence of government and business perspectives. There was a perception that the Chun regime, unlike its predecessor, was insufficiently sensitive to business interests. This was reflected in the official turn towards economic liberalisation when business was highly insecure in the aftermath of the 1980 downturn. For the first time in two decades, the state was not explicitly committed to the expansionary economics from which business had reaped enormous benefits. Business was wary of the consequences of reduced subsidies and intensified competition that was explicit in Chun's liberalisation programme. That President Chun was more receptive to the opinions of US-trained economic advisers than to those of industrialists with practical experience seemed to be another manifestation of his government's detachment from business concerns (by contrast, President Park was personally highly attentive to the views of top industrialists).

7   In 1961 the military regime organised the leading business groups into the Association of Korean Business, which later became the Federation of Korean Industries.

The government's commitment to scaling down support for business led industrialists to question the utility of political–economic exchanges. The donations they were being forced to give to maintain Chun's political machine, the Democratic Justice Party, cut into very slim profit margins and brought few tangible benefits in return,[8] while massive amounts of funds were evidently being siphoned off by the president's entourage. Such behaviour further exacerbated Chun's legitimacy problem (he was the instigator of a bloody coup). The dissolution in 1985 of Kukje, the country's eighth largest business group, was allegedly triggered by the group owner's refusal to make political donations. The alienation of the Hyundai group founder Chung Ju-Yung from Chun and his successors also dates from this time. Working with pro-interventionist bureaucrats, business waged a lobbying campaign against liberalisation (with dire threats of a return to recession) during the early 1980s. As it turned out, government support was scaled down very slowly while the top business groups became the main beneficiaries of the partial liberalisation. But the experience of the early 1980s was a turning point in business perceptions of the state as a benevolent protector.

Policy differences between government and business became open in the aftermath of democratisation. As before, economic liberalisation was the main point of contention. The roles, however, were now reversed. Recovered from the 1980 crisis and sensing massive opportunity (primarily from control of financial institutions and from direct access to international capital markets), business now demanded swifter liberalisation. By contrast, having seen the problem of economic concentration exacerbated by the partial liberalisation of the early 1980s (and the ineffectiveness of anti-monopoly measures), government maintained its cautious approach. Even the Kim Young-Sam government (1993–98) with its guiding slogan of 'globalisation' (commonly understood to mean the completion of economic liberalisation and democratisation) pursued a balanced approach of gradual liberalisation with economic deconcentration measures. As a mark of growing sophistication, the business campaign for speedier liberalisation drew its intellectual rationale from the concepts of neoclassical political economy. Ironically, business, for decades the principal beneficiary of state patronage, was now arguing for the operation of a free market undistorted by political-economic collusion. By contrast, government seemed more favourably disposed to a Japanese 'model' of advanced capitalism. From being united behind economic nationalism, government and business now articulated competing versions of economic internationalism.

The balancing of economic liberalisation with deconcentration measures also reflected a changing official perspective on business. The Chun

8   Woo (1991), p. 199.

regime (1980–87) had already explicitly recognised the negative efficiency and distributional implications of economic concentration but did little to correct those imbalances. Under electoral pressure, democratic governments had to be seen to be taking pro-active measures against economic concentration and social maldistribution and to be recognising the claims of the previously excluded labour movement. Such anti-business populism could be seen in the campaigns against land concentration in 1989 (Public Concept in Land) and against corruption in 1993 and in the attempts to bring labour into some form of tripartite body from 1988. The internal conflict within government over the nature of business power was reflected in the divergent views between key agencies (for example, the Fair Trade Commission and the Korea Development Institute) but the direction was clear, the dual alliance of state and business would have to give way to an accommodation of wider social interests.

Democratisation had a politicising impact on the business sector, which moved from political quiescence under authoritarianism to active electioneering by 1992. For business, democratisation meant having to adopt a more proactive attitude to fostering beneficial relations with the state. Business could no longer rely on a benevolent state whose support was guaranteed on the basis attaining performance targets and regular donations to the ruling party. In the less favourable policy environment, business had to seek special relationships with sections of the state that were sympathetic or which could be bought. In other words, the alliance of state and business became fragmented into alliances of *chaebol* groups and their allies inside the state. These particularistic relationships were reinforced by ties of marriage between business and state elites. There were other reasons why democratisation should have made business more politicised. Competitive politics allowed business to make choices about which party or individual to support while elections increased the political sector's demand for campaign funds. Business discontent could now be articulated openly. The decision by the founder of the Hyundai group to run as a candidate in the 1992 presidential contest (he garnered a respectable 16 per cent of the votes cast) was the most extreme manifestation of business politicisation.

On his inauguration in February 1998, President Kim Dae-Jung (DJ) pledged to transform Korean economic and political life according to his blueprint of 'democratic market economy'. Claiming that his election as the candidate of the opposition party in December 1997 represented Korea's first real democratic transfer of power, President Kim announced his intention of completing the dual transition of democratisation and economic liberalisation. This did not seem very different from the previous government's 'globalisation' policy. On the other hand, DJ was more internationalised than his predecessor from his long stints abroad (in exile and by choice). He had long established a favourable image abroad for his opposition to dictatorship. According to Bruce Cumings, DJ's idealistic notions about market economy (see below) made him 'the IMF's man in Seoul'.[9] DJ certainly saw himself as more profound than a professional politician. To domestic opponents, he was something of a demagogue.

In his opposition to military authoritarianism, Kim came to be identified with populism. Kim's 'populism', however, was quite distinct from the traditional quasi-authoritarian, statist types commonly associated with Latin America in the 1940s and 1950s. He rejected the growth versus democracy trade-off that was used to justify the authoritarian developmental state of the 1970s and 1980s. Kim argued that the high growth rates were being achieved at the cost of serious market and social distortions such as business concentration, underdevelopment of small business, corruption, skewed distribution and alienated labour force. Such distortions, he argued would impair Korea's long-term growth potential. In his view, the authoritarian political system would sap the competitive dynamism of the capitalist system itself and reduce national welfare. This was because market discipline could not function properly in the absence of democratic accountability. The material and ideological gap between the bureaucratic–capitalist elites and the rest of society would also widen in the absence of accountability. In placing much of the blame for Korea's economic woes on the absence of accountability of government-business relations, the president's analysis of the 1997 crisis had parallels to the IMF's 'cronyism' diagnosis.[10]

Restructuring of Government–Business Relations

Despite safeguards (such as the strengthening of anti-monopoly measures) partial economic liberalisation under the authoritarian regime coincided with the worsening of economic concentration. The experience of economic reform under the authoritarian regime in the 1980s showed that, if liberalising reforms were to be successful, they needed to be reinforced by measures of a political kind (that opened up the lobbying activities and other anti-competitive activities of the business groups to scrutiny). The need to restructure government–business relations was all the more necessary given the democratic governments' commitment to accelerated liberalisation. The prospective gains from liberalisation (that is, from the privatisation of public monopolies) created powerful incentives for business to try to influence the process by means legal or otherwise. Democracy provided the popular mandate for transparency and other far-reaching measures to be implemented. It gave rise to popular demands for fairer

9   Cumings (1998), p. 60.
10   Kim (1985, 1999).

distribution and criticism of the malpractices stemming from government patronage of the business sector. The crisis of 1997 reinforced this with an international mandate from the IMF but the post-1997 experience reveals the business groups' capacity for resistance even under the most unfavourable of circumstances. This section will examine the restructuring of government–business relations with reference to the measures implemented to make that relationship more consistent with competitiveness and public perceptions of honesty. The status of the government–business relationship vis-à-vis other societal forces (especially labour) will be considered in the next section.

There were aspects of continuity in the measures tried by the two governments of the first democratic decade with their authoritarian predecessors. Like their authoritarian predecessors, the two democratic governments after 1987 both began with a strong sense of financial propriety. Both presidents Roh Tae-Woo and Kim Young-Sam declared at the beginning of their terms of office that they would not receive any money from business. While the Roh government was noted for its switch away from labour repression and for the adoption of redistributional policies (in the form of social welfare and housing development), its term of office coincided with the saturation of the political process by business money. Election campaigns were characterised by massive expenditures. The Suso land development scandal of 1990 showed the ease with which business groups could circumvent regulations (in this instance forbidding the development of land on the greenbelt of Seoul) by using corruption. It also demonstrated the limitations of the anti-land accumulation campaign (Public Concept in Land) launched in 1989 in response to public unease over the spiralling land price. (Similar measures for forcing the leading business groups to divest land had failed at the beginning of the 1980s.) As for President Roh's own integrity, the marriage connection between the first family and that of the owner of the Sunkyong business group was accompanied by the ascent of that group to become the fifth largest business group in Korea.

The Kim Young-Sam government also began with bright hopes. Soon after his inauguration in 1993, the president launched a vigorous anti-corruption campaign which led to the dismissal of several top bureaucrats and ruling party functionaries. This was followed by other significant measures. Passed in August 1993, the long awaited real name reform prohibited the holding of bank accounts under assumed names, a practice long synonymous with corruption and tax evasion. This measure would later lead to the exposure of the slush funds extracted from business and held by former presidents Chun and Roh (ironically Kim Young-Sam himself fell under suspicion as being the chief beneficiary of those funds, amounts of which filtered through to other political bosses as well). A law placing limits on electoral campaign expenditure of US$112,000 per candidate was also passed in 1993 but was flawed by the absence of limits on the amount that the party headquarters could spend on the candidate's behalf. Not surprisingly, it did not prevent the irregularities that were alleged to have marked the April 1996 national assembly election (in which it was widely believed that candidates spending under two billion won [c. US$2.5 million] would be defeated).[11] Concern about economic concentration led to the enactment of stricter anti-monopoly measures but no measures were taken to reform the internal authority structures of the business groups (despite there being much academic debate about the future evolution of the groups and their appropriate form of 'corporate governance').

By mid-term, the limits of the Kim Young-Sam government's measures were evident as corruption scandals involving senior figures erupted. In 1997, the problem went to the very top of the government with the disclosure of the connection between President Kim's son and the boss of the bankrupt Hanbo conglomerate. The controversy centred on the first family member's use of his influence with senior bank officials to secure $6 billion worth of credit for a steel plant of dubious commercial merit. The staggering amount obtained by Hanbo, a second tier conglomerate, was a pointer to the ability of business groups to secure favourable treatment by illicit means. Another was the problem of 'financial tech', the lucrative activity whereby the conglomerates manipulated the rapidly growing financial sector. The sharp deterioration of the economy in the last year of the government coincided with the bankruptcy of a number of second and third tier *chaebol* groups. It highlighted the ease with which the *chaebol* could circumvent checks on unsound borrowing. Then the financial crisis of November 1997 brought this problem to international attention under the label of 'cronyism'.

In a nutshell, the IMF's diagnosis of the Korean crisis was that the existence of collusive or cronyistic relationships between government and business distorted financial markets. The apparent signal that loans were in effect being bankrolled by the Korean government lowered foreign investors' perceptions of risk and encouraged them to lend recklessly. As the condition of financial rescue, the IMF called on the Korean government to complete liberalisation and to introduce safeguards against abuse of the liberalisation process that had done so much to bring about the crisis. These conditionalities were fully accepted by the Korean reformers and used to build up the domestic momentum for restructuring.[12]

There were parallels between the IMF's and Kim Dae-Jung's visions of Korean capitalism's future. Under DJ's 'democratic market economy' blue-

11   Koh (1997), pp. 1-9.
12   Mathews (1998).

print, the centralised and highly collusive capitalism of the Korea Inc. type would have to give way to a more market-coordinated and accountable form of capitalism. Capable of standing by itself within a proper regulatory framework, Korean capitalism would have less need and less opportunity to enter into illicit collusion with politicians and other public officials (a German NGO had listed Korea as the second most corrupt of 19 leading export nations).[13] The dominance of the major business groups would be offset by competition from smaller groups, small and medium enterprises, and crucially, TNCs. In the political realm, more space would be opened up to progressive and reform minded forces to hold the economic elites responsible. In effect, a form of economic pluralism would prevail. The condition of economic freefall favoured reform since the business sector no longer had recourse to the traditional argument that growth would be endangered. There was strong public expectation that the root causes of the crisis (widely perceived to be the failings of the business and governing elite) be permanently eradicated. The huge amounts of public cash being injected into the financial system (to rescue the troubled banks that had lent heavily to the business groups) was another factor strengthening the hand of the reformers.

The new government announced a series of restructuring measures based on five principles of corporate reorganisation: enhanced transparency in corporate governance; elimination of cross-loan guarantees; improved financial structures; concentration on core businesses; and tougher legal responsibility for management.[14] These measures were tantamount to a complete overhaul of the internal workings of the business groups and their relationship with the state. The new emphasis on financial discipline and propriety was reinforced by the institutional changes. A new financial watchdog, the Financial Supervisory Commission, was created in April 1998. To combat the problem of official corruption, the new government also planned to introduce an agency modelled on Hong Kong's effective Independent Commission Against Corruption.[15]

The course of reform since 1998 appears to be consistent with previous attempts to overhaul the government–business relationship, that is, ambitious (re)declarations of intent, but very slow progress in the face of resistance from the leading business groups and resort to panic measures by the state. This is evident from a review of the extent of reform in accordance with corporate transparency and concentration of business groups on their core competencies, two key principles of corporate reorganisation specified above.

13   China was ranked as the most corrupt. See Transparency International, *1999 Bribe Payers Index*, www.transparency.de.
14   See Jang (1999), pp. 14–19.
15   Lee (1999).

Despite almost four decades of growth, the corporate structure of the Korean business groups had hardly changed. At the end of the twentieth century that structure continued to resemble the Japanese *zaibatsu* type dismantled after 1945. This structure centred on the group chairman (usually a direct descendant of the founder), in whose hands rested the final power of decision-making. The chairman's powers also included possession of the real accounts (as opposed to the published versions) of the group's myriad activities and the ability to control the group on the basis of relatively small equity holdings (because of the dependence on debt financing). These powers made the group chairmen indispensable to the functioning of their groups and the economy as a whole. A number had been implicated in corruption scandals during the 1990s (including the chairmen of the Hanbo and Daewoo groups), but their crucial role meant they were liable only to symbolic punishment.

Making transparent the secretive finances of the business groups was a difficult process. Even external auditors could not establish an accurate picture of group finances, without which potential investors dared not risk their capital.[16] The absence of reliable financial indicators meant that the reported improvements in financial soundness (as measured by the debt-equity ratio) had to be treated cautiously.[17] This was underlined by the collapse of the Daewoo group with debts of $70 billion in July 1999. Meanwhile some top group chairmen were busily making plans to transfer their businesses to their children. The completion of the father-to-son succession in the leading Samsung group through the untaxed transfer of shares, was completed in the face of official emphasis on corporate transparency and the professionalisation of management.[18] The recent intra-family succession over the control the Hyundai group showed just how much power continued to be wielded by the founding families.

There was resistance from the leading business groups to the swap deals through which participation in the leading industrial sectors would be rationalised.[19] Unwilling to concede key industries to their rivals, leading business groups became bogged down in their negotiations over the terms of industrial transfers (namely the apportionment of debts). As of late-1999, only two major deals (LG's transfer of semiconductors to Hyundai and the transfer of Daewoo electronics to Samsung) had been completed. A similar reorganisation effort had been tried in the early 1980s and had

16   Combs (1999).
17   Jane Fuller, 'Sluggish Pace of Reform Persists', *Financial Times Survey: South Korea*, 19 October 2000, p. iv.
18   'Samsung Completes Father to Son Succession Scheme', *Korea Herald*, 9 October 1999.
19   IMF (2000), pp. 103–8.

also failed and some policy advisers were advising the government to abandon this policy.[20] Meanwhile, the top groups continued to expand ambitiously (the very cause of the economy's near collapse in 1997) and cherry-picked key industries from the weaker groups (such as Hyundai's acquisition of Kia's car division). Humbled by bankruptcy, the smaller *chaebol* or 6–64 group (as denoted by their ranking) were more compliant than the top five groups which were kept afloat by their cash-rich divisions (such as Samsung's semiconductors division, Hyundai cars, Daewoo Securities) and by the continuing bias shown towards them in the allocation of bank finance (while the government was propping up the banks). With the brunt of the recession borne by small and medium industry, the concentration of private economic power was actually accentuated in the first two years of DJ's government.

The beginning of the collapse of the Daewoo group in the summer of 1999 led the government to announce additional measures for corporate reform on 25 August 1999, including the appointment of outside directors. Tough tax audits were conducted against leading groups including Samsung, Hyundai and Hanjin (Hanjin group, owner of Korean Air, was fined a record $445.8 million).[21] The legendary tycoon Kim Woo-Chung was also forced to resign the chairmanships of Daewoo and the Federation of Korean Industries. Impressive as these measures appeared, they highlighted the gaps existing in corporate supervision. In response to the government's tougher line, the Federation of Korean Industries (the conglomerates' umbrella organisation) ominously warned that the fragile recovery was being jeopardised by excessive government intervention.[22]

The experience of the Kim Dae-Jung government exhibits recurring problems faced by governments seeking to restructure their relationship with business. First, the business groups resorted to tactics of resistance they had used in the past two decades: voicing concerns that reforms would jeopardise the recovery; demanding that other sectors (government, labour) reform first; and stalling in the expectation that recovery would weaken the pressure for reform. Second, the experience of reform highlighted the business groups' capacity for resistance even in moments of extreme weakness. The groups calculated (correctly) that the government was reluctant to take stern measures that could jeopardise the viability of the leading groups and in doing so delay the recovery. As in the past, the leading groups were well aware that their financial fragility gave them leverage over government. Third, as in the past, finding it difficult to reform the

---

20 Yoo (1999), pp. 57–8.

21 'Chaebol Stunned by Government's Hard Line on Reform, Hefty Tax Fines,' *Korea Herald*, 6 October 1999.

22 'Chaebol Breakup a Risky Policy, Report Says,' *Korea Herald*, 18 October 1999; 'State Intervention Named as Worst Economic Policy,' *Korea Herald*, 20 December 1999.

leading business groups, government imposed punitive measures on second-tier groups (such as the fine on Hanjin, or the dissolution of Kukje group in 1985) in the attempt to maintain credibility. Fourth, the fierce competition between the leading business groups that was once a source of dynamism has now become an obstacle preventing industrial reorganisation along more rational lines. This was evident from the leading groups resistance to the swap deals. It shows that the excesses of the 1970s Big Push still plague policy reformers a generation on.

The Political Context of Government–Business Relations

As we have seen, democratisation affected government–business relations in various ways: business could now criticise (and even challenge) government policy openly; it could seek close particularistic relationships with individual officials to compensate for the dilution of the state's pro-business orientation; and government had to balance business interests against the objectives for redistribution and labour inclusion. On the other hand, there were some constants in the political environment that democratisation left unchanged between 1987 and 1997. First, the regional concentration of political power remained undisturbed, that is with the representatives of the industrialised southeastern Kyongsang region. Second, the ruling political coalition was extended rather than replaced as a consequence of the three party merger of 1990 that led to the incorporation of two opposition parties into government (on the basis of their regional and ideological affinity). Third, despite some tentative openings (such as the Non Aggression Pact of 1991), the continuing tension with North Korea helped to maintain the right-wing orientation of public opinion, leaving little space for the emergence of ideologically progressive political parties. For example, the success of the labour movement in wresting major concessions on wages and conditions in 1987–88 did not lead to the creation of a labour based political party capable of challenging the dominant mode of competition centred around regional political bosses.

The election of Kim Dae-Jung represented Korea's first ever peaceful alternation of power. It also meant the transfer of executive power from the prosperous Kyongsang region (the home region of presidents Park, Chun, Roh and Kim Young-Sam) to the underdeveloped southwestern Cholla region. With his power rooted in the less populous region, Kim Dae-Jung (or DJ) was the political boss most prepared to forge pan-regional political alliances and in so doing open the political arena up to ideological and issue-based competition. The assembly election results of April 2000 showed the extent to which DJ's effort of pan-regional alliance building had been successful. The results showed the old Kyongsang–Cholla divide to be more alive than ever. The Kyongsang region was as implacably anti-DJ as ever (DJ's Millennium Democratic Party was defeated in 64 of the 65 contests there). DJ's support in his native Cholla province also remained solid. On the other hand, the gains the MDP made in the populous Seoul–Inchon–Kyonggi area, and in the Kangwon and Chungchong regions, showed that there was the beginnings of a pan-regional electoral coalition. Chungchong was the home region of the archconservative Kim Jong-Pil (who first entered politics as a leader of the 1961 coup) who was now being deserted by his own regional voters, especially the young. While DJ's presidency may have reinforced the traditional Kyongsang–Cholla divide, DJ was extending his support base beyond his traditional regional stronghold. With the growth of population in the Seoul metropolitan area, and with the advanced ages of the regional political bosses (including DJ himself), there is every prospect for the further erosion of regional dominance in Korean politics and for more contestation along ideological lines.

The political context of government–business relations was influenced by the inclusionary policies of the DJ government. In seeking to reach beyond his regional base, and in his longstanding criticism of the excesses of authoritarian developmentalism, DJ had a long record of association with progressive activists and intellectuals.[23] This association helped to draw organised labour into a social pact for economic recovery, a Rubicon that previous democratic governments would not cross (previous hopes for such an alliance were wrecked by bouts of mini-repression in 1990 and 1995). Another source of the social pact was the need to reform the labour market in line with IMF conditionalities. Labour groups and business had blamed each other for the decline of economic competitiveness throughout the 1990s and that impasse was responsible for the failure of labour market reform (Kim Young-Sam's attempt in the winter of 1996–97 had provoked massive strikes). The resulting Tripartite Agreement for Fair Burden Sharing tied labour cooperation to improvements in legal status and to the restructuring of the business sector. This signalled a transition from the old dual alliance of state and business (or 'corporatism without labour') to some form of societal corporatist arrangement, a first for Korea (and for industrialising Asia for that matter)

The social pact was an agreement by which organised labour accepted redundancies (which was now made easier than in the 1997 version of the law)[24] in exchange for enhanced political rights, state social counter-meas-

---

23   For example, Lee Jin-Soon, an adviser to DJ, had been a member of the Citizens' Coalition for Economic Justice.

24   In the aftermath of the strikes of early 1997, a revised version of the labour law was passed. This version provided more safeguards for labour but its workability was untested.

ures and structural reform of big business, including its internal governance. The labour unions reluctantly accepted the necessity of lay-offs, employment flexibility and other productivity-enhancing measures. In return, the business sector agreed to put its own financial house in order and to implement lay-offs only in the last resort and after the appropriate consultation with the labour unions. The pact was also consistent with DJ's 'democratic market economy' blueprint, which envisaged a politically empowered labour movement that was also economically responsible. The formal inclusion of labour into the economic decision-making process marked a departure from the old pro-business bias when labour repression was intensified during economic crises.

In spite of its high ideals, the pact failed to work effectively for a number of reasons. The labour unions did not perceive the burden sharing to be fair. Corporate governance reform proceeded very slowly.[25] The labour organisations became convinced that business was merely taking advantage of the crisis to shed workers without making any genuine improvements to their own internal workings that did so much to bring the crisis about.[26] Such mistrust would bring about standoffs like the one that paralysed Hyundai Motors at Ulsan (one of Korea's premier export plants) in June–August 1998. The dispute was only halted when the government intervened to moderate the group's redundancy plans, a halfway house that satisfied neither the objectives of management (downsizing as permitted under the new labour law) nor labour (job security). The pattern of reactive labour protest and mutual recrimination, tentative government crackdowns followed by ad hoc compromises unsatisfactory to either side resembled the sequence of events following the previous government's abortive labour law reforms of December 1996. Neither labour nor business seemed quite ready to be 'incorporated'.

Apart from the fairness of burden sharing, the labour unions were also discontented over their exclusion from the making of key economic decisions such as the swap deals. Progress on the extension of political rights was slower than the labour unions expected. For example, the right of laid-off workers to join a union, while being acknowledged in principle by the tripartite presidential advisory panel in September 1998, had its implementation postponed until 2000 (ostensibly owing to opposition from the Justice Ministry). Despite these complaints, the social pact delivered many of the concessions organised labour had been demanding over

25   In fact, the ultimate aims of corporate governance reform (such as managerial decision-making determined by share price) did not necessarily accord with labour interests in safeguarding employment. For example, labour unions joined the Daewoo group in resisting the acquisition of the motors division by US giant General Motors in late 1999.

26   Song (1999), pp. 23–4.

the past decade. These included extension of organisation to the government sector (for instance, partial trade union rights were granted to teachers in December 1998), legalisation of the more radical Korea Confederation of Trade Unions, multiple unionisations at the workplace, and the permission of third parties to enter disputes. Business had previously opposed these measures.

Even though it was not very successful at consensus building or at modifying the behaviour of the most powerful business groups, the social pact and other political openings helped to facilitate challenges to the conservative mainstream from critical social forces. DJ's presidency has made it easier for the labour unions and progressive civic groups to participate in political activities.[27] Underpinning this change is the 'sunshine' policy of positive engagement with North Korea (which enabled the historic summit between DJ and North Korean leader Kim Jong-Il to take place in June 2000). This has helped to moderate the fear factor on which half a century of right-wing dominance was built. Reforms of the past two years have enhanced the capacity for independent action of the progressive groups that had long been attached to DJ's coat tails. This broadening of the political spectrum was reflected in the activities of civic organisations and in the formation of a labour-oriented party to contest the 2000 national assembly elections.

The relaxation of restrictions on political participation opened the way for civic groups and labour unions to assume more active roles in party politics.[28] This was apparent from the formation of an alliance of civic groups (Citizens' Alliance for General Election [CAGE] 2000) aimed at securing a clean legislative election in 2000. It became a vocal critic of the impasse over legislative reform and the irresponsible and self-interested behaviour of the professional politicians in raising their own incomes while calling for belt-tightening and in voting for bigger public allowances for their campaign expenditures. In the campaign against the political class, CAGE 2000 took the unprecedented step of publishing a blacklist of unfit candidates (individuals allegedly tainted by past corruption or other illegal acts), a list that included Kim Jong-Pil.[29] The civic alliance also pressed the government to relax further the constraints on their political activities (the revision of the election law in January 2000 had already eased the political restrictions on civic groups)[30] as well for revi-

---

27   There is a growing literature on this subject cast in terms of 'democratic consolidation'. For example, see Kim (2000) Seong (2000).

28   For background on civic groups including the CCEJ, see Lee (1992).

29   'Civic Groups, Political Circle Set to Clash Over Rejection Drive,' *Korea Herald*, 13 January 2000; 'Rejection Campaign to Change Korea's Political Landscape Once and For All,' *Korea Herald*, 26 January 2000.

30   'Civic Groups' Deem Politicians' Election Law Insufficient,' *Korea Herald*, 1 February 2000.

sion of the 1948 National Security Law (a demand that has gained momentum after the June 2000 leaders' summit).

Spokesmen for CAGE 2000 claimed to have forced unsuitable individuals out of the political process. They claimed that 70 per cent of blacklisted candidates in the key Seoul-Kyonggi region were defeated (including the vice-president of the conservative United Liberal Party) and that two-thirds of all blacklisted candidates were defeated at the April 2000 assembly elections.[31] The main parties also de-selected some candidates given adverse publicity by the civic alliance (the opposition claimed that the alliance was an extension of the governing party). On the other hand, complaints about campaign violations exceeded the 1996 level despite there being fewer seats up for election.[32] The all time low turnout of 57.2 per cent showed the extent of public apathy towards the political process.[33]

The campaign against unworthy candidates also coincided with other civic movements including the campaign to bring accountability to the business groups on behalf of small stockholders by using the new corporate governance legislation. There was also the launch of a left of centre political party (Democratic Labour Party), a party based on the support of organised labour. The relaxation of restrictions on organised labour under the terms of the social pact made possible their participation in politics. A constitutional court ruling of November 1999 opened the way for the KCTU to provide financial support to the DLP. Headed by Kwon Young-Kil, a former journalist and labour activist, the party espoused broad aims (such as the completion of democratisation, democratic economy and peaceful reunification) not so different from the populist slogans commonly used by Kim Dae-Jung. Previous attempts to form progressive parties had failed miserably but there were grounds for expecting the DLP to fare better than its hapless predecessors: public dissatisfaction with the established politicians; a freer role for the labour unions and other support groups; and the change in Korean society to accommodate more progressive ideas. As it turned out, the prediction of capturing ten seats in the April election[34] proved excessively hopeful. Winning 1.2 per cent of the national vote, the party came close to winning seats in the industrial heartlands of Changwon and Ulsan (ironically, Chung Mong-Joon, a scion of the Hyundai business empire also won a seat there as an independent). Of the 27 labour-friendly candidates backed by the more moderate Federation

---

31   'Nation's Largest Civic Alliance Calls Election Revolution a "Success",' *Korea Herald*, 14 April 2000.

32   'Rival Camps Locked in Close Contest,' *Korea Times*, 12 April 2000.

33   'Opposition GNP Remains Largest Party at Assembly,' *Korea Times*, 14 April 2000.

34   'Editorial: A Progressive Voice. Formation of Labour Party,' *Korea Herald*, 2 February 2000.

of Korean Trade Unions and running for the mainstream parties, 21 were elected, of whom seven were former labour activists.[35]

Conclusion

New democracies have experienced serious difficulties in containing the abuses of business power associated with economic liberalisation. In part this reflects the weaknesses in the rules of economic and political governance commonly theorised by neoclassical political economists under the heading of 'second generation' development problems (such as loopholes in the business regulatory mechanism, weaknesses of corporate governance, lack of bureaucratic transparency, retention of discretionary bureaucratic powers that invite business lobbying). The problem, however, is more than simply one of 'institutional design'. Another vital dimension is the role of effective countervailing social forces, forces whose existence depends not only on the extent to which liberal-democratic rules pertain but also the whole ideological tenor of the political elites. Atul Kohli has commented on the tendency of the neoliberal economic consensus to keeps substantive social and economic issues off the political agenda in the new democracies. The result is a degeneration into a form of 'twin track' democracy dominated by squabbling for office between likeminded politicians, who in the absence of substantive issues, seek to differentiate themselves on the basis of personal competence and integrity.[36] Meanwhile public apathy from the political realm is rife in the absence of real issues.

Korea's political life has elements of this situation: dominance of the regional and boss politics in which DJ himself has played a key role; the trading of accusations between political parties; and the irrelevance of the legislature as an effective body for democratic scrutiny (that body has always served primarily as voting fodder for political bosses and as a channel for the politically upwardly mobile). But the Korean situation under DJ diverges from the neoliberal democratic pattern in key respects. While embracing the neoliberal demands for the completion of liberalisation and institutional redesign, DJ's government has eschewed the path of social exclusion. Instead he has pursued a parallel agenda of opening to labour and other progressive groups. The existence of a benign and sympathetic government has enabled these forces to operate more freely then ever before. Historically, such groups have played an important role in Korea's recent social transformation (for instance, the impact of unofficial labour activists in transforming the state-dominated labour organisations during

---

35 Federation of Korean Trade Unions, '21 Candidates Backed by the FKTU Win,' www.fktu.org.kr.
36 Kohli(1993).

the 1970s and 1980s, and the role of democratic activists). In other new democracies, parties and leaders traditionally associated with populism and redistribution have sought to deactivate labour and other popular organisations believing them to be antithetical to the pursuit of market economics.[37] By contrast, DJ's government has fostered such forces in the belief that they represent essential counterweights that maintain the vitality and accountability of the liberalised capitalist system. Thus, the ideological tenor of the government may be as important as rules in regulating business behaviour in new democracies.

---

[37] For studies of this phenomenon in Latin America see Murillo (2000) and Gibson (1997). On a Sri Lankan case study see Moore (1997).

Bibliography

Abreu, A., Gitahy, L., Ramalho, J. and Ruas, R. (1999) 'Industrial Restructuring and Inter-Firm Relations in Brazil: A Study of the Auto-Parts Industry in the 1990s,' *Occasional Papers*, no. 21 (London: Institute of Latin American Studies).

Addis, C. (1997) 'Cooperação e desenvolvimento no setor de autopeças,' in G. Arbix and M. Zilbovicius (eds.), *De JK a FHC — A reinvenção dos carros* (São Paulo: Scritta).

Addis, Caren (1998) *Taking the Wheel. Autoparts Firms and the Political Economy of Industrialization in Brazil* (Philadelphia: Penn State Press).

Addison, J.T. and Chilton, J.B. (1993) 'Can we Identify Union Productivity Effects?,' in *Industrial Relations*, vol.32, no.2, pp.124-32 (Winter).

Ahn, G.S. (1996) 'Trends in Korean Income Distribution: Conflicting Estimates and their Evaluations,' in J.W. Lee et al., *Industrial Relations and the Lives of the Workers in Korea* (in Korean) Seoul: Seoul Institute of Economic and Social Studies).

Amadeo, E. (1998) 'Dez pontos sobre a situação recente do mercado de trabalho,' *Notas sobre o Mercado de Trabalho*, no. 5, August 1998 (Brasília: Ministério do Trabalho).

Amann, E. (1995) 'Defensive Modernisation: Brazilian Industry Responds to the Challenge of Market Liberalisation,' Manchester Brazililan Research Group, University of Manchester.

Amann, E. (2000) *Economic Liberalisation and Industrial Performance in Brazil* (Oxford and New York: Oxford University Press).

Amann, E (2002) 'Globalisation and Technological Sovereignty: The Case of Brazil', *Quarterly Review of Economics and Finance*, November.

Amann, E. and Nixson, F. (1999) 'Globalisation and the Brazilian Steel Industry: 1988–97,' *Journal of Development Studies*, August

Amsden, Alice (1989) *Asia's Next Giant: South Korea and Late Industrialization* (Oxford and New York: Oxford University Press).

Amsden, Alice and Hikino, Takashi (1994) 'Project Execution Capability, Organizational Know-How and Conglomerate Corporate Growth in Late Industrialization,' *Industrial and Corporate Change*, vol. 3, no. 1, pp. 111–48.

Andrade, Amarante de, Silva Cunha, M.L. da and Tavares Gandra, G. (1999) *Restructuring the Brazilian Metallurgical Sector* (Banco Nacional de Desenvolvimento Econômico e Social — BNDES).

Anfavea (1999) *Anuário Estatístico* (São Paulo: Anfavea).

Arbix, G. (1997) 'O consórcio modular da VW: um novo modelo de produção,' in G. Arbix and M. Zilbovicius (eds.), *De JK a FHC — A reinvenção dos carros* (São Paulo: Scritta).

Arestis, P., Palma, G. and Sawyer, M. (eds) (1997) *Capital Controversy, Post-Keynesian Economics and the History of Economics — Essays in Honour of Geoff Harcourt*, vol.1 (London, New York: Routledge).

Bacha, Edmar and Welch, John (1997) 'Privatização e financiamento no Brasil, 1997–99,' in João Paulo dos Reis Velloso (coord.), *Brasil: desafios de um país em transformação* (São Paulo: Fórum Nacional, José Olympio Editora).

Baer, W. (2001) *The Brazilian Economy* (New York: Praeger).

Baltar, P., Dedecca, C. and Henrique, W. (1996) 'Mercado de trabalho e exclusão social no Brasil,' in C. Oliveira and J. Mattoso (orgs.), *Crise e Trabalho no Brasil* (São Paulo: Scritta).

Bank of Korea (BOK) (2000) *Financial Statement Analysis for 1999* (Seoul).

Bank of Korea (BOK) website, http://www.bok.or.kr

Barker, Wendy Joan (1990) 'Banks and Industry in Contemporary Brazil: Their Organization, Relationship, and Leader,' PhD dissertation, Yale University.

Batista, Paulo Nogueira Jr. (1999) 'Vaticínios e surpresas,' *Folha de São Paulo,* 16 December.

Bebchuk, Lucian and Roe, Mark (1999) 'A Theory of Path Dependence in Corporate Ownership and Governance,' *Stanford Law Review,* vol. 52, no. 1.

Berger, Susan (1996) 'Introduction,' in S. Berger and R. Dore (eds.), *National Diversity and Global Capitalism* (Ithaca: Cornell University Press).

Betcherman, Gordon, Dar, Amit, Luinstra, Amy and Makoto, Ogawa (2001) 'Labor Adjustment, Non-Standard Work and Employment Programs: Korea in an OECD Context,' in Funkoo Park, Young-bum Park, Gordon Betcherman and Amit Dar (eds.), *Labour Market Reforms in Korea: Policy Options for the Future* (The World Bank, Korea Labor Institute).

Blaine, M. (1993) 'Profitability and Competitiveness: Lessons from Japanese and American Firms in the 1980s,' *California Management Review*, vol. 36, no. 1.

Blank. R.M. and Freeman, R.B. (1993) 'Evaluating the Connection between Social Protection and Economic Flexibility,' *Working Paper Series*, no. 4338 (Cambridge, MA: National Bureau of Economic Research, April).

Bonelli, Regis (1998) 'Las estrategias de los grandes grupos económicos brasileños,' in W. Peres (ed.), *Grandes empresas y grupos industriales latinoamericanos* (Mexico City: Siglo XXI).

Bora, Bijit, Lloyd, Peter and Pangestu, Mari (2000) 'Industrial Policy and the WTO,' *UNCTAD Study Series on Policy Issues in International Trade and Development*, no. 5.

Brennan, M. (1995) Corporate Finance Over the Past 25 Years, *Financial Management*, vol. 24, no. 2.

Brittan, S. (1997) 'Asian Model R.I.P.,' *Financial Times*, 4 December 1997.

Bruschini, C. *O Globo*, 8 March 1998.

Burchill, Scott (1998) 'Human Nature, Freedom and Political Community: an Interview with Naom Chomsky,' in *Citizenship Studies*, vol. 2, no.1 (February, Oxford).

Burton, J. (1998) 'Boxed into a Corner,' *Financial Times*, 23 November.

Cardoso, A. (1999) *Sindicatos, trabalhadores e a coqueluche neoliberal* (Rio de Janeiro: FGV).

Cardoso, Fernando Henrique (1964) *Empresario industrial e desenvolvimento económico no Brasil* (São Paulo: Difusão Européia do Livro).

Cardoso, Fernando Henrique (1978 [1969]) *Política e desenvolvimento em sociedades dependentes: ideologias do empresariado industrial argentino e brasileiro* (Rio de Janeiro: Zahar), 2nd edition.

Carvalho, Ruy de Quadros and Bernardes, Roberto (1998) 'Cambiando con la economia: la dinámica de empresas líderes en Brasil,' in Wilson Peres (ed.), *Grandes empresas y grupos industriales latinoamericanos* (Mexico City: Siglo XXI).

Chandler, Alfred. Jr. (1990) *Scale and Scope* (Cambridge, MA: Harvard University Press).

Chandler Alfred, Amatori, Franco and Hikino, Takashi (eds.) (1998) *Big Business and the Wealth of Nations* (Cambidge: Cambridge University Press).

Chandler, Alfred, Amatori, Franco and Hikino, Takashi (1998b) 'Historical and Comparative Contours of Big Business,' in Alfred Chandler et al. (eds.) *Big Business and the Wealth of Nations* (Cambidge: Cambridge University Press).

Chang, H-J. (1993) 'The Political Economy of Industrial Policy in Korea,' *Cambridge Journal of Economics*, vol. 17, no. 2.

Chang, Ha-Joon (1994), *The Political Economy of Industrial Policy* (Basingstoke: Macmillan)

Chang, Ha-Joon (1998) 'South Korea: The Misunderstood Crisis,' in K.S. Jomo (ed.), *Tigers in Trouble: Financial Governance, Liberalization and Crises in East Asia* (London: Zed Books), pp. 226–9.

Chang, Ha-Joon (1998a) 'Korea: The Misunderstood Crisis,' *World Development*, vol. 26, no. 8.

Chang, Ha-Joon (1999), 'Industrial Policy and East Asia: The Miracle, the Crisis and the Future,' paper presented at the World Bank workshop on 'Re-thinking East Asian Miracle,' San Francisco, 16-17 February.

Chang, H-J. (2000) 'The Hazard of Moral Hazard: Untangling the Asian Crisis,' in *World Development*, vol.28, no.4., pp.775–88.

Chang, Ha-Joon and Park, Hong-Jae (1999), 'An Alternative Perspective on Government Policy towards Big Businesses in Korea: Industrial Policy, Financial Regulation and Political Democracy,' paper prepared for the project on 'The Korean *Chaebols* in Transition: Restructuring Strategy and Agenda,' organised by the Korea Economic Research Institute (KERI)

Chang, H-J. and Park, H-J. (2000) 'An Alternative Perspective on Government Policy towards the *Chaebol* in Korea: Industrial Policy, Financial Regulations and Political Democracy,' in S-H. Jwa and I. Lee (eds.), *Korean* Chaebol *in Transition: Road Ahead and Agenda* (Seoul: Korea Economic Research Institute).

Chang, H-J. and Singh, A. (1993) 'Public Enterprise in Developing Countries and Economic Efficiency,' *UNCTAD Review*, no. 4.

Chang, Ha-Joon and Yoo, Chul Gyue (2000) 'The Triumph of the Rentiers?,' *Challenge*, January–February.

Chang, H-J. and Yoo, C.G. (2002) 'The Triumph of the Rentiers? — The 1997 Korean Financial Crisis in Historical Perspective,' in J. Eatwell and L. Taylor (eds.), *International Capital Markets: Systems in Transition* (Oxford, New York: Oxford University Press).

Chang, H-J., Park, H-J. and Yoo, C.G. (1998) 'Interpreting the Korean Crisis: Financial Liberalisation, Industrial Policy and Corporate Governance,' *Cambridge Journal of Economics*, vol. 22, no. 6.

Chang, Sea-Jin and Choi, Ungwhan (1988) 'Strategy, Structure and Performance of Korean Business Groups: A Transactions Cost Approach,' *Journal of Industrial Economics*, vol. 37, no. 2, pp. 141–58

Chang, Sea-Jin and Hong, Jae-Bum (2000) 'Economic Performance of Group-Affiliated Companies in Korea: Intra-Group Resource Sharing and Internal Business Transaction,' *Academy of Management Journal*, vol. 3, pp. 429–48.

Choi, Sung-Rho (1999), *30 Big Business Groups of Korea in 1998* (Seoul: Centre for Free Enterprises) (in Korean).

Claessens, S., Djankov, S. and Lang, L. (1998) 'Corporate Growth, Financing and Risks in the Decade before East Asia's Financial Crisis,' *Policy Research Working Paper*, no. 2017 (Washington, DC: World Bank).

Clark, John (2000) 'Competition Policy and Regulatory Reform in Brazil,' (Paris: Organization for Economic Cooperation and Development).

Combs, Gifford (1999) 'The Role of International Finance in Korea Economic Reconstruction and Reunification,' *NBR Analysis*, vol. 10, no. 5 (December) [National Bureau of Asian Research].

Corbett, J. and Jenkinson, J. (1994) 'The Financing of Industry, 1970–89: An International Comparison, Discussion Paper,' no. 949, Centre for Economic Policy Research, University of London.

Corden, M. (1998) 'Sense and Nonsense on the Asian Crisis,' The Sturc Lecture, delivered on 8 November 1998, at the Paul H. Nitze School of Advanced International Studies, Johns Hopkins University.

Corsetti, G., Pesenti, P. and Roubini, N. (1999) 'Paper Tigers? — A Model of the Asian Crisis,' *NBER Working Paper*, no. 6783.

Crafts, Nicholas (2000) 'Globalization and Growth in the Twentieth Century', *IMF Working Paper 2000/44*.

Cumings, Bruce (1998) 'The Korean Crisis and the End of "Late" Development,' *New Left Review*, vol. 231.

Dantas, V. (1990) 'Modernização defensiva,' *Automação e Indústria*, no.43

Davis, Gerald, Diekmann, Kristina and Tinsley, Catherine (1994) 'The Decline and Fall of the Conglomerate Firm in the 1980s,' *American Sociological Review*, vol. 59, no. 4, pp. 547–70.

Demigruc-Kunt, A. and Maksimovic, V. (1996) 'Stock Market Development and Firm Financing Choices,' *The World Bank Economic Review*, vol. 10, no. 2.

Dicken, P. (1992) *Global Shift* (London: Paul Chapman Publishing).

Departamento Intersindical de Estatística e Estudos Socios Econômicos (DIEESE) (2000) 'Mapa da população negra no mercado de trabalho' (São Paulo).

Desep/CUT (1999) 'O papel econômico do salário mínimo,' *Resenha DESEP 15* (São Paulo: Desep).

Diniz, Eli (2000) *Globalização, reformas econômicas e elites empresariais* (Rio de Janeiro: Editora FGV).

Dosi, Giovanni (1998) 'Organizational Competences, Firms Size and the Wealth of Nations,' in Alfred Chandler, Franco Amatori and Takashi Hikino (eds.) (1998), *Big Business and the Wealth of Nations* (Cambidge: Cambridge University Press).

Drazen, A. and Masson, P. (1994) 'Credibility of Policies versus Credibility of Policy Makers,' *The Quarterly Journal of Economics*, August.

ECIB (1993) *Estudo de competitividade da indústria brasileira* (Rio de Janeiro: UFRJ–UNICAMP–FDC–FINEP).

Eggertson, T. (1990) *Economic Behaviour and Institutions* (Cambridge: Cambridge Surveys of Economic Literature).

Ernst, D. (1999) 'How Globalization Reshapes the Geography of Innovation Systems: Reflections on Global Production Networks in Information Industries,' paper prepared at the DRUID 1999 Summer Conference on Innovation Systems, 9–12 June, Rebild, Denmark

Evans, Peter (1979) *Dependent Development* (Princeton: Princeton University Press).

Evans, Peter (1995) *Embedded Autonomy: States and Industrial Transformation* (Princeton: Princeton University Press).

Feldstein, M. (1998) 'Refocusing the IMF,' *Foreign Affairs*, vol. 77, no. 2.

Feijó, C. and Carvalho, P. (1997) 'Old and New Trends in the Productivity Growth of Brazilian Industry,' *Anais do XXV Encontro Anual da ANPEC* (Recife: ANPEC).

Ferraz, J., Kupfer, D. and Haguenauer, L. (1997) *Made in Brazil: desafios competitivos para a indústria* (Rio de Janeiro: Campus).

Ferraz, João Carlos, Iootty, Mariana and Rocha, Frederico (2000) *Desempenho das fusões e aquisições na indústria brasileira na década de 90* (Río de Janeiro: Instituto de Economía, Universidade Federal de Río de Janeiro — IE/UFRJ).

Field, Karl J. (1995) *Enterprise and the State in Korea and Taiwan* (Ithaca and London: Cornell University Press).

Financial Supervisory Commission (FSC), website, http://www.fsc.go.kr

Fligstein, N. (1991) 'The Structural Transformation of American Industry: an Institutional Account of the Causes of Diversification in the Largest Firms, 1919-1979,' in W.W. Powell and P.J. DiMaggio (eds.), *The New Institutionalism in Organizational Analysis* (Chicago and London: The University of Chicago Press), pp. 311–36

Fligstein, Neil and Freeland, Robert (1995) 'Theoretical and Comparative Perspectives on Corporate Organization,' *Annual Review of Sociology*, no. 21, pp. 21–43.

Franco, Gustavo (1999a) 'The Real Plan and the Exchange Rate'; mimeo, (Rio de Janeiro: Pontifícia Universidade Católica do Rio de Janeiro — PUC/RJ).

Franco, Gustavo (1999b) '*O desafio brasileiro — ensaios sobre desenvolvimento, globalização e moeda*' (São Paulo: Editora 34).

Frankel, J. (1998) 'The Asian Model, the Miracle, the Crisis and the Fund,' a speech delivered at the US International Trade Commission, 16 April.

Frankel, Jeffrey, A. (2000) 'Globalisation of the Economy', *NBER Working Paper 7858*.

Fritsch, W. and Franco, G. (1991) 'Trade Policy Issues in Brazil in the 1990s' (Rio de Janeiro: Pontifícia Universidade Católica do Rio de Janeiro — PUC/RJ), Working Paper no. 268.

Fuller, Jane (2000) 'Sluggish Pace of Reform Persists,' *Financial Times Survey: South Korea* (19 October).

Furman, J. and Stiglitz, J. (1998) 'Economic Crises: Evidence and Insights from East Asia,' *Brookings Papers on Economic Activity*, no. 2.

Garrido, Celso (2000) 'The Large Private National Mexican Corporations in the Nineties' (Mexico City: Universidad Autónoma Metropolitana).

Gereffi, Gary (1990) 'Big Business and the State,' in Gary Gereffi and Donald L. Wyman (eds.), *Manufacturing Miracles* (Princeton: Princeton University Press).

Gerlach, Michael (1992) *Alliance Capitalism: The Social Organization of Japanese Business* (Berkeley: University of California Press).

Gerschenkron, A. (1962) *Economic Backwardness in Historical Perspective* (Cambridge, MA: Harvard University Press).

Giambiagi, Fabio (1998) 'Brazil: Handling the Crisis,' BNDES-Economic Department (December).

Giambiagi, Fabio (1999) 'O câmbio e a Europa de 1992,' *Estado de São Paulo*, 9 January.

Giambiagi, Fabio and Além, Ana Cláudia (1999) '*Finanças públicas — teoria e prática no Brasil*' (Rio de Janeiro: Editora Campus).

Gibson, Edward L. (1997) 'The Populist Road to Market Reform: Policy and Electoral Coalitions in Mexico and Argentina,' *World Politics*, vol. 49, no. 3 (April), pp. 339–70.

Gitahy, L., Leite, M. and Rabelo, F. (1993) 'Relações de trabalho, política de recursos humanos e competitividade,' in ECIB (1993) *Estudo de competitividade da indústria brasileira* (Rio de Janeiro: UFRJ –UNI-CAMP–FDC–FINEP).

Goldstein, Andrea (1998) 'Politics and Economics of Privatization: The Case of Argentina,' *Canadian Journal of Latin American and Caribbean Studies*, vol. 23, no. 45.

Goldstein, Andrea (1999) 'Brazilian Privatization: The Rocky Path from State Capitalism to Regulatory Capitalism,' *Industrial and Corporate Change*, vol. 8, no. 1.

Goldstein, Andrea (2001) 'From National Champion to Global Player: Explaining the Success of Embraer,' Centre for Brazilian Studies, Oxford University, *Working Paper*, no. 17.

Goldstein, Andrea and Giuseppe Nicoletti (1996) 'Italian Privatizations in International Perspective,' *Cuadernos de Economía*, vol. 33, no. 100.

Gonçalves, R. (1999) *Globalização e desnacionalização* (São Paulo: Paz e Terra).

Greider, W. (1997) *One World, Ready Or Not: The Manic Logic of Global Capitalism* (New York: Simon and Schuster).

Grimshaw, D. and Rubery, J. (1998) 'Integrating the Internal and External Labour Markets,' *Cambridge Journal of Economics*, vol.22, pp. 199–220.

Guillén, Mauro (1999) 'Corporate Governance and Globalization: Arguments and Evidence against Convergence,' mimeo, The Wharton School and Department of Sociology, University of Pennsylvania.

Haagh, L. (1998) 'Re-Democratisation, Labour Relations and the Development of Human Resources in Chile,' D.Phil thesis, Oxford, England.

Haagh, L. (1999) 'Training Policy and the Property Rights of Labour in Chile: Social Citizenship in the Atomised Market Regime,' in *Journal of Latin American Studies*, vol. 31, part II, May.

Haagh, L. (2001) 'The Challenge of Labour Reform in Korea: a Review of Contrasting Approaches to Market Enhancement,' in *Labor Market Reforms in Korea: Policy Options for the Future* (Washington: The World Bank), pp. 386–419.

Haagh., L. (2002a) *Citizenship, Labour Markets and Democratization – Chile and the Modern Sequence* (Basingstoke: Palgrave-St.Antony's).

Haagh, L. (2002b) 'Human Resources and De-Centralisation in Chile,' in L. Haagh and C. Helgø (eds.), *Social Policy Reform and Market Governance in Latin America* (Basingstoke: Palgrave-St. Antony's), pp. 47–76.

Haagh, L. (2002c) 'The Emperor's New Clothes — Labour Reform and Social Democratisation in Chile,' *Studies in International Comparative Development*, University of Berkeley, vol. 38, no.1, May.

Haagh, L. (2004) 'Market Neutrality and Social Policy — Unemployment Insurance and Resistance to Comprehensive Learning in Chile,' in K. Weyland (ed.), *Learning from Foreign Models in Latin American Policy Reform* (Washington, DC: The Woodrow Wilson Center).

Haagh, L. (forthcoming), 'Labour Relations and Welfare Reform in the Korean Transition to Democracy,' in J.S. Valenzuela (ed.), *Labour Movements in Transitions to Democracy*, manuscript.

Harris, M. and Raviv, A. (1991) 'The Theory of Capital Structure,' *The Journal of Finance*, vol. 46, no. 1.

Hay, D (2001) 'The Post-1990 Brazilian Trade Liberalisation and the Performance of Large Manufacturing Firms: Productivity, Market Share and Profits,' *Economic Journal*, July.

Hayek, van F.A. (1984) *1980s Unemployment and the Unions — The Distortion of Relative Prices by Monopoly in the Labour Market*, Hobart Papers, no.87 (London: The Institute of Economic Affairs).

Hirschman, A.O. (1970) *Exit, Voice and Loyalty* (Cambridge: Cambridge University Press).

Hirschmann, A.O. (1993) 'The Rhetoric of Reaction — Two Years Later,' in *Government and Opposition*, vol. 28, no.3, pp. 292– 314.

Hirsh, B.T. (1992) 'Firm Investment Behaviour and Collective Bargaining Strategy,' in *Industrial Relations*, vol. 31, no.1, pp. 95–121, Winter.

Hobsbawm, E.J. (1979) 'The Development of the World Economy,' *Cambridge Journal of Economics*, vol. 3, pp. 305–18.

Hou, C.M. and Gee, S. (1993) 'National Systems Supporting Technical Advance in Industry: The Case of Taiwan,' in R.R. Nelson (ed.), *National Innovation Systems: A Comparative Analysis* (Oxford: Oxford University Press).

Hur, Jai-Joon (2001) 'Expanding the Coverage of Korea's Unemployment Insurance,' Funkoo Park, Young-bum Park, Gordon Betcherman and Amit Dar (eds.), *Labour Market Reforms in Korea: Policy Options for the Future* (The World Bank, Korea Labor Institute).

IBGE (1995) *Pesquisa Nacional por Amostragem de Domicílios* (Rio de Janeiro, IBGE).

IDEA (1998) 'Currency Crises and Contagion Aftershocks: How, Why and What Next?,' January.

ILO (1999) 'Denmark: Flexibility, Security and Labour Market Success,' Per Kongshøj-Madsen, *ILO Employment and Training Papers*, no.53, Geneva, Switzerland.

International Monetary Fund (IMF — 2000) 'Republic of Korea: Economic and Policy Developments,' *IMF Staff Country Report No. 00/11* (February), pp. 5–6.

International Monetary Fund (IMF — 2000a) *International Financial Statistics* (CD-Rom)

Jang, Ha-Sung (1999) 'Corporate Governance and Economic Development: The Korean Experience', paper presented at

International Conference on Democracy, Market Economy and Development, Seoul, 26–7 February, www.democracy-market.org, pp. 14–19.

Jeong, J. (1995) 'The Failure of Recent State Vocational Training Policies in Korea from a Comparative Perspective,' in *British Journal of Industrial Relations*, vol. 33, no. 2., June (London), pp. 237–52.

Jeong, J. (2000) 'Skill Formation of Engineers in Large Korean Firms and Analysis from a Comparative Perspective,' in *International Journal of Training and Development*, vol. 4, no.1, pp. 66-78.

Johnson, Chalmers (1987) 'Political Institutions and Economic Performance: The Government–Business Relationship in Japan, South Korea, and Taiwan,' in Frederic C. Deyo (ed.), *The Political Economy of the New Asian Industrialism* (Ithaca: Cornell University Press).

Jones, L.P. and Sakong, I. (1980) *Government, Business and Entrepreneurship in Economic Development: The Korean Case* (Cambridge, MA: Harvard University Press)

Julius, D. (1990) *Global Companies and Public Policy: The Growing Challenge of Foreign Direct Investment* (London: Pinter).

Kang, Soon-Hie and Lee, Byung Hee (2001), 'Evaluating the Training for the Unemployed in Korea,' in Funkoo Park, Young-bum Park, Gordon Betcherman and Amit Dar (eds.), *Labour Market Reforms in Korea: Policy Options for the Future* (The World Bank, Korea Labor Institute).

Khan, Mushtaq (1995), 'State Failure in Weak State: A Critique of New Institutionalist Explanations,' in J. Harris, J. Hunter and C.M. Lewis (eds.) (1995) *The New Institutional Economics and Third World Development* (London and New York: Routledge).

Khanna, Tarun (2000) 'Business Groups and Social Welfare in Emerging Markets: Existing Evidence and Unanswered Questions,' *European Economic Review*, vol. 44, nos. 4–6, pp. 748–61.

Khanna, Tarun and Palepu, Krishna (1997) 'Why Focused Strategies may be Wrong for Emerging Markets,' *Harvard Business Review*, July–August, pp. 41–51.

Khanna, Tarun and Palepu, Krishna (1998) 'The Future of Business Groups in Emerging Markets: Long Run Evidence from Chile,' mimeo, Harvard Business School.

Kim, Dae-Jung (1985) *Mass Participatory Economy: A Democratic Alternative for Korea* (Cambridge, MA: Harvard University — University Press of America).

Kim, Dae-Jung (1997) *Shimin Kyungje Iyaki* (Stories of Economics for Citizens) (Seoul: Sanha).

Kim, Dae-Jung (1999) *DJnomics: A New Foundation for the Korean Economy*, www.democracy-market.org.

Kim, Kyong-Dong (1976) 'Political Factors in the Formation of the Entrepreneurial Elite in South Korea,' *Asian Survey*, vol. 16, no. 5, pp. 465–77.

Kim, Sun-Hyuk (2000) 'Civic Mobilization for Democratic Reform,' in Larry Diamond and Doh-Chull Shin (eds.), *Reform and Democratic Consolidation in South Korea* (Stanford: Hoover Institution Press), pp. 279–303.

Kindleberger, C. (1996) *Manias, Panics, and Crashes*, 3rd edition (London and Basingstoke: Macmillan).

Kogut, Bruce and Walker, Gordon (1999) 'The Small World of Firm Ownership in Germany: Social Capital and Structural Holes in Large Firm Acquisitions,' mimeo, The Wharton School.

Koh, B.C. (1997) 'South Korea in 1996: Internal Strains and External Challenges,' *Asian Survey*, vol. 37, no. 1, pp. 1–9.

Kohli, Atul (1993) 'Democracy Amid Economic Orthodoxy: Trends in Developing Countries,' *Third World Quarterly*, vol. 14, no. 4.

Kongshøj Madsen, P. (1997), 'Transitionalle arbejdsmarkeder – et generelt perspektive på det rummelige arbejdsmarked,' in *Arbejdsmarkedspolitisk Årbog* (Copenhagen, Denmark), pp. 94-101,.

Kopits, George and Symansky, Steven (1998) 'Fiscal Policy Rules,' *Occasional Paper*, no. 162 (International Monetary Fund — IMF).

Korea Labor and Society Institute (KLSI) Survey, 1999, Korea Labour and Society Institute.

Korean Labour and Society Institute (KLSI) (1999a) *Employment Structure and Trade Union Policy in Korea* [in Korean] (Seoul, Korea: Korea Labour and Society Institute).

Korean Metal Workers' Federation (1999) 'Result of the Fact-Finding Survey of Collective Agreements' [in Korean] (Seoul: Korean Metal Workers' Federation).

Korean Metal Workers' Federation (1999a), *Koyongkucho Pyônhwawa Nodongchohap-ui Koyongchông Chaek* (Seoul: The Korean Metal Workers' Federation).

KOSDAQ website, http://www.kosdaq.or.kr/

Kregel, J. (1998) 'Yes, "It" Did Happen Again — the Minsky Crisis in Asia,' a paper presented at the conference on the 'Legacy of Hyman Minsky', December, Bergamo.

Krueger, A.O. (1983) *Trade and Employment in Developing Countries, Vol. 3: Synthesis and Conclusions* (Chicago: Chicago University Press).

Krugman, Paul (1979) 'A Model of Balance of Payment Crises,' *Journal of Money, Credit, and Banking*, vol. 11.

Krugman, Paul (1998a) 'What Happened to Asia?,' mimeo., Department of Economics, Massachusetts Institute of Technology, internet, web.mit.edu, home-page of Paul Krugman.

Krugman, Paul (1998b) 'Fire-sale FDI,' a paper presented at the NBER Conference on Capital Flows to Emerging Markets, 20–21 February 1998.

Lall, S. (1994) '"The East Asian Miracle" Study: Does the Bell Toll for Industrial Strategy?,' *World Development*, vol. 22, no. 4, pp. 645–54

Lall, S. (1995) 'Paradigms of Development: the East-Asian Debate,' Plenary paper to Queen Elizabeth House 40th Anniversary Conference: the Third World after the Cold War (Queen Elizabeth House, Oxford University, July).

Lall, S. (1998) 'Selective Industrial and Trade Policies in Developing Countries: Theoretical and Empirical Issues,' a paper prepared for 'Project on Economic Policymaking and Implementation in Africa: a Case for Strategic Trade and Selective Industrial Policies,' organised by the IDRC (International Development Research Centre), Nairobi Office

Lane, Timothy et al. (1999) 'IMF-Supported Programmes in Indonesia, Korea and Thailand: A Preliminary Assessment' (International Monetary Fund)

Lavinas, L. *O Globo*, 8 March 1998.

Lee, Jay-Min (1999), 'East Asian NIEs' Model of Development: Miracle, Crisis and Beyond,' *Pacific Review*, vol. 12, no. 2

Lee, Jay-Min and Eo, Woon-Sun (2000) 'Economic Crisis and Bankruptcy of Chaebols,' *Kyungje Baljun Yonku* (Seoul: Studies of Economic Development), vol. 6, no. 1 (in Korean)

Lee, Jin-Soon (1999) 'Anti-Corruption Measures of the "Government of the People",' paper presented at *International Conference on Democracy, Market Economy and Development*, Seoul, 26–7 February, www.democracy-market.org.

Lee, Joohee (2000) 'Income Assistance and Employment Creation through Public Works in Korea,' paper presented at the International Conference on Economic Crisis and Labor Market Reform: The Case of Korea, 18-20 May, sponsored by the World Bank, the Korea Labor Institute and KED.

Lee, Su-Hoon (1992) 'Transitional Politics of Korea, 1987–1992: Activation of Civil Society,' *Pacific Affairs*, vol. 66, no. 3, pp. 351–67.

Leff, Nathaniel (1978) 'Industrial Organization and Entrepreneurship in the Developing Countries: The Economic Groups,' *Economic Development and Cultural Change*, vol. 26, no. 4 (July), pp. 661–75.

Leite, M. (1994) 'Reestruturação produtiva, novas tecnologias e novas formas de gestão da mão-de-obra,' in M. Oliveira et al. (eds.), *O mundo do trabalho* (São Paulo: Scritta/Cesit/Mtb-PNUD).

Little, I., Scitovsky, T. and Scott, M. (1970) *Industry and Trade in Some Developing Countries* (Oxford and New York: Oxford University Press).

Low, L. (1998) *The Political Economy of a City-State: Government-made Singapore* (Oxford University Press).

Maeil Business Newspaper, various issues (Seoul: Korea).

Markwald, R. (2001) 'O impacto da abertura comercial sobre a indústria brasileira,' XIII Fórum Nacional, Rio de Janeiro.

Mathews, John A. (1998) 'Fashioning a New Korean Model Out of the Crisis: The Rebuilding of Institutional Capacities,' *Cambridge Journal of Economics*, vol. 22, no. 6, pp. 747–59.

Mattoso, Jorge (1995) *A desordem do trabalho* (São Paulo: Scritta).

Mattoso, Jorge (2000) 'As desculpas que saíram de moda,' *Gazeta Mercantil*, 5 June 2000 (São Paulo).

Mayer, C. (1988) 'New Issues in Corporate Finance,' *European Economic Review*, vol. 32.

Mayer, C. (1990) 'Financial Systems, Corporate Finance, and Economic Development,' in R. Hubbard (ed.), *Asymmetric Information, Corporate Finance, and Investment* (Chicago: University of Chicago Press).

McCraw, Thomas (1998) 'Government, Big Business and the Wealth of Nations,' in Alfred Chandler, Franco Amatori and Takashi Hikino (eds.), *Big Business and the Wealth of Nations* (Cambidge: Cambridge University Press).

McKinnon, R. and Pill, H. (1998) 'International Overborrowing — A Decomposition of Credit and Currency Risk,' *World Development*, vol. 26, no. 7.

McKinsey Global Institute (1999) *Produtividade no brasil: a chave de desenvolvimento acelerado* (Rio de Janeiro: Campus).

Mesquita Moreira, Mauricio (1999) 'Foreigners in an Open Economy: Recent Impacts on Productivity, Concentration and External Trade,' mimeo, BNDES Economics Department.

Ministério do Trabalho (1998) 'Emprego no Brasil: diagnóstico e políticas' (Brasília: Ministério do Trabalho).

Ministry of Finance and Economy (MOFE — 1999) 'The Road to Recovery: Korea's Ongoing Economic Reforms'.

Ministry of Finance and Economy (MOFE — 2000), *The White Paper on Operation of Public Funds* (in Korean).

Ministry of Labor, Republic of Korea (1997), Press release on the new Labor Laws in Korea.

Ministry of Labor (1999) *Trends in Employment Insurance*, KLI, vol. 4, no. 1.

Mirza, H. (1986) *Multinationals and Growth of the Singapore Economy* (New York: St. Martins Press).

Mishkin, Frederic (1999) 'International Experiences with Different Monetary Policy Regimes,' *NBER Working Paper*, no. 7044.

MOCIE (Ministry of Commerce, Industry and Energy) website, http://www.mofe.go.kr

Mody, A. (1989), 'Institutions and Dynamic Comparative Advantage: Electronics Industry in South Korea and Taiwan,' *Cambridge Journal of Economics*, vol. 14, pp. 291–314

MOFE Website, http://www.mofe.go.kr

Montero, Alfred (1997) 'State Interests and Business Coalitions for the Privatization of Brazilian Steel, 1990–94,' paper presented at the annual meeting of the American Political Science Association.

Moore, Mick (1997) 'Leading the Left to the Right: Populist Coalitions and Economic Reform,' *World Development*, vol. 25, no. 7, pp. 1009–28.

Moreira, Maurício Mesquita (1999) 'A indústria brasileira nos anos 90. O que já se pode dizer?,' in Fabio Giambiagi and Maurício Mesquita

Moreira (orgs.), '*A economia brasileira nos anos 90*' (Banco Nacional de Desenvolvimento Econômico e Social — BNDES).

Moreira, M. and Correa, P.G. (1996) 'Abertura comercial e indústria: o que se pode esperar e o que se vem obtendo' (Rio de Janeiro: BNDES), *Textos para Discussão*, outubro.

Munck, R. (1984) *Politics and Dependency in the Third World: The Case of Latin America* (London: Zed Books).

Murillo, M.V. (2000) 'From Populism to Neo-liberalism: Labour Unions and Market Reform in Latin America,' *World Politics*, vol. 52 (January), pp. 135–74.

National Science and Technology Board (NSTB) (1999) 'National Survey of R&D in Singapore 1998'.

National Statistical Office (NSO) website, http://www.nso.go.kr

Neri, M., Camargo, J.M. and Reis, M.C. (2000) 'Mercado de trabalho nos anos 90: fatos estilizados e interpretações,' Texto para Discussão No 743 — IPEA, julho de 2000 (Rio de Janeiro: BSB).

Obstfeld, M. (1994) 'The Logic of Currency Crises,' *Cahiers Economiques et Monetaires*, vol. 43.

OECD (1986) *Flexibility in the Labour Market — the Current Debate — a Technical Report* (Paris: OECD).

OECD (1992) *Technology and the Economy — the Key Relationships* (Paris: OECD).

Pacific Economic Cooperation Council (PECC) (1999) *Pacific Science and Technology Profile*, sixth issue

Pagano, U. (1985) *Work and Welfare in Economic Theory* (Oxford, New York: Basil Blackwell).

Park, Won-Am (1996) 'Financial Liberalization: The Korean Experience,' in T. Ito and A. Krueger (eds.), *Financial Deregulation and Integration in East Asia* (Chicago: University of Chicago Press).

Park, Duck-Jay, Park, Jonghee, Yu, Gyu-Chang (2001), 'Assessment of Labor Market Response to the Labor Law Changes introduced in 1998,' in Funkoo Park, Young-bum Park, Gordon Betcherman, Amit Dar (eds), *Labor Market Reforms in Korea: Policy Options for the Future* (The World Bank, Korea Labor Institute).

Park, Funkoo and Joohee, Lee (1999) 'The Social Impact of the Financial Crisis: Labor Market Outcomes and Policy Responses in Korea,' unpublished manuscript, August (Seoul: The Korea Labour Institute).

Park, Young-Bum (1994) 'State Regulation, the Labour Market and Economic Development: The Republic of Korea,' in G. Rodgers (ed), *Workers' Institutions and Economic Growth in Asia*, pp.156–9 (Geneva).

Park, Young-bum (2001) 'Feasibility of Introducing a Non-Contributory Cash Benefits System for the Unemployed in Korea,' in Funkoo Park, Young-bum Park, Gordon Betcherman, Amit Dar (eds), *Labor Market Reforms in Korea: Policy Options for the Future* (The World Bank, Korea Labor Institute).

Park, Yung-Chul (1998) *Financial Liberalization and Opening in East Asia: Issues and Policy Challenges* (Korea Institute of Finance).

Pauly, Louis and Reich, Simon (1997) 'National Structures and Multinational Corporate Behavior: Enduring Differences in the Age of Globalization,' *International Organization*, vol. 51, no. 1.

Pinheiro, A. and Almeida, G. (1994) *Padrões setoriais de proteção na economia brasileira* (Rio de Janerio: IPEA).

Pinheiro, A. and Moreira, M. (2000) 'O perfil dos exportadores brasileiros nos anos 90: quais as implicações de política,' *BNDES Texto Para Discussão*, no. 80

Pires, J. and Piccinni, M. (1999) 'A regulação dos setores de infra-estrutura no Brasil,' in F. Gambiagi and M. Moreira (eds.) *A economia brasileira nos anos 90* (Rio de Janeiro: BNDES).

Pochmann, M. (1999) *O trabalho sob fogo cruzado* (São Paulo: Editora Contexto).

Pochmann, M. (2000a) *A batalha pelo primeiro emprego* (São Paulo: Publisher Brasil).

Pochmann, M. (2000b) 'Os jovens excluídos do mercado de trabalho,' *Gazeta Mercantil*, 1 July 2000 (São Paulo).

Pochmann, M. (2000c) 'Mudanças (para pior) no mercado de trabalho,' *Gazeta Mercantil*, 15 August 2000 (São Paulo).

Pochmann, M. (2000d) 'O desemprego no governo Cardoso,' *Folha de São Paulo*, 2 August 2000 (São Paulo).

Posthuma, A. (1997) 'Autopeças na encruzilhada: modernização desarticu-lada e desnacionalização,' in G. Arbix and M. Zilbovicius (eds.), *De JK a FHC — A reinvenção dos carros* (São Paulo: Scritta).

Puga, Fernando Pimentel (1999) 'Sistema financeiro brasileiro: reestruturação recente, comparações internacionais e vulnerabilidade à crise cambial,' *Texto para Discussão*, BNDES, no. 68 (March).

Pyo, H.K. (1998) 'Excess Competition, Moral Hazard and Industrial Trauma in Korea (1997–1998),' a paper presented at the conference on *The Aftermath of the Asian Crisis*, 13–14 May, Washington, DC.

Radelet, S. and Sachs, J. (1998) 'The East Asian Financial Crisis: Diagnosis, Remedies and Prospects,' *Brookings Paper on Economic Activity*, no. 1, pp. 1–90.

Radelet, S. and Sachs, J. (1998a), 'The Onset of the East Asian Financial Crisis,' Working Paper, Harvard Institute for International Development.

Reich, Robert B. (1990) 'Who Is Us?,' *Harvard Business Review*, January–February.

Rodrik, D. (1998), 'King Kong Meets Godzilla: The World Bank and The East Asian Miracle,' *Policy Essay no.11* (Overseas Development Council).

Ruiz, Ricardo (1997) 'The Restructuring of Brazilian Industrial Groups between 1980 and 1993,' *Cepal Review*, no. 61.

Ryan. P. (1994) 'Training Quality and Trainee Exploitation,' in R. Layard, K. Mayhew and G. Owen (eds.), *Britain's Training Deficit* (Aldershot: Avebury).

Ryan, P. (1995) 'Trade Union Policies towards the Youth Training Scheme: Patterns and Causes,' in *British Journal of Industrial Relations*, no. 33, no. 1 (London, March), pp. 1–35.

Ryan, P. (2000) 'Publicly Funded Training for Unemployed Adults: Germany, the UK and Korea,' presentation at the Conference on Financial Crisis and Labor Market Reform in Korea, organised by the World Bank and the Korea Labor Institute, Seoul, May 18–20.

Schamis, Hector (1999) 'Distributional Coalitions and the Politics of Economic Reform in Latin America,' *World Politics*, vol. 51, no. 2.

Schneider, Ben Ross (1991) *Politics within the State* (Pittsburgh: University of Pittsburgh Press).

Schneider, Ben Ross (1997–98) 'Organized Business Politics in Democratic Brazil,' *Journal of Interamerican Studies and World Affairs*, vol. 39, no. 4.

Schneider, Ben Ross (1998) 'Elusive Synergy: Business-Government Relations and Development,' *Comparative Politics*, vol. 31, no. 1.

Schneider, Ben Ross (1999) 'The Desarrollista State in Brazil and Mexico,' in Meredith Woo-Cumings (ed.), *The Developmental State* (Ithaca: Cornell University Press).

Schumpeter, J. (1934) *The Theory of Economic Development* (Cambridge MA: Harvard University Press).

Schumpeter, J. (1943) *Capitalism, Socialism and Democracy* (New York: Harper).

Schwartzman, S. (ed.) (1995) *Science and Technology in Brazil: A New Policy for a Global World* (Rio de Janeiro: Fundação Getúlio Vargas).

Seong, Kyoung-Ryung (2000) 'Civil Society and Democratic Consolidation in South Korea: Great Achievements and Remaining Problems,' in Larry Diamond and Byung-Kook Kim (eds.), *Consolidating Democracy in South Korea* (Boulder, CO: Lynne Rienner), pp. 87–109.

Shin, Inseok and Hahm, Joon-Ho (1998) 'The Korean Crisis — Causes and Resolution,' paper presented at the East-West Center/Korea Development Institute Conference on the Korean Crisis, Honolulu, 8 August.

Shin, Jang-Sup (1996) *The Economics of the Latecomers: Catching-Up, Technology Transfer and Institutions in Germany, Japan and South Korea* (London and New York: Routledge).

Shin, Jang-Sup (1999) *A Third Way for the Korean Economy* (Seoul: Joong-Ang Media Books) (in Korean).

Shin, Jang-Sup (2000) 'Corporate Restructuring after the Financial Crisis in South Korea: A Critical Appraisal,' a paper prepared for the annual meeting of the Korea Economic Association, August, Seoul, Korea.

Siffert Filho, Nelson and Souza e Silva, C. (1999) 'Large Companies in the 1990s: Strategic Responses to a Scenario of Change,' mimeo, BNDES Economics Department.

Sikkink, Kathryn (1991) *Ideas and Institutions: Developmentalism in Brazil and Argentina* (Ithaca: Cornell University Press).

Silva, Eduardo (1996) *The State and Capital in Chile* (Boulder: Westview Press).

Silva, O. (1999) *A decolagem de um sonho: a história da criação da Embraer* (São Paulo: Lemos).

Singh, A. (1992) 'The Stock-Market and Economic Development: Should Developing Countries Encourage Stock-Markets?,' *UNCTAD Discussion Paper*, no. 49 (Geneva: UNCTAD).

Singh, A. (1994) 'How do Large Corporations in Developing Countries Finance Their Growth?,' *Finance and the International Economy*, vol. 8.

Singh, A. (1995) 'Corporate Financing Patterns in Industrialising Economies: A Comparative International Study,' *IFC Technical Paper*, no. 2 (Washington, DC: International Finance Corporation).

Singh, A. (1998) 'Savings, Investment and the Corporation in the East Asian Miracle,' *Journal of Development Studies*, vol. 34, no. 6.

Singh, A. (1999) '"Asian Capitalism" and the Financial Crisis,' in J. Michie and J. Grieve Smith (eds.), *Global Instability — The Political Economy of World Economic Governance* (London: Routledge).

Singh, A. and Hamid, J. (1992) 'Corporate Financial Structures in Developing Countries,' *IFC Technical Paper*, no. 2 (International Finance Corporation).

Smith, N. (1997) '*Det effektive, rummelige og trygge danske arbejdsmarked?*' in *Arbejdsmarkedspolitisk Årbog* (Copenhagen, Denmark), pp.102–19,.

Solow, R. (1990) *The Labour Market as a Social Institution* (Cambridge, MA, Oxford: Basil Blackwell).Song, B.N. (1997) *The Rise of the Korean Economy* (New York: Oxford University Press).

Song, Ho-Keun (1999), 'Labour Unions in the Republic of Korea: Challenge and Choice,' *ILO Discussion Paper 107* (Geneva: ILO), pp. 23–4.

Standard & Poor's (1999) 'Bank Industry Risk Analysis: Brazil,' Bank System Report (December).

Steinbruch, Benjamin (1998) 'O novo capitalismo brasileiro,' *Folha de São Paulo*, 26 May.

Stiglitz, J. (1996) 'Some Lessons from the East Asian Miracle,' *The World Bank Research Observer*, vol. 11, no. 2.

Stiglitz, J. (1998) 'Sound Finance and Sustainable Development in Asia,' a speech delivered at the Asian Development Forum, 12 March 1998, Manila, the Philippines.

Stiglitz, J. (2001) *The Rebel Within – Collected Essays by Joseph Stiglitz at the World Bank*, edited and introduced by H-J. Chang (London: Wimbledon Publishing Company).

Strachan, H.W. (1976) *Family and Other Business Groups in Economic Development: The Case of Nicaragua* (New York: Praeger).

Suzigan, W. and Villela, A. (1997) *Industrial Policy in Brazil* (Campinas: Unicamp).

Taylor, L. (1998) 'Capital Market Crises: Liberalization, Fixed Exchange Rates and Market-driven Destablization,' *Cambridge Journal of Economics*, vol. 22, no. 6.

Teixeira Lima, E. and Carvalho, M. (2000) 'Ações para acelerar a expansão de exportações,' *Revista do BNDES*, December.

The World Bank (1993) *The East Asian Miracle: Economic Growth and Public Policy* (New York: Oxford University Press).

Toh, M.H. and Tan, K.Y. (eds) (1998) *Competitiveness of the Singapore Economy* (Singapore: World Scientific/SUP).

Transparency International (1999) *1999 Bribe Payers Index*, www.transparency.de.

Trebilcock, C. (1981) *The Industrialization of the Continental Powers 1780–1914* (London: Macmillan).

Trends in Employment Insurance (various years) Korea Labor Institute.

Velasco Jr., Lucio (1997) 'A economia política das políticas públicas: fatores que favoreceram as privatizações no período 1985/94,' BNDES, *Textos para Discussão*, no. 54.

Vernon, Raymond (1963) *The Dilemma of Mexico's Development* (Cambridge, MA: Harvard University Press).

Villarim de Siqueira, Tagore (1999) 'Concentration of Ownership in Brazilian Quoted Companies,' mimeo (BNDES Economics Department).

Wade, R. (1990) *Governing the Market: Economic Theory and the Role of Government in East Asian Industralization* (Princeton: Princeton University Press).

Wang, Yoon-Jong (1997), 'Performance of Korea's Overseas Firms,' in Yoon-Jong Wang (ed.) (1997) *Current Status and Performance of Korea's Foreign Direct Investment* (in Korean), Korea Institute of Economic and

Weeks, John. (1999) 'Wages, Employment and Workers' Rights in Latin America, 1970–98,' *International Labour Review*, vol. 138, no. 2 (Geneva: ILO).

Whitley, Richard D. (1992) *Business Systems in East Asia* (London: Macmillan).

Williamson, O. (1985) *The Economic Institutions of Capitalism* (New York: The Free Press, New York).

Wong, Poh-Kam (2000) 'The Role of the State in Singapore's Industrial Development,' paper presented at workshop on 'Industrial Policy, Innovation, and Economic Growth,' organised by the Scandinavian Academy of Management Studies in Copenhagen, Denmark

Woo, Jung-En (1991) *Race to the Swift: State and Finance in Korean Industrialization* (New York: Columbia University Press).

World Bank (1993) *The East Asian Miracle: Economic Growth and Public Policy* (Oxford and New York: Oxford University Press).

World Bank (1992, 1995, 1997) *World Development Reports* (Oxford: Oxford University Press).

Yearbook of Labour Statistics, Labour Ministry of Korea, various years.

Yoo, S.M. (1997) 'Evolution of Government-Business Interface in Korea: Progress to Date and Reform Agenda Ahead,' Working Paper, no. 9711 (Seoul: Korea Development Institute).

Yoo, Seong-Min (1999) 'Corporate Restructuring in Korea: Policy Issues Before and During the Crisis,' *KDI Working Paper 9903* (February 1999).

You, J-I. and Chang H-J, (1993) 'The Myth of Free Labour Market in Korea,' in *Contributions to Political Economy*, vol., no. 12, pp. 29–46.

You, J-I (1997) 'Globalization, Labor Market Flexibility and the Korean Labor Reform,' in *Seoul Journal of Economics*, vol. 10, no. 4, pp.341–72.

You, Shi-Wang (2000), The Role and the Future of KOSDAQ (in Korean), paper presented at Venture Symposium organised by Samsung Economic Research Institute, March, Seoul.